MW00638740

Kabbalistic Cycles and
The Mastery of Life

SOME OTHER TITLES FROM FALCON PRESS

Joseph Lisiewski, Ph.D.
Israel Regardie and the Philosopher's Stone
Ceremonial Magic and the Power of Evocation
Kabbalistic Handbook for the Practicing Magician
Howlings from the Pit
Christopher S. Hyatt, Ph.D.
Undoing Yourself With Energized Meditation & Other Devices
Radical Undoing: Complete Course for Undoing Yourself (DVDs)
Energized Hypnosis (non-book, CDs & DVDs)
To Lie Is Human: Not Getting Caught Is Divine
The Psychopath's Bible: For the Extreme Individual
Secrets of Western Tantra: The Sexuality of the Middle Path
Christopher S. Hyatt, Ph.D. with contributions by
Wm. S. Burroughs, Timothy Leary, Robert Anton Wilson et al.
Rebels & Devils: The Psychology of Liberation
S. Jason Black and Christopher S. Hyatt, Ph.D.
Pacts With the Devil: A Chronicle of Sex, Blasphemy & Liberation
Urban Voodoo: A Beginner's Guide to Afro-Caribbean Magic
Antero Alli
Angel Tech: A Modern Shaman's Guide to Reality Selection
Angel Tech Talk (CDs)
Peter J. Carroll
The Chaos Magick Audio CDs
PsyberMagick
Phil Hine
Condensed Chaos
Prime Chaos
The Pseudonomicon
Israel Regardie
The Complete Golden Dawn System of Magic
The Golden Dawn Audio CDs
The Eye in the Triangle

**For up-to-the-minute information on prices and
availability, please visit our website at
http://originalfalcon.com**

Kabbalistic Cycles and The Mastery of Life

by

Joseph C. Lisiewski, Ph.D.

Foreword by
Christopher S. Hyatt, Ph.D.

THE *Original* FALCON PRESS
TEMPE, ARIZONA, U.S.A.

Copyright © 2004 by Joseph C. Lisiewski, Ph.D.

All rights reserved. No part of this book, in part or in whole, may be reproduced, transmitted, or utilized, in any form or by any means, electronic or mechanical, including photocopying, recording, or by any information storage and retrieval system, without permission in writing from the publisher, except for brief quotations in critical articles, books and reviews.

International Standard Book Number: 978-1-935150-87-9
ISBN: 978-1-61869-870-4 (mobi)
ISBN: 978-1-61869-871-1 (ePub)
Library of Congress Catalog Card Number: 2004115685

First Edition 2004
Second Printing 2006
Third Printing 2010
First ebook Edition 2012

This story is based on true events. Names and locations have been changed when necessary to protect the identity of the participants.

Cover by Linda Joyce Franks

The paper used in this publication meets the minimum requirements of the American National Standard for Permanence of Paper for Printed Library Materials Z39.48-1984

Address all inquiries to:
THE ORIGINAL FALCON PRESS
1753 East Broadway Road #101-277
Tempe, AZ 85282 U.S.A.
(or)
PO Box 3540
Silver Springs, NV 89429 U.S.A.
website: http://www.originalfalcon.com
email: info@originalfalcon.com

DEDICATION

This book is lovingly dedicated to my darling wife, Darlene, who has so understandingly put up with my bizarre ways throughout the decades.

TABLE OF CONTENTS

ILLUSTRATIONS

To the Reader

E very man and woman who truly desires success and fulfillment in this world must have access to some method or methods which, if not actually guaranteeing success and fulfillment, will at least provide the tools necessary to help them make the manifestation of their deepest desires much, much more certain. For the most fortunate and usually the most successful, those methods are locked deep in their subconscious minds, and are tapped into automatically, turning both daily humdrum as well as sporadic critical situations to their advantage. Such people frequently credit their intuition, a feeling, or perhaps a simple hunch to their never-ending stream of good luck. But to others like you and I who were not endowed with such automatic intuitive faculties, other methods must be discovered to enable us to turn the tide of events in our favor.

We can spend many years or even decades, in search of such methods or systems, and even then we all too often fail to find this elusive, dependable method. All too often, the seeker who has traveled the ways of Astrology, Numerology, and divinatory practices ranging from the Tarot and I Ching to Pendulum question and answer schemes, is left with the attitude that none of it works, at least, not so that it can be *depended* on when the chips are down and it's really needed! Unfortunately, for the most part, their final evaluation is right.

Does this mean that you and I have to trust our fate to blind luck? Or do we keep on searching for some *practical*, realistic means of reading the inevitable, sometimes subtle, sometimes dramatic, occult influences that are woven into the fabric of everyday mundane and worldly issues that cross our path? Are we doomed to take our best shot employing our purely analytical and reasoning faculties, which means that at any given moment we never have sufficient information to make the oft touted rational decision? A decision that grants us a higher probability of success? Are we so subject to the psychological influences that are believed to operate behind astrology and the various forms of divination that we can never be certain of the actual psychic influences those systems do influence, or our interpretation of them?

And what about our attempts to make sense of and weave any number of the popular forms of modern day psychology into a workable system we can use to decipher, interpret, analyze, and deal with the eventualities of daily life? How do we as untrained psychologists or psychiatrists even begin to understand that *any* given event and our psychological response to it can be interpreted *differently* according to the vast number of psychological schools of thought, each of which postures it has the answer!

How is it even remotely possible for the modern day individual to learn enough of the theoretical basis underlying these schools, such that he or she can find which school's theoretical framework is in closest agreement with his or her own subconscious processes, conscious views, and perceptions of the world? Of course, we can't. So for better or worse, we are left searching for some occult influence that we can manipulate in one way or another, in order to make our lives count. Let me make this perfectly clear right now. There is nothing wrong with this. It is, in my opinion, a completely human need.

Whether occult or other hidden influences are actually a part of the tapestry of daily mundane or sporadic critical events, or are strictly part of our subconscious belief systems or, most probably a combination of both, does not really matter. What matters is that at some level we *think* and *act* on the supposed existence of these external and internal influences, treating them with all of the respect and caution we grant any of the physical forces that effect us every day, such as electricity and gravity.

But if the truth be known, after all of the arguments for or against these so-called occult forces are said and done, the hard fact remains. Anyone who has lived in the real world of people, places and things, knows instinctively that something is operating behind the continued successes of the lucky, and the perpetual failures of the unlucky. So what does the average, well-meaning, hardworking, diligent, I-won't-take-no-for-an-answer man and woman do, who is trying to succeed amidst the every widening and deepening chaos of daily life?

Actually, that is what this book is about. It's about proving to you that we are *not* subject to the nebulous, shadowy methods of modern day psychology. Nor are we desperate slaves to the uncertain, rustic, complex ploys of the New Age, with all of the doubts and fears that particular brand of insanity can produce in us. For thirty-two years, using that most ancient of philosophical traditions— the Kabbalah, and a planetary system of hours employed by magicians and occultists for the past five hundred years—and wedding the two through a new concept, I have produced *a dependable system of 'prediction' that the reader can use anywhere, anytime, for any event—whether mundane or spiritual—no matter how suddenly it arrives.* This method, which I refer to simply as the **Method of Kabbalistic Cycles**, has been used daily, sometimes hourly, over and over, for decades, and not only by me and those close to me, but literally by hundreds of others to whom I have taught this method.

Those of us who have employed the principles of this **Kabbalistic Cycles and the Mastery of Life System** as I called it throughout the years, have not only found it works consistently and accurately, but we have also found it *gives us priceless insights into the motivations of others.* In short, it provides us with the tools with which we can chart our own course in life, and be much more than relatively or fairly certain of the results. If you have had enough of all the 'ologies,' 'isms' and 'ics' out there, and are still looking, then look no further. You have finally found the System of life mastery that can make all the difference in your personal, professional, and spiritual or **psychic life**, as I will refer to this part of your nature throughout this book. And I am very, **very** serious about this.

FOREWORD

My first encounter with the idea of the "Kabbalistic Cycles System" occurred during the early Fall of 1987. In those days, Dr. Joseph Lisiewski and his wife were living in Scottsdale, Arizona, and it was my custom to drive from my residence in Los Angeles to their home and spend several days with them every so often. Although our times there were always very productive, this one time Joe confided in me about a special project he had been working on for (at that time) twenty-one years. This was a mathematically-based system using the Glyph of the Tree of Life—the essential theological doctrines of the Kabbalah—combined with a geometrical interpretation of what he called "Flow" up and down the Tree. All was somehow wedded together through the symbolism of the twenty-two cards of the Greater Arcana of the Tarot, as a means of both determining and literally *directing* the forces of the Tree itself. In other words, this system of his appeared to consciously control and direct the very forces that underlie all Creation.

We discussed the fact that our late friend, teacher, and colleague, Israel Regardie, always felt the Tree was neither employed correctly nor extended more fully into the daily life of both practicing occultists as well as lay people. Like myself, Joe had discussed this matter with Regardie many times. When Joe originally presented his work on this Kabbalistic Cycles System (which he began working on in 1966) to Regardie in 1978 and again in the years to follow, their conversations on this matter would always end on the same note. Regardie always had his hands full with other things, but he still felt that people needed a better way to use the occult forces that exist "out there" and in their own psyches to aid them in their daily lives. So, since he didn't have the time, he would always encourage Joe to figure this one out.

Joe took Regardie's encouragements seriously, trying to determine if such a system could indeed be either found or constructed. It would take him another eleven years after our 1987 discussion before he had all of the proof he needed that the system he discovered—as he insists, not constructed—was complete, and had been thoroughly tested. Joe then spent an additional six years further testing and fine-tuning his system before he felt it was good enough and dependable enough for anyone—experienced occultist or lay individual—to use with confidence, effectiveness, and efficiency. This book is the result of those thirty-two years of intense experimental and theoretical labours.

The underlying theme of *Kabbalistic Cycles and the Mastery of Life* is really very simple:

(1) None of us have the *control* over our own lives that we not only want, but deserve, by virtue of our Divine birthright.

(2) As a consequence of the lack of control, the extent of certainty with which we live from moment to moment is somewhere between zero and none.

In reality, we are continually walking on eggs, waiting for the next shoe to drop. Each day is a pale reflection of the previous one. There is always the presence of doubts and uncertainties, not knowing what to do or when to do it. We cannot effectively evaluate apparent opportunities that cross our paths, decipher the hidden intentions or motives of others, or know how to handle problems that suddenly drop into our laps. Yet we have the temerity to call this Life? and Living? Not according to Dr. Lisiewski.

With this straightforward, complex Kabbalistic Cycles System transformed into simplicity itself, he has provided more than a simple roadmap for the individual. He has provided his readers with markings along the way, knowledge of the lay of the land, and full directions on how to undertake the journey of life. Now the individual can travel on their own terms, directing, interpreting, and controlling every condition, event, situation, and circumstance that arises.

How is this possible? Remember: Knowledge is Power! Here lies the knowledge of the Kabbalistic forces that underlie and weave their magic throughout all of Creation— from the movement of the largest galaxies and star systems, to the smallest subatomic particle, to the situations that confronts each human being daily. All is integrated into one system, presented here for the man or woman who has had enough of being buffeted about by circumstance, so they have the answers they have been looking for. These answers will enable them to direct the universal forces on their own behalf and, in so doing, will grant them the confidence, certainty, and control they have every right to demand from Life itself. That's what this book is about.

To the best knowledge of Dr. Lisiewski, my own, and so many others to whom he privately taught this Kabbalistic Cycles System, there is no other occult system or method like it in the world, past or present. This system is completely new. It is unique. And it is a true discovery. Use it if you choose, but especially if you are serious about living life free from fear, worry, guilt, doubt, and uncertainty, and are determined to take hold of the Certainty and Control that is yours for the taking.

— Christopher S. Hyatt, Ph.D.
November 2004

CHAPTER ONE

The Purpose of This Book

"Every day, in every way, I am getting better and better." Such were the inspiring words of Emile Coué,[1] one of the famous New Thought Movement personalities whose brand of applied psychology was actually the precursor to the positive thinking phenomenon so well known today. His idea was to use positive affirmations as a means of programming the subconscious (or unconscious if you will), in an effort to have that vast storehouse of knowledge and power manifest the wants, needs, and desires of the practitioner in his or her life.

As with so many of these occult methods of the New Thought Movement, it worked. Such commonly known methods still do work, but only to a point. Unfortunately, times have changed from the earliest years of the twentieth century when these and other methods of individual control over one's environment were being worked out. Year after year, generation after generation, new governmental, commercial, industrial, and others-oriented vested interests entered into the life stream of the average individual. Once in place, these external factors added layer upon layer of extraneous, energy and time-consuming complexities to daily life.

Such early life-controlling and life-determining methods which worked easily then became mired down by this layering effect. Over time their results became negligible at best. Having seen national and world events unravel, and having witnessed new trends throughout the first few years of the twenty-first century that add more and more layers upon the needlessly mad, ever-growing complexity of daily life, those of us who can recall a time as short as fifty years ago, now face a world we no longer know, and cannot understand. This is not because we lack the mental ability but because the madness of the times is utterly beyond comprehension and reason, and therefore outside of our noblest efforts to even modify, let alone control.

Daily, hourly, we find ourselves in a world populated by every type of naysayer, controlling influence, would-be demigod, and self-styled authority in this and that field of endeavor, whose only purpose is to throw up every obstacle they can into our paths; to create every brush fire possible; to consume the last vestige of energy we have; to extract from us not simply the last dollar and shred of self-sufficiency we possess, but to push us so far down into their purposely designed hells, that we can barely close our eyes at night in any type of peace, in order to prepare for yet another day of *their* madness.

But amidst the chaos out there, there is more than hope for those of us who want to regain maximum control over our lives; for those of us who want to make our lives count, both personally and professionally; for the minority who want to lay their heads down at night, confident that the past day has moved them even closer to their most cherished goals, as they ready themselves for another day of continued victory and progress.

How does one actually attain to such a high and noble control over one's life, while the lives of others and all of society is unraveling around them? By learning the natural laws governing the cycles of the universe. And don't be swayed by the dialectical materialist who wears the familiar, friendly face of your president, boss, husband or wife, or postman. YOU are affected by those same cyclic laws of Creation, as are the smallest forms of animate and inanimate matter.

These occult laws governing the cycles of the universe of which I speak, are as ordered and regular as your heartbeat. They are extensions if you will, of the physical laws that we physicists so love to tout and lay claim to understand so very well. But since they do not *readily* lend themselves to laboratory measurement and the scientific method of analysis—although in fact, a surprising number of them do—artificial lines of demarcation were drawn between the *apparent* physical laws we manipulate through our understanding of them, and these more ethereal, quasi-laws that influence and effect both the inanimate and animate, just as much as the physical laws do.

Ironically, however, these occult laws of cycles are not so easy to manipulate, at least not through the prevailing knowledge found in astrology, I Ching divination, numerology, crystal gazing, geomancy, pendulum forecasting, or even through the tarot. Why? Because of two operational conditions that reflect back on the laziness and shallowness of the contemporary human mind.

The first operational condition is that an effective 'Subjective Synthesis' must be built up within the subconscious (or unconscious) mind of the individual. This all-important concept was rigorously developed and thoroughly discussed in my first book, *Ceremonial Magic & The Power of Evocation*.[2] The reader would do well to consult a copy of that book, and learn the details of this all-important subjective synthesis state. Suffice it to say here that the state of subjective synthesis is that subconscious constellation of beliefs and ideas that govern most of our conscious actions, ideas, and mental perceptions of our personal universe: the outer world we see, act toward and react to, and the inner world of our psychic nature that we are barely conscious of.

When these subconscious beliefs and ideas are structured through our *conscious effort* into a unified whole, each part supporting the other in a particular framework— that is, a given belief about something—the subconscious mind directs the outcome according to those beliefs. A few pages ago I said whether occult or other hidden influences are actually part of the tapestry of daily mundane or sporadic critical events, or are strictly part of our subconscious belief systems or most probably, a combination of both, does not really matter. I went on to say that what matters is that at some level we *think* and *act* on the supposed existence of these external and internal influences, treating them with all of the respect and caution we give to any of the physical forces that affect us every day, such as electricity and gravity.

The fact is, it is my personal opinion, that it is *not* the subjective synthesis itself that produces the phenomenal results attained through the use of this **Kabbalistic Cycles and the Mastery of Life System.** Rather, it is the construction of an effective subjective synthesis which actually allows the efficient subconscious use of the occult or hidden laws that exercise such powerful influence over our lives.

As to the question of Free Will, Destiny, Purpose, or any of the other religious-based, life-defeating, socially-controlling dictums that consume so many lives, I am not in the least bit interested. It is enough that we—you and I—are here, now, and that we have determined our own ideals, our own goals, and our own life-courses, and are actively seeking ways to fulfill our very real in-the-here-and-now desires and needs.

This is just the point of this first operational condition being discussed here. All too often we cringe at the idea of having to **work**. We reel at the idea of having to exert—in this case—a substantial intellectual effort to *learn* something new, and in so doing, build our subjective synthesis thought-by-thought, as is required in the Kabbalistic System laid out for you in this book. We back off from the mental effort required to apply what is given here, and keep accurate notes of the conditions in our lives that we apply these Kabbalistic Cycles to, all of which then enables us to say, "The System works!"

Why do we take such a lazy view? It might surprise you to learn that our flippant and often cowardly attitude toward such work is due to having been taught that we have rights in everything, including our right to an easy and carefree life. If any destructive subjective synthesis exists within the subconscious minds of most people, it is this one. But then, it was easy to build this. Everyone else, especially the government, says this, so it must be true. But was it really easy?

It's true. It takes effort to build any state of subjective synthesis. If you look back over your life and your utter discontent with where you are now and the general state of your life, I am willing to bet you will find you had to work hard at it for years to try to convince yourself things were not as you saw them but as others told you they were, and the present conditions of your life *exactly* mirror the state of this subconscious belief system.

So it is up to you. Prepare to learn, to work, and as a result, to succeed in your life. That is, if you have the belly for it. I say this as a justified warning because as has happened to so many who suddenly had success thrust upon them as a result of their own efforts, handling your success may not be as easy as you think. The lives of such people as Elvis Presley, Marilyn Monroe, Judy Garland, Ingrid Bergman, and more movie stars, political figures, and 'ordinary' successful people than one cares to count, are examples of our general state of un-preparedness. So be certain to build into your subjective synthesis constructive thoughts of how you will handle your success as you work this System, or you will simply replace one set of agonies with another.

As to how to build handling success into your subjective synthesis in a rational and highly effective manner, I suggest the reader obtain the book, *The Master Key System*, by Charles F. Haanel.[3] Its principles and practical guidance are solid, effective, and more than helpful to not only learn how to handle success, but to obtain it as well. When used in conjunction with the book, *Undoing Yourself With Energized Meditation and Other Devices* by Christopher S. Hyatt, Ph.D.,[4] the individual will not only be prepared for success, but will find an entirely new self buried deep within. This new self can use the Kabbalistic Cycles System so well as to utterly transform his or her life.

The second operational condition that breeds a slothful attitude as we work at hammering out a system that will help us in our daily lives, is due to carrying over the attitude we have developed toward orthodox science itself.

As it took centuries for the physical laws to be discovered, examined, and carefully formulated, so too does this process apply to these occult laws. But science, having drawn the line between what could be easily and realistically measured, didn't bother to include these seemingly more elusive, more nonphysical laws. As a consequence, their evolution has been slower, and has resulted in the separate systems of divination, self-help, and every -ology, -ism, and -ic that abounds today. Just as the study of the physical laws has produced carefully defined systems which treat different physical phenomena, so too what is needed here is an eclectic synthesis of occult laws into one unified, working system.

This is exactly what I intend to show you is contained within the covers of this book: an eclectic system of occult laws that will allow you to live your life on your terms, making as few blundering errors and missteps as possible, so you can expand outward, and live the good life in the here and now. I encourage the reader to sit back, but *not* relax! Pick up a tablet and pen, calm your mind, and prepare to learn. And then, **work!**

CHAPTER TWO

Randomness, Order, and the Need for Personal Control in Daily Affairs

You may be asking yourself why we need to wade through a whole chapter on the need to control our daily affairs, since the need is an obvious one. Actually, this need may not be as obvious as you might like it to be. Why do I say this? Because if it was so, you would not be reading this book. And why not? Because your life would already be exactly what you want it to be, and you would have no need for this written instruction. Your control would be an established fact, and you could pretty much design your affairs and their outcomes almost exactly the way you want them to be.

The reason for this chapter is that I intend to school you in the way things happen. Actually, the way things seem to happen; how the idea of randomness is introduced into this picture; but instead, how an actual order and pattern underlies all phenomena, including your daily life and affairs; and how to produce the level of control you need to turn your life around.

In the learning process, this chapter will go a long way toward helping you build your subconscious belief system of subjective synthesis which when structured properly so that each part of it supports the other, it will enable you to work the Kabbalistic Cycles System efficiently, effectively, and perhaps in time, automatically. All of this will work toward the betterment of your overall life condition. Fair enough?

My first task is to convince you that there are really few earth-shaking, life-changing random events in your life. In fact, you have more control over your life *right now* than you are aware of. Yes, you have been taught otherwise by those who raised you, and who exerted the strongest influence upon you during your early years from childhood throughout your late teens. You were taught that 'things just happen,' and the best you can do is 'to make the most of them.' In other words, you were taught that all of life is a chaotic, open-ended, free-for-all. You were schooled in the idea that it was random.

In reality, the people who drilled this life philosophy into you were as disorganized, unthinking, and reactionary as were the people who made up their lives. How else could they instruct you any differently? It will serve you no useful end either to be angry with them, or to blame them for who you are at this moment, and as a result, what position you currently find yourself in. I also intend to convince you that even during those early years *you* had the wherewithal to stop the influence they exerted upon you. *You* had the ability to strike out on your own and build the type of life you wanted to live as far back as you can remember. Surprises you, doesn't it?

The bottom line of a designed, purposeful life is that in the end, the individual has no one to blame for his or her current state of being and position in life other than themselves. There is a dynamic, psychic, intelligible reason for this, which you might even be able to ferret out by the end of this chapter. If not, it will be clearly explained by the time this presentation is concluded.

Webster's Unabridged Dictionary defines 'randomness' as: "Occurring by chance; without any aim or method." Let's take a hypothetical example of a series of events that can occur in the life of almost any adult, and see just how much 'randomness' is actually involved.

You wake up in the morning, and have to rush through your daily ablutions, because last night you just couldn't tear yourself away from that football game (or other television show or involvement). You knew you'd be tired if you

didn't but hey! the game (or show) was just too good, and
you had to see how it ended. Now you find that you didn't
shave properly (or put your makeup on just right), and
while occupied with this irritating thought, you are frustrated, because you know deep down that you are to
blame for staying up late.

You spill the milk for your cereal over your pants (or
skirt). You rush to change, knowing you're falling further
behind your time as you do. While wondering if you can
make it to your job on time, you begin a familiar self-
dialogue. "Damn, anyway! Why does *everything* happen
to *me*! Just once I'd like to catch a break! But no! The
breaks *always* go to *someone else*! Not to me! *Life is just
so unfair*, I'd like to pack it all in!"

Sound familiar? Sound like the trumpet of randomness
echoing louder and louder throughout your structured,
mental belief system—your subjective synthesis—that
exists beyond your conscious level of awareness? The
belief system that determines how you view yourself,
other people, and the world around you? The belief system
which acts upon you by producing your thoughts and
emotions, which are then played out through your actions,
and that now has been reassured that these events were all
randomly produced, making you their victim?

And since your world is a series of you-never-know-
what-is-going-to-happen-next, the world of others just has
to be the same, and you are about to go out into that free-
for-all, floating crap game again, in order to earn your
daily bread? Is this the type of random state of affairs that
is forced upon you daily in ever increasing numbers,
types, and variations? I'm certain you can see there was no
randomness involved here whatsoever.

Like the well-known domino effect, a single decision,
an event that went against your better judgment, and
worse, went against your past *experience* of similar situations, provided the dynamic series of conditions that got
you into the situation you are in now. All of this could
have been avoided by simply relying upon your past *experience* in similar situations, and by *exercising control* over

your emotions, and not allowing them to override your own experience. Of course there are random events that do not fit the simple model given in the above. But if you look beneath the surface, I assure you that many, if not most, of these obviously random events are not random at all.

What do I mean? How about that automobile of yours that didn't start last winter. You thought the battery was dead, but it turned out to be the alternator. "Well, that's not my fault! It just gave out!" Or did it? Didn't that small red light on your dashboard light up a few times during the fall? And didn't you cancel that scheduled appointment you had with your mechanic a few days after that because "Well, I wanted to go shopping instead and take the family out for a good time." It is simple examples like this that illustrate that if you will just look a bit below the surface, the randomness of many upsetting and frustrating events are not random at all. They are the *effects* of having neglected to exercise control over their *causes* when these causes appeared.

Are there genuine random events? Ones that you are not responsible for in any way whatsoever, that could not have been prevented no matter how hard you tried? Of course there are. Life is filled with them. But in the main, these type of conditions are few and far between, and do not drastically effect you on a daily basis, but rather, usually come upon you by surprise. That is, their causes are genuinely and completely out of your control.

The weather; other people's spontaneous feelings and behavior; new legislation designed behind closed doors and thrust upon you; the errors of others; increasing government bureaucracies; employer downsizing and changes leading to the loss of your job; family issues; the list goes on and on. But overall, what is so very important is that you *skill* yourself in recognizing the difference between truly random events—those whose production you have or had no control over whatsoever—and those that you ultimately caused yourself.

And the requirements for developing this supposed superhuman skill? They are neither mystical nor occult. Rather, all that is required is that you:

- Cease your mental laziness, and force yourself (at first) to look below the surface of those daily frustrating, upsetting, time-and-life consuming events, to identify the real *cause* of your dilemma. This also mandates that you—
- Take *responsibility* for your decisions and actions—or the lack of them!—and stop wallowing in that comfortable state of guilt which affords you the cozy feeling of being the victim.

You will be surprised how quickly you will reach a vastly superior level of self-confidence, while achieving a justified feeling of greater control over your own life. Along with these two powerful personal tools will issue an expanded sense of freedom as you learn to separate the genuinely random events of your life from those that were self-inflicted, and learn to handle the former by using the Kabbalistic Cycles System offered in this book.

And what about order? If our lives are largely filled with self-induced causes of misery and anxiety, added to by external events and the actions of others over which we have no control, how can there be any order in our own personal universe? The answer to this may seem mystical or occult at first glance, but if you follow my explanation closely, I think you will find the answer to be somewhat more straightforward than you originally thought. I say somewhat because the human mind commonly learns new things by first making comparisons to old constructs— concepts and ideas it is already familiar with and has filed away.

This comparison process is a two-edged sword, and the side that cuts away from you is usually the one requiring you to break out of old mental and habit patterns in order to learn new ideas. This is rarely easy to do. With that said, we can look more closely into the actual nature and extent of the randomness, structure, order, and the need for control, that actually surrounds your entire life. Imagine the top of a billiard table. The surface of the table is covered with a fine velvet-like material that has an extremely small coefficient of friction. The ball can move across the surface of the table so effortlessly, it is as if there was no friction between it and the table surface to slow it down. This allows the force that the billiard player applies to the ball through his cue to be imparted almost exclusively to the ball, causing it to go exactly where it is supposed to go as fast as it can. Of course the table top itself is as flat and level as possible, so no other force can substantially interfere with the movement of the balls.

Let our table have four raised, sharp edges surrounding the flat playing surface with marks at equal distances along the length of the edges. These marks are what I will call *Geometric Wells*, because a ball, making contact with the edge of the table at any of these marks, rebounds from that point in a perfect, predetermined, geometric angle. In this way, the billiard player can *control* the angle which the cue ball will travel, attempting to sink as many of the balls as possible into six pockets around the table.

It is this innocuous game that provides a powerful insight into the so-called randomness, structure, order, and the need for control in life. While being metaphorical at first glance, it will be found to be highly informative and pragmatic as it is examined more closely.

Even from a cursory examination of such a simple game, it is not difficult to see that much if not most of the randomness that occurs is under the potential *control* of the player. Such playing factors as stroke-length; the force with which the cue stick hits the ball; the angle between the cue; the way the fingers hold the stick; the ability to judge angles and see the final result of the carry-through— all can be brought under the *control* of the player through the use of analysis, concentration, and practice. It is the same with daily life.

The randomness that you have been taught since childhood as the *rule* for your life is—for the most part—a

convenient lie, designed by others to remove the control
you have over your own life, and place it in the hands of
some quasi-being in the clouds, under the domain of laws
of chance or the government, or most usually, under *their*
control. But as you saw from the earlier examples and
those yet to follow, and as you will soon see for yourself,
these qualities of analysis, concentration, and practice, will
be developed in you using the **Kabbalistic Cycles and the
Mastery of Life System**, enabling you to minimize the
randomness in your life, and gain the *control* over it that
all of us so desperately seek.

In terms of your life structure, just as the four edges of
the billiard table provide a framework for the table surface
—the area of play—so too does the individual's personal
universe provide a framework for his or her area of play,
or daily life. And just what is a this oft touted personal
universe? *It is the sum total of your physical, mental,
emotional, and psychic states of awareness that make up
the conscious, self-determining you at any given moment.*

It is a fact that at any given moment you can exercise
control over any of these states of awareness simply by
deciding to. If you have heartburn, you can take an
antacid. If your mind is fuzzy, you can take a break from
what you are doing, go for a walk, take a nap, and thereby
revive it. If you are upset with your child, spouse, friend,
or neighbor, and are about to go off on them, you can pull
up, walk away, calm down, and return to the problem
after you have exercised your conscious control over your
emotions.

If the senses beyond your five physical senses—the so-
called paranormal senses or faculties—are breaking in on
your consciousness in an uncontrolled fashion and playing
hell with your perceptions of people, things, and life in
general, you can control these too. You can, for example,
seek some training in a form of passive control such as
meditation, whereby you learn to let this inner energy
discharge itself safely, as you simply sit and watch these
impulses within you neutralize themselves.

In any of these cases, it is always *you* who has the ultimate control over those facets of your being, and hence, over your life. So your life structure and your personal universe is always under your direct control to some self-determining degree, whether you want to admit this to yourself or not.

What about the order that was discussed briefly earlier? How does this illustration of billiards extend itself to our understanding of a very fundamental truth which all governments, groups, societies, and most other individuals would have you believe does not and cannot exist in your life? The truth is that order can be brought into your life more easily than you think. It is there for the taking.

We return to the perfectly flat, nearly frictionless surface that allows the billiard balls to move so effortlessly and powerfully toward those geometric wells on the edges of the table. That same level area of play can be created by the individual through the use of analytical thinking in daily affairs, concentration on the task at hand, and practice in applying the first two to any life condition. Why is this? Because analytical thinking forces the individual to see the condition or event for what it actually is, and what forces or factors are really at work in it, instead of what others tell them, or would have them *believe* are operating behind or in a given condition.

When the lucid insight into the situation, brought about by analytical thought, is then wedded to concentration on the matter, *a new state of being is reached.* This state is one the individual will never forget, and which can be repeated at *will.* When this clarity of inner comprehension of such magnitude bursts in upon the mind, an automatic and *always successful* plan for dealing with the condition arrives along with it. It is as if the plan comes from somewhere *outside* of the individual. As this practiced state becomes more frequent in the individual's life, their playing surface or area of play which is their daily life, becomes as level as that of the billiard table. That is, it becomes as predictable and manageable as does the travel of a billiard ball toward one of the geometric wells. Use of the **Kabbalistic**

Cycles and the Mastery of Life System is designed to serve two purposes:

1. It will force the reader's mind into an analytical mode of thought, while gently coaxing the necessary level of concentration.
2. When the analytical thought and concentration are joined through the *application* of the Kabbalistic System itself to any given life event, then an *automatic and always successful plan* will emerge within the mind of the individual, providing him or her with the control over their life they so desperately need and justifiably deserve.

As to the billiard balls, they can be likened to the goals, desires, and aspirations of the individual, as well as to the individual components or events that make up any life condition or situation. Thus, the physical, mental, emotional, and psychic force applied by the individual through the use of the Kabbalistic System can be powerfully transmitted to those goals or events, and effectively direct success.

But what of those geometric wells? How do they fit into this metaphor, and how can we can understand their use in manifesting our will as often as we choose? This is where our metaphor achieves a transformation and takes on the properties of an analogy, one that is extremely applicable to understanding the very basis of the Kabbalistic System presented in this book.

Specifically, the geometric wells of the billiard table correspond to those occult forces that operate in the background, but which influence our lives and daily affairs every bit as much as do those silent, almost-unnoticed marks on the top our billiard table's edges. In this case however, rather than using some so-called New Age mumbo-jumbo to direct our goals and desires toward these occult forces, or more usually, rather than culling them down to achieve them for us, we apply these background energies in an orchestrated way to the problem to be overcome, the goal to be reached, or the desire that is to be fulfilled, all the while remaining the self-determining, self-controlling, conscious beings we truly are.

Consequently, we do not surrender up our goal, our desires, or our wills, by turning our responsibility for manifesting our own creations in our own lives over to some spiritual being or mystical power, as so many of the pop nonsense approaches out there are trying to sell. I guarantee you this. It takes as much precision, analytical thinking, concentration, and practice to use these hidden forces accurately, as it does for the billiard player to direct a ball toward a given geometric well so he can achieve his desired end and win the game. There is no difference here either in our discriminate use of these occult forces so we can win our game, which is the game of life.

As to control, it has already been pointed out to you that you already have it, but due to the propaganda you have been fed most if not all of your life, you have been led to believe you don't have it. When you believe you lack it, you don't use it, and thus allow truly random events and the daily frustrations, impositions, and demands of others to reinforce your belief that they were right all along.

You are the victim of a bummer of a life. Oh really!? You have just as much intrinsic control over yourself at this point, as does the billiard player getting ready to make that special shot. It is the express purpose of this book to convince you of this. As you learn the system taught here, you will be able once and for all, to allay your deepest fears and secret misgivings that you are the plaything of random external and internal events, when you move knowledgeably, intelligently, continually, toward creating the life you want for yourself and for those important to you.

I would like to make a special comment at this point about the concentration part of practicing the analytical thinking/concentration formula discussed here. Do not be fooled by the nonsense you may have come to believe are the conditions necessary to bring about this intense, yet completely natural state. You do not need burning incense, nor do you need to sit in a torturous yoga asana (position).

You do not need to chant an unintelligible word or series of words, supposedly derived from some ancient and strange tongue, or dress in special robes. *All you need to activate concentration is your desire for the object or for a specific result.* This *energy of desire* will reveal the inner mystery so many schools of the New Age would have you believe takes months or years of visualization practice before this gift is conferred upon you. That inner mystery is simply *focus.* The more intense your desire, the more charged with psychic energy of one-pointed intent, the more powerful and directed your focus becomes.

You will find this does not involve visualization or scrying, or any such foolishness as it is preached today. Rather, this focus is *a refined perception of cognition.* It produces a *crystallization of clarity of awareness* through which the end you seek, or the desire you are attempting to manifest becomes so fixed and bright to your mind, emotions and senses, that for you **nothing** exists outside of you and it. That is the entire secret behind concentration.

As you will find out, this is easier to achieve and sustain than you might think possible, especially when you know how to employ those occult forces that pervade and express themselves through all matter, all time, all space, and all human affairs. This knowledge alone, gained from experiencing the accuracy of this system, will forever remove your doubts, and place in your hands one of the most powerful of all human mental abilities that can be easily imported into any other area of your life.

In closing this chapter, I would like to explain something else that, once you have made it part of your mental armada, will go very far toward assisting you to build your own subjective synthesis while gaining *direct* control over your own actions and reactions in your daily life.

It is no mysterious secret, yet it might as well be, because it is something all of us have heard at one time or another. Yet, for some reason, we continually fail to use it. We prefer to suffer and destroy our lives, a little piece at a time, each and every day. It is as if the Christian saying 'Suffering is good for the soul,' has become our delicious justification for victimizing ourselves. Because in truth, that is exactly what we do when we play the role of the victim and martyr ourselves on someone else's cross.

This secret that is so necessary, and which I strongly suggest you ponder carefully as often as you can, is: **No thing or no one can produce an effect within you unless you allow them to.**

All too often we hear the words, "He never does what I ask! He makes me so mad, I could burst!" Or, "She just won't let up! Nag, nag, nag! That's all I ever hear! She's destroying my life!" Then there is the frequent, "I don't know how to handle my boss! He's so demanding, nothing I do is good enough! I never know what to expect!" And let's not forget those all-time favorites, "Why is it always me! Life is just so unfair!" and, "If only my luck would change! Then everything would be alright!"

The hard fact is there is no 'he' or 'she,' there is no 'boss,' there is neither 'unfairness,' nor 'luck.' There is only *you*. Somewhere in *your* mind, *you* have granted power over you to the he's, the she's, the tyrannical bosses, and the ideas of fairness, unfairness and luck. They determine your feelings about yourself and about them, the kind of day you had, and the type of life you will have. You have turned control of your personal universe over to them.

The surprising thing is, it only takes a counter-thought to any of these self-defeating statements to rob them utterly of the power you gave them over you and your life. Yes, you will have to repeat this counter-thought over and over until your subconscious mind accepts it and acts upon it. But after a while, you will find that the he's and she's suddenly become more understanding toward you. That ogre of a boss now seems like just another individual trying to get a fair day's work done.

The unfairness that pressed in upon you from every side, now is seen to be due to your reaction to what you could not control directly, or which you *chose* not to control when you could have. The absence of the good luck you complained about is now understood to be due to action without thought, or acting with insufficient information. In fact, you are in control of every facet of your inner and outer life, and you will come to realize this.

Things not in your best interest will still most certainly continue to occur. But in all cases, *you* control *how they will act upon you,* and in turn, *how you will react to them.* You will be surprised how many of these negative instances will turn out in your favor after all, and how ordered your life will become and in the way you want it to be, as if by 'magic.'

I would like to recommend a book that will help you over this hurdle easily and masterfully, as well as over the obstacle of doubt that is certain to rear up, which will be examined later on. *A New Guide to Rational Living,* by Ellis and Harper,[5] will provide all you need to turn your life around when it comes to control. You might argue, "Hey! I thought this book is about Kabbalistic Cycles and the Mastery of Life! What's this psychological stuff?"

The answer to this is, yes, this book is about Kabbalah and how to use these Cycles, as I call them, to enable you to genuinely master your daily life. But what you may not realize at this point is that Kabbalah includes many correspondences and attributions, all of which, when understood and used properly, will enable you to *build* the life you want. In keeping with this, I have just given you one of those corresponding Kabbalistic tools. In fact, this book could be properly assigned to the Sephiroth Hod and Yesod. The mediating influence, or the result of combining these two influences, being the Path that connects these two Kabbalistic Intelligible forces.

In this case, their mundane result would be 'happiness and contentment.' But we will get to this and the Kabbalistic Cycles themselves in due time. Suffice to say at this point, I wanted to diffuse those possible objections that all too often arise in a reader's mind, simply because they never encountered material that does not fit in conveniently with New Age pabulum. It is all too easy to use your own partially formed, negative subjective synthesis as the lens through which to view and incorrectly pass judgment on new material.

CHAPTER THREE

The Physical and Psychological Basis of the Need for Certainty and Control

Certainty and Control. If ever two words defined and created human history, these are those words. It only takes a little thought to realize that the two are inextricably connected. The need for control is based upon the desire for certainty, and the desire for certainty demands control as the means and method by which this all too human desire can be achieved. If viewed in this light, it becomes obvious that as with the age-old question, "Which came first, the chicken or the egg?" clearly, the desire for certainty arose within mankind as a first impulse.

As a normal human being, you rarely have an opportunity to explore the basis of these underlying causes of the need for certainty and control in life. I say underlying because if truth be known, all of your worldly desires, wants, and needs are actually effects founded upon these two critical, psychologically-structured, life-elements. That is, everything from your inner emotional needs to your external material wants are based upon these two overwhelming psychic forces.

From your need for approval from others, right down to a stable, well-paying job; all are based to some extent upon this need for certainty and the subsequent control that flows from it. When the process works correctly, it enables you to attain the object of your heart's desire. But for most people, this pleasant picture of the working process is only theoretical. Indeed, there are so many hurdles for them to cross, that the process itself becomes lost in the shuffle, and is rarely ever acted upon. What type of hurdles? Here is an illustration.

Amidst the daily ebb and flow of life, you are constantly bombarded on every side by other vested interests that have you questioning if those things you deeply desire are truly in your best interest. This may come from the family who feels financially and socially threatened by your desire to go back to night school to finish that degree you gave up in order to have and support them; to a boss who is worried that the new ideas you are generating now, without that degree, are making his superiors wonder just who is really running the department he is supposedly in charge of; to the next door neighbor who feels threatened when he is told of the new educational goal. After all, for the past twenty years his opinions were just as good as yours because, well, both of you were high school graduates, and just regular Joe's after all, living the same cozy, ignorance is bliss part of the American Dream.

Let's not forget your spiritual involvements and maybe even affiliations that teach you that the world and all of its trappings are simply a veil of tears, while the expounders of such pseudo-self-righteous, hypocritical dogma live the high life in every way possible. Or how about society that tells you from every possible direction that at your age, you should be content to bounce your grandchildren off your knee! Going back to school? A degree? Nonsense! That's not what life is about! You should be content with what you have!

Put very simply, the louts and other members of the social herd have consumed your time, mental and emotional energy, and have successfully managed to sway you from your life's deepest goals more often than you care to admit. At this point, do yourself a favor. Put this book down, sit back, and let your mind roam at will through its corridors of despair; the ones so dimly lit by the final flickering embers of the dreams and goals you sacrificed for the approval and acceptance of those you inwardly know you despise, and yet fear beyond measure. Facing up to *your* part in this pathetic fiasco is the *first* step in extricating yourself, and in enacting your dreams.

The idea that your dreams, wants, desires, and goals are actually based upon your need for certainty and control, can be clearly seen by even the most casual study of history. The anthropological and archeological evidence of the most remote of prehistoric times has finally been woven into the logical fabric of this particular historical episode. Such depictions as presented in the recent award-winning television documentary, *Walking with Cavemen*,[6] reveals that the **need for certainty** in human life began as a **biological reaction** to the dangers of the physical world.

In those earliest days of the human saga, our ancestors and the other humanoid species that did not survive, faced the most hostile and unsympathetic environment imaginable. Certainty became the mechanism by which they could at least try to assure to some small degree that they would survive in their hostile world. But it was not as easy as that. For millions of years, their developing but highly limited thought process prevented them from recognizing the need for Control.

It wasn't until much later that the concept of control dawned upon them and that with this control, a higher degree of certainty could be established that would increase their chances for seeing the next sundown or the next sunrise. Throughout the millennia, their observations of the conditions that defined their environment acted upon them to spark the first glimmerings of connective, cause-and-effect related thought.

They slowly began to realize that certainty to some extent was only achievable if, for example, they banded together into groups. The combined effort of many men hunting, many women bearing young, preparing the food and producing clothing, increased the good of all to a large measure. They came to understand that the lone individual could neither feed or clothe himself properly in order to survive for any length of time. As a given group moved on to new hunting grounds, the new dangers they faced sparked still further cause-and-effect connections, all bringing about new reactions to these latest unique environmental dangers and conditions.

Since the races were in their developmental stage, new realizations initiated by their new reactions, became the stuff of the genetic code that was gradually being developed and passed down to successive generations. This hard-wiring enabled them to pass instinctive reactions down to their offspring, providing them with a foundation for survival that originally was not present in the earliest humankind. Over eons, these qualities—along with further cause and effect thinking—led to more brain and nervous system development: an advanced form of hard-wiring that developed the cortical or thinking area of the brain.

At this point—somewhere around 10,000 B.C.E.—these human-type beings finally realized that without control, their hard-wired need for certainty only provided them with probabilities for survival and growth at best. It took another 5,000 years or so before the honing of this insight could be passed down mechanically by teaching it to successive generations. The hard-wiring due to biological reactions to environmental conditions had taken root, and developed the thinking area of the brain. As a result, the splendor of the civilizations of Egypt, Persia, Syria, and other Mediterranean peoples arose. From this point on, history has recorded the rest.

While attainment of desires, wants, and goals of individuals in these developing civilizations continued to expose them to more physical danger than we see today, the aspirations of the ancients still received their fair share of opposition from others. Competition for food, land, and suitable mates was still at the top of the list. But as times progressed, and farming replaced hunting as both the foundation of, and as a working metaphor for a working society's structure, the more the basic desires mentioned were replaced or became at least as equal as the newly emerging desires for prestige, political power, material wealth, and learning.

As societies continued to evolve and become more complex, the essential survival desires were ultimately replaced almost completely by the more socially materialistic, psychologically-based urges and longings. Just as the physical dangers of the external world produced a conscious awareness of the need for certainty, and in time initiated the need for control to guarantee that certainty while hard-wiring it into the brain, so too did the newly emerging psychologically-based desires and goals become hard-wired into the human brain. The result is the civilization we have today.

What all of this means, besides helping you build a rock-solid subjective synthesis, is that the desires, goals, and wants you have now—just as you are at this very moment—are the effects of your own *biologically-induced hard-wiring, evolved over time to now include psychologically-based needs and desires*. This is essentially the same hard-wiring mental matrix that enabled your distant ancestors to have longings and desires for survival, and later, for emotional, mental, and psychic growth and development.

Despite all of the ravings and interference from any individual, group, government, or institution, you have the *biological right* to your goals, needs, and desires: a new concept and term used here for the first time as far as I am aware. This means that you as a conscious, thinking, self will-determining, self will-directing individual, do not need permission from anyone to attain whatever you deeply desire, and whatever gives *meaning* and *purpose* to your life. Your wants are not a matter of so-called morality, nor of ethics—whatever convenient contrivances those words may hold—depending upon the would-be master who would dissuade you from your goal.

But am I referring to just any desire, perceived need, or goal? Of course not. An individual must be extremely careful when determining what his or her goals and desires truly are. They must not be confused with the arbitrary whims, capricious feelings, illogical notions, or conceited fancies that plague all of us at times. The fortunate part of this determination process is that each and everyone of us does know within our hearts of hearts, what our genuine desires and goals are.

Many times however, these genuine desires can be literally felt as standing at sword's point to our fanciful ideas, flights of fantasy, and egotistical needs. That feeling is your Guardian at the Threshold, as it is sometimes referred to in occult circles, and it will be your best friend and most useful tool at these times. In all cases of its action, this Guardian will produce an uncomfortable reaction in the mind, and a quickening queasiness in the pit of the stomach. When this happens, do not act on the impulse that awakened the Guardian. Rather, when time permits, lock yourself away in some quite place, and begin an examination of your desire, your inner motivations that lie behind it, and the end result the fulfillment of that desire will bring into your life.

Such a self analysis will quickly prove to you the truth of the maxim, "Be careful what you wish for, because you just might get it!" The diligent reader will find that the goals and desires that are important to them are so connected to something within, that the prospect of life without their attainment will be unimaginable. And yet, a number of these inner directed desires, if I may call them that, will be found to be the most simple of all, while many others will be profound and complex.

It is as if nature strikes a balance within the deepest strata of the individual, so that both he or she and the world at large, will benefit from the manifestation of the ends sought. While the further exploration of this problem is beyond the scope of this present book, the diligent reader would do well to study the works recommended below. Some will provide keen insight through an analytical, unemotional process of discernment, while others will address the most basic of human emotions in a gentle, yet clear way. Both of these approaches will go a long way to help the reader avoid the self-sabotage of their most genuine desires and goals—ones that are sure to rear up as the process of self-unfoldment progresses.

As to the recommended readings. First there is *Self-Analysis*, by Karen Horney.[7] This is the only effective text I know of on the subject of self-analysis, at least as far as the classical psychoanalytical procedure is concerned. While cautioning the reader against the limits of the self-analysis process due to the nature of the ego, its techniques for getting to that point are second to none. After that point—as people who have spent twenty years or so going through professional analysis will tell you—the process then becomes redundant and ineffective.

Psychology. The Briefer Course, by William James,[8] is an excellent survey course in the basic practical workings of the subconscious mind. In truth, it provided the working principles for the New Thought Movement that sprang up in the early decades of the twentieth century, the different schools of which are still quite active to this day.

An Elementary Textbook of Psychoanalysis by Charles Brenner,[9] is perhaps the most concise exposition of the nature of the subconscious (unconscious) mind from the Freudian perspective. While Freud's conclusions on the individual being able to be either helped or to help himself out of his psychological quagmires are, in my opinion, fatalistic to a fault, the basic theoretical underpinnings of his work will serve as an excellent reference point, and prevent the reader from getting carried away with some of the more romantic conclusions expounded by William James. Balance is, after all, the most powerful function you can build into your subjective synthesis, and these two views will insure that balance.

Optimal Thinking by Rosalene Glickman,[10] is a book of critical thinking applied to achieving goals and desires. In essence, it arms the reader with the applied logic needed to tunnel through obstacles and reach any serious goal. It is the fulcrum that allows the practical application of James' philosophy and Freud's theories, to achieve a balance. It will also go a long way toward recognizing your self-sabotaging mechanisms, thus aiding you in all areas of life.

I don't know if *The Einstein Factor*, by Win Wenger and Richard Poe[11] will truly prove to be 'a proven method for increasing your intelligence,' as its marketing claims. I do know it provides a wealth of intellectual tools that will provide you with a keen and realistic look into your own mental processes. As such, I highly recommend it.

Maximum Achievement by Brian Tracy[12] is a book that at first sight appears to be one of those pop, quick-fix, self-help expediencies found in any contemporary bookstore. In point of fact, it's just the opposite. It uses modern day language to convey what some will call occult principles, and it does so in such a way as to force the reader to truly and genuinely define not only their deepest goals, but to take charge of their life, while offering them a blueprint to follow to actualize those goals. It also has a unique discussion on the power of the subconscious mind, and the role emotions play in the overall mental/emotional goal-achieving process.

Finally, there is a curious book you probably never heard of: *The Way of a Pilgrim* and *The Pilgrim Continues His Way*, translated by Helen Bacovcin.[13,14] This is a mystical story of the highest caliber. You don't have to concern yourself with the fundamental tenet of the book, the Jesus Prayer, or the Prayer of the Heart. Rather, this true story will provide the inner guidance and direction the astute reader is sure to need, as he or she begins to touch that Divine Center that exists within each of us. The reader will find that this book and the powerful lessons it teaches are every bit as important in attaining goals and desires in this life, as are the philosophical and magical principles contained within the system of Kabbalistic Cycles itself.

CHAPTER FOUR

Exoteric and Esoteric Systems for Increasing Certainty and Control —

An Overview

I n using the term Exoteric, I am referring to a standard dictionary definition of the word meaning: "Comprehensible to or suited to the public; popular." By contrast, the same dictionary source defines the word Esoteric to mean, "Meant for or understood by only a specific group, synonym: mysterious."[15]

Before we explore these concepts and see how they can effect your daily life, let me briefly recap what you have learned to this point. Why is this necessary? Because nothing succeeds solidifying new learning like repetition and rephrasing at critical junctures.

Up to this point, it was established that we humans have a biologically-based need for certainty, and that over millions of years of evolution we found that this need could best be fulfilled through the control of internal and external conditions. We define those conditions as ones that lead to achieving goals necessary for our survival, and fulfilling the desires necessary for our continued growth.

We have also seen that as civilization advanced and developed, the goals, needs and desires of individuals changed to where it is today, with longings diametrically opposed to those of our earliest ancestors. We have also seen how and why our former exclusive physically-based yearnings have today become predominantly psychologically-based, and that as much as our physically-based yearnings became hard-wired into us, so too are our psychologically-based desires and goals equally hard-wired into our cortical scheme. We have concluded that indeed we have a **Biological Right** to every goal, desire, and need that each of us determines is essential for our continued physical survival, as well as for our intellectual development, emotional stability, psychic growth, and overall happiness. If you think about it, you might agree that we humans have traveled a very hard road to get to this point.

It is as if the dawning of the conscious faculty in us has become both our cross to bear, as well as the singular road that leads to the fulfillment of our dreams. It was the advent of this colossal realization in mankind that drove various members of both ancient and modern civilizations to devise systems that would lend control over life's events, so certainty could be established and those important goals and desires could be achieved.

That's what this chapter is about: the exploration of several of these systems in use today. It is necessary that you, the reader, who is beginning to build a subjective synthesis even while reading this book, have more than just an idea of the various systems available. You also need to know what ideas these systems are based upon, and how they work.

Why? The answer to this may be the most important of all. To prevent the most destructive force in human nature from either slowly chipping away or outright destroying your newly formed subconscious belief system that will enable you to effectively use the Kabbalistic Cycles System as taught here. The name of that force is *doubt*. Make no mistake about it. If you have even a grain of doubt about any endeavor, that doubt will eventually manifest itself as the final result of all of your earlier positive efforts.

"That's not fair! This guy is making mountains out of mole hills!" you might object. "Life can't be as one-sided as that!" Oh, no? Let's take two common everyday examples, and see just why life *is* fair, and in fact, why you have no one to blame but *yourself* for the final negative outcome of your overall noble efforts! You've been on the job for a few years now. While you may not have earned any awards as employee of the month or the year, you have been dependable, hard-working, and have built a reputation for being a valuable, productive employee. Then, as so often happens in life, some strange event occurs. Maybe your boss became suddenly ill. Or there was an increase in business that allowed management to begin those new expansion plans it has been talking about for years. Or maybe you hit upon some idea that wound up helping the company in some significant way, and all of a sudden you find yourself standing out from the crowd of your fellow workers. You didn't intend for it to happen, it just did.

One day your boss calls you into his office—or his boss calls both of you into his—and announces that they would like to send you to night school at the local college or university. They want you to get a certificate in this or that, or another degree, so that you can take over when your present boss retires, or in some other way goes up the corporate ladder. Of course, there's a whopping pay raise that goes along with it right now if you accept the offer, and an even bigger raise when you complete the courses or program they want you to take. In short, you are rising from the ranks of lowly worker to middle management!

They ask you to think it over and let them know your decision within a week. Fair enough. You're exhilarated—at first. And why not? You've been waiting for a chance to show them what you're made of for as long as you can remember. Now you have the chance. "Of course I can do it!" you tell yourself. "All it involves is some night school a few times a week, some studying, taking a few tests. Nothing could be as hard as my daily grind on the job—so sure, I can handle it! No problem! This is a once in a lifetime opportunity and I'm going to make the most of it!"

Your confidence level is at an all-time high, and you're ready to make something more out of your life. You discuss your good luck with your mate or significant other, family, friends, and anyone who is important to you who will listen. And even, even with someone you despise, because you want to really irritate them. Then guess what? To your utter surprise, everyone is supportive of you! Why not! You're going to get a fat pay raise right now, just for going back to school! Why, everyone will benefit in one way or another from that alone!

A few days later you announce to management that you are the one they have been looking for, and you accept their offer. You can't wait to begin classes and get your new show on the road! So, you get your pay raise now. It's the beginning of summer, and classes won't start for another eight weeks. In the meantime, besides the extra money, you are enjoying the prestige and envy that goes along with having become the chosen one. Life is great. Or is it?

A few weeks go by, and you receive the information package from the school, fill out the forms, and are careful to check-mark the little box on the application for admission that says your tuition and all fees are being paid by your employer. How good and important you feel, as you should! Another couple of weeks pass, and you receive your registration package. You've been accepted, your company paid the eleven-hundred-and-some-odd dollars for your first two courses, and the outlines for each course are enclosed. But, there's time to look at it.

One day in early August—school's only three weeks off now—you pick up the outlines of the courses and begin to study them seriously. "Gee, I didn't think introductory engineering (or management or accounting) courses were this **hard**! I can't even pronounce some of the words, let alone know what they're talking about! Are they serious?" A little shiver goes through you—the first *doubt*. But you're a grown-up now, and you dismiss it from your mind, *after* arguing with yourself for an hour.

"After all, the teachers are bound to clear up the things I don't understand. It's just a matter of going to class, taking notes, studying, and taking the tests. Nothing to it!" you reassure yourself. "Heck, after all, I did that for twelve years in public school." (and maybe even two or four years in college.) But the next day, at work, images of those twelve years or college days begin to flash through your mind. All of a sudden, the warm, fuzzy memories that normally define those good old days have faded. You see yourself as you truly were, not having done well on many tests. "That's right! I always had a psychological block against taking tests!"

You suddenly remember the long nights studying subjects that were not far from what you will be studying now. They were **hard** subjects you just managed to pass, but never could make any sense out of. Let's not forget the low marks you were afraid to show your parents on your report card either, or the way your classmates viewed you and a few other dummies. "I'm older now," you tell yourself as you wipe the sweat off your forehead, and cool your flushed face with a folded paper fan. "I'll get through this. Have to!"

As the final three weeks before school start to slip by, you notice the work at your job has piled up on your desk. Not because you couldn't do it: you've been doing it for years! But now you're having a rough time of it because the memories of past failures have been flooding your mind. Memories that somehow have come to include many, many other kinds of failures besides your earlier school days.

And you are not the only one who has noticed your drop in productivity. So has your boss. He spoke to you a few times about it and even asked if there was anything wrong that he could help you with. Of course, you could not tell him because that's all you need is for him to find out! So you muddle along, figuring they will cut you some slack in your daily work at the office (or plant or factory) since you are going back to school—and they do.

The first several weeks of classes pass. It went well at first. The bad memories of past academic problems and other difficulties that somehow became associated with those problems and failures subsided. Then something happens on the job that you didn't count on: added responsibility. Your boss didn't tell you they would expect you to begin using your newly acquired knowledge, no matter how basic it is. Their expectations precipitate more work you can't handle.

Memories of those other life difficulties have been reoccurring all along as well, slowing you down even more, while being tied to those still surfacing memories of past academic problems. Everything has intensified. As if things were not bad enough, those night school subjects picked up the pace in order to cover all of the material. Not that you couldn't handle both the job and the studies, if you really tried. If only those damn memories would stop causing you to *doubt* yourself!

The process spirals out of control, and by the end of October, you finally tell your boss you can't do it anymore. "I've had problems with the books before" you explain, "but I thought they were over. I keep remembering the failures I had in school. I just can't get them out of my head. I don't think, or, I *doubt* I can learn this new material. They're going too fast too. And with all of my work here, well, I'm burned out." Then you try to save what little face you have left to save—and maybe your job too—by adding "If I have to choose, I choose my job first. I'm sorry." The company is disappointed, reduces your pay to the original salary, and forgives your failure. You are returned to your former position in the office, factory, or plant, where you spend the rest of your working life being humiliated day in and day out, in one way or another, by the people whose envy you rejoiced just a few months ago.

See what a little doubt will do? Everyone of you can identify with at least some of the elements in this example, and I am willing to bet that not a few of you have a numb feeling inside right now from recollections of your own school and general life failures this story stirred up. All caused by that first flickering ember of *doubt.*

Just in case there are readers who cannot relate to the former academic example, or for those who are more romantically disposed, let's take a look at something everyone can identify with to some extent. You and your wife—or husband, lover, or significant other—have a loving relationship. Both of you have enjoyed the relationship for sometime now, and are quite comfortable with each other. Trust is the name of the game, and the order of the day.

One evening you get home early, only to find your partner talking softly but excitedly, and giggling (or laughing) to someone on the telephone. You can't make out the words, but the tone is one of softness or endearment—you can't be sure. At least it sounds this way to you. Surprised, he or she quickly hangs up, and seems nervous afterwards, like a kid caught with their hand in the cookie jar, is your immediate analysis of the situation.

You're taken aback at the surreal picture you just stepped into. Somehow it doesn't feel right. What's going on here? is the next thought to enter your mind. A tiny *doubt* about your partner's loyalty has crept into your consciousness. Your partner offers an awkward "Hello!" and then what seems like to *you*, a very suspicious, "I didn't expect you home so early!" The scene is uncomfortable, and both of you know it and are fully aware of the other's suspicions. "Who was that on the phone?" you ask in a cautious and yet somewhat demanding tone.

"Uh. Just one of the girls (or guys). You know." The unnatural setting begins to fade as your partner changes the subject to small talk, and you begin to feel better and relate the events of your day. The night wears on and there is an unspoken something between the two of you that *you* can feel, and which you're certain your partner can feel as well. Now you think his or her normal actions and talk are dodges to cover up for what's *really* going on behind your back. Finally, as the night wears on, you put the matter out of your mind, convinced you read too much into it.

You won't admit it to yourself the next day at work, but you just so happen to manage to leave work earlier than normal, and breaking every speed limit on your route home, walk in early. There's no one there, much to your surprise. But beneath the lingering air freshener, you could swear you smell the fading aroma of a cigar (or see a tissue

lying on the edge of the coffee table with a smudge of lip-
stick on it you are sure is not your partner's color.) "What's
going on?" shoots through your mind. "I'm no fool! It
doesn't take a genius to see she (or he) is carrying on
behind my back! Well, when she (or he) gets home, we'll
settle this matter once and for all! If that's the way she (or
he) wants it, then that's the way it'll be!" Of course, your
faint shadow of *doubt* grew. It has convinced you that you
know what's been going on behind your back for a long,
long time.

"Why was I such a fool not to see it sooner?" you mut-
ter under your strained breath, and between the beats of
your furious, pounding heart, as you race up to the bed-
room in a huff, throw open your suitcases, and hastily put
your worldly belongings into them. "Just wait! I *thought*
there was something going on all along! I could *feel* it!
Now I *know* I was right all along!" You race back down-
stairs, your heart in your throat, waiting for the front door
to open and admit your partner.

You're braced for the inevitable confrontation, and the
valley of tears that both of you are about to be plunged
into. A million thoughts run through you mind at warp
speed, the good times together, the love, the trust. How
could she (or he) do this to you? What did you do wrong?
How did it all happen? Just then the telephone rings. It's
your partner. You break out in a cold sweat, as you feel the
blood drain from your face. You didn't expect him or her
to call, and are caught off balance. The voice on the other
end sounds neutral, neither warm and inviting, or hostile
and belligerent.

"I have to see you right away. I'm at Joe's Bar and
Grill. Please come as soon as you can. It's very important!"
You manage to grunt out, "I'll be there as soon as I can,"
and in a daze, hang the phone up. You were right—that is,
your doubt was right. Why didn't you listen to those
promptings it has been giving you all along? "This is it!"
you say aloud to yourself. "She (or he) has put two-and-
two together, and wants a confrontation in a public place.
Probably has her (or his) lover right there, just in case.

Brace yourself, this is it!" The world around you has slipped into a bizarre state of non-reality. Your guilt, fear, confusion, anger, and hate have turned your mind inward upon itself. You don't know how you made it the five miles to Joe's, but here you are. As you approach the front door, you don't see anyone inside. Now you're really upset. Your mind can no longer ask any questions of itself you are so sick with the chain of events. When you open the door and step inside, balloons begin to fall from the ceiling. As they drift through a snow shower of confetti, people jump out from all directions yelling, "Surprise, Bill (or Gale)! Happy Birthday!"

That telephone call, the cigar aroma or lipstick-smudged tissue, and the absence of your partner when you got home today, were the last minute preparations for your surprise birthday party. The one you completely forgot about because of your *doubt*. Can you imagine what would have happened—due to your doubt-energized suspicions—if your partner would have come home and tried to lure you to the surprise party personally? I am certain the reader can imagine the rest.

Have I made my point clear? Any doubt, no matter how seemingly insignificant at first, will erode your subjective synthesis—your subconscious belief system—about any given matter in your life, if you allow it to. It will marshal together all of your weaknesses, from painful memories of past failures and difficult times, to the most negative of human emotions that have survived the development of our rational thinking ability, and which still play hell with our lives today. This doubt will destroy that which you most want and cherish above all else. A grim conclusion, but as you know from your own experience, one that is most true.

How can you eliminate doubt in any area of your life, and principally in those areas that are most certainly dominated by your subjective beliefs? If you think about it, and go back over those successful ventures, experiences, and victories you have had in the past—and your involvement with their current counterparts in which you continue to excel to this very day—you will find the process of eliminating doubt quite rational and easy after all. All it requires is:

1. Knowledge.
2. Understanding.
3. Intellectual and Emotional Acceptance of similar past failures.
4. Experience and Experiential Knowledge.
5. Application.
6. Self-Trust.

After learning the details of a particular situation or field of interest, and thinking it through from various angles, you come to understand just what it is about. But that is not enough. (Actually, with only knowledge and understanding, doubts will quickly and frequently arise from what you have learned, and the understanding that flows from the learning. Why does this occur? It occurs due to that portion of your mind that refuses to learn new things. It is your ego, the part of you that wants to just play, have fun, and not be accountable for anything. You see, when you learn new material of any kind, this ego knows it must be brought under further control if you are to use this new knowledge and understanding, and it initially objects to this.)

Next, it is important that you go back into your memory to literally dig up your failures in similar circumstances, and accept them for what they were: painful experiences that occurred during earlier periods of your life. During your younger days—even as 'long ago' as last week—you were not as skilled and proficient in handling life's matters well. The intellectual part of this acceptance comes easily. But when you try to accept these failures *emotionally*—that is, accept the emotions that are tied to them—you will find you will have to struggle with them for awhile.

If you continue with this struggle while following the principles laid down in the classic text, *A New Guide to*

Rational Living, that I cited in chapter two, I assure you that within a few short weeks you will discharge most if not all of that painful emotional energy tied to those destructive memories.

Now you must gain experience in the issue, whether it is taking those night school courses, or living with a partner, or whatever. This experience will open up a new kind of knowledge for you, knowledge not found in a book. This *experiential knowledge* can only arise from experiencing the condition itself. Then it becomes necessary for you to apply these new features of your life stream. That is, they must be put into action—*applied* to the task at hand.

For instance, in the case of the employee whose doubt destroyed his opportunity for the life he wanted, the individual in that example could have applied his or her new course knowledge and understanding of the material to their daily work immediately. If it required some extra hours without pay, so be it. After all, that person was trying to build a new life! Doing so, the course material would have made more sense, and with the doubt all but vaporized, things would have fallen into place more easily than many would believe. Finally, the individual would have found that the combination of the new knowledge, understanding, acceptance of past failures, the experience gained and the experiential knowledge that arose from it, along with the application, would have actually triggered self-trust automatically. An entirely new life would have 'magically' opened up to them.

Now you see why this seeming digression from the main topic of this chapter was necessary. *Unless the reader understands the essential nature of the human mind in these matters of control, certainty, and building a new life by the use of the Kabbalistic Cycles, all of the 'meat' material of the Cycles' chapters will avail them nothing.* With this new insight into the mental processes and phenomena that you will be involved with—and which you actually have been involved with throughout your life whether you knew it or not—we can move on to the core material of this chapter proper.

At the beginning of this chapter I noted that the word Exoteric is generally defined as comprehensible to or suited to the public; popular. In the arena of the human need for certainty and control, the methods and techniques that have evolved to satisfy these drives are often referred to as 'the ways of the world.' Everyone of us knows them more or less, because we really haven't pinned them down or given them much thought. They are the generalities you hear and all too often use yourself, to account for someone else's good, usually at your expense.

These would include phrases like, "It's not what you know, it's who you know," or, "The one thing you can say about luck is that it's sure to change," and, "Guess my best wasn't good enough!" Sayings like these are actually the products or *effects* of social and personal *causes* that are rooted in the Exoteric System itself. Even though this system was designed for achieving certainty by supposedly allowing you to exercise control over your own internal conditions (goals, desires, wants), and the external conditions (job, family, friends) that will enable you to fulfill those dreams of yours, it has produced these side effects that serve as props when the system doesn't work.

This being the case, it is always better to have more than a general idea about any issue or matter; especially if your life revolves around it, or depends upon it in some significant way. Of course, the need for certainty and control in achieving what you want in life is no exception, so we are going to take a closer look at these social and personal devices now.

EXOTERIC SYSTEMS

• **It's not what you know, it's who you know!** This is one of my all-time favorites. It's a like an antonym, and a self-serving reason (excuse) at the same time. Just as opposites are shown by, for example, the word 'wet,' which is an antonym of the word 'dry,' this phrase is meant to deride someone by implying he or she is not as good as you, and yet, got the job, promotion, or what have you. At the same time, it acts as a self-serving reason for your failure. You were the better candidate—and of course your listener knows this!—but, well, you just didn't know the right people. But underlying the superficial use of this cliché in daily life, is a call to action.

This exoteric method of increasing certainty is telling you that if you learn to 'know the right people' your fortune can most assuredly be made. You'll climb the corporate ladder, attract the best, prettiest (or handsomest) mate, get the right house, have the most respectful and brightest children—the list goes on and on. Naturally, this social method leading to the good life requires that you become who you are not. But then, that's not so hard to do. Or is it.

Just because this approach requires you to smile when you don't feel like it, laugh at the simplistic, moronic jokes of your boss at the company party and on a daily basis, spend what little free time you have down at the office looking busy, or playing golf with your supervisor—none or all of these and a host of other 'techniques' *really* don't make you a phony. Or do they? And don't forget. These same 'who you know' or 'right people' people—even though you humiliated yourself countless times in order to get them to like you—will still require that *you do them a favor first*. This is actually the largest part of paying your dues to belong to their right people club.

But, you may ask yourself, "How can I do anything of any significance to help them? I'm trying to be accepted and approved of by them, so they can help me! Heck! I'm a nobody right now, so how is this thing going to work in *my* favor?" The answer, of course, is that it can't. Yes, the right people will use and abuse you for their own tawdry, little ends. But when you have given them all you have to give; when the last shred of your integrity, dignity, and self-confidence has been martyred by *you* on their altar of 'making it to the top,' and that big job, promotion, or favorite son (or daughter) title is now the big prize on their country club stage of life, you can rest assured—you won't get it.

Why? For all the reasons just discussed. You see, the right people are not the fools or supplicating kind you thought they were. They are good at what they do, that's how they got there. They will use you and what you have to offer, and in the end, give your brass ring to some other favorite son or daughter to keep it in the club. Let's face it. All of us have been there. Each and every one of us has humiliated ourselves to some extent or another, trying to play this loser game. Despondent, self-rejected from having bastardized our finest qualities, we turned away, but always trying to find another sure fire ways-of-the-world (Exoteric System) method for getting the Good in this life that we have earnestly and diligently worked toward for decades.

• **Hard Work.** This, by far, is the greatest lie ever foisted upon the diligent, struggling individual. It is the literal coin-of-the-realm through which companies, corporations, institutions, and governments carry on their daily activities of 'providing equality for all.' It is based upon yet another glaring deception in the promenade of the American Dream: that there is justice for all. How many times have you heard—from childhood through the present day—"If you keep your nose to the grindstone and work hard, you'll succeed! You'll make it right to the top! I guarantee it!"

Yet you work and work. You even help your company out by taking your vacation time when it is best for them, rather than when you want it. You may have increased your overall efficiency, and become more effective at your job, and have been complimented for it. You have been told what a valuable employee you are, and the next time that pay raise comes along, you're in for a surprise. Of course the surprise does come. You receive the exact same raise percentage as everyone else, including that guy (or gal) across the hall who has been given a written warning that one more foul up, and they will be fired.

You might even go so far as to complain to your boss, and ask what happened. His stoic reply, "I know. Sorry. It's the economy. Times are tough. It's all *they*—notice how he suddenly separated himself from the management he is an integral part of—could afford. But don't worry! *Next time....*" But that next time never comes.

Or a new position has opened up in your company. It was made for you. It requires all of the talents, skills, and abilities you have amply demonstrated day in and day out for years. Your boss winks at you and smiles when you tell him you are going to apply. You're a cinch to get it. Why did they even ask for applicants to fill it, you wonder? Surely, they know what I have been doing! Of course. It's that blasted Equal Opportunity Employment thing again. Oh well. No one is better for that position than me, EOE or not. The company would never actually hire someone from the outside to comply with such a stupid, unfair practice.

Then the announcement comes. In your company's quest to fly the American flag higher, their new politically correct, socially responsible strategies demanded they hire the right kind of individual from the outside. But there is good news for all—even for you, crushed by the news. This new hiring policy paid off! Because of this strategic move, the company landed a whopping new government contract! Everyone will benefit—sooner or later. That is, after they drive the last nail in your coffin of human trust by coming to you and asking you to train the new person for that new position.

Eventually you learn. It may take five years, or ten, or twenty, but you learn that where you are now is where you will be when retirement time comes around. They will give you that equally cliché-ish gold pocket watch if you're lucky, a pat on the back, and then "See ya!"

Or maybe after five or ten years at company A, you didn't quite learn your lesson, and thought the grass would be greener on the other side. So you switched to company B. Well, after another five or ten years there, bringing your skills from company A to your new job, and working as hard and diligently as you could for your new savior, I'm willing to bet you finally learned the truth. Hard work gets you a hand-to-mouth paycheck, and that is all. No glory, no admiration, no big promotions, no job security, no place in the corporate, factory, or assembly line sun.

So you finally settle in, accept your lot in life, and become another faceless name in the work-a-day world. Hard work only helps those directly above you in any position in life. Yet by no means am I advocating anything less than a fair day's work for a fair day's pay. But remember, the old-time ethic of hard work has been butchered beyond all recognition in this so-called New America, and it will *never* give you *equal* reward for *equal* effort.

• **"You need more education!"** Yes, in one form or another, all of us have heard this one, and will throughout our lives. From your employer who has to prove to newly emerging businesses that his people are up to the task of doing their type of work; to your mate, family member, or other interest who has encouraged you to better yourself in order to bring home more money for this-and-that 'necessity' of life; right through to yourself, wondering if perhaps more education might not be the way to go to make your life better in so many ways.

Somewhere in those four small words—You need more education—must lie the Keys to the Kingdom of happiness and success. In truth, those four words most definitely *can* contain those Keys. More education is a priceless asset to any individual if it is used for: self-enrichment; to train the mind to be more analytical and to genuinely appreciate the finer things in life such as a good book or the wonders of nature; or to acquire some specialized knowledge to start a business or to indulge in some hobby or activity that provides one with happiness and contentment.

Certainly, education can most definitely help the hard working person to further their skills or professional career. But here, only if certain conditions are fulfilled, and those to the letter. The example of the young man or woman who was offered advancement by taking a night school course was one instance. In such a case, by doing 'A'—getting the certificate or degree—the individual would get 'B'—the promotion and pay raise, while attaining no small measure of job security.

All too often however, we humans have a way of playing very hurtful games with ourselves. Here, it would be the game of I Won't Tell if You Won't Tell. That is, rather than sitting down with your employer and discussing the possibilities of obtaining more relevant education at your own expense, you deceive yourself into believing that if you gain further education in the area in which you are working, they would have to give you a promotion, raise, and pretty much whatever else you wanted within reason. Notice, by within reason, I mean *your* reason.

In ninety-nine out of one hundred cases, such blindsiding will always result in tremendous disappointment, along with a huge college or Vo Tech student loan to be repaid. I caution the reader not to laugh at this scenario. This game is more prevalent than you might think. It doesn't simply apply to those people caught up in the work-a-day world of nine-to-five, but to any activity.

For instance, consider the case of the college student who thinks the bachelor degree isn't enough, and goes merrily on for a masters or a doctorate without having the slightest idea what the employment or academic markets are like now, or what the projected needs of those markets are likely to be when they finally get their advanced degree. Or how about the scenario of the weekend mechanic who thinks that after a few years of auto shop at the local Vo Tech school he can open his own garage and become a success overnight.

Of all the Exoteric Systems for increasing certainty through establishing control, this method is by far the best and most effective. But as I warned, it has very specific conditions attached to it, all of which must be carefully and rationally considered and planned before this technique will yield successful and favorable results for the individual.

There are, of course, an almost infinite number of other Exoteric Systems out there. From, "Save your money," to "Invest your money *wisely*," to what I call the Bookstore Traps that promise you *the* answer as to how you can—in effect—increase your certainty by controlling others, albeit indirectly. This can include such books and tapes as *How to Win Friends and Influence People,*[16] all the way to such books as *How to Hypnotize Yourself and Others.*[17] Such approaches fall into the cheap trick category, as I call it.

While an exhaustive account of these ploys are beyond the scope of this book, I have provided you with what I have found to be the most common and most damaging of the Exoteric Systems. In the process of highlighting these systems, I think you will find your subjective synthesis to be that much better off. I say this because now those ill-defined ideas and concepts upon which these lies are built, have been exposed a little. With some work on your part—that is, **thinking this material through**—this understanding will quickly find its way into your subconscious belief system. And along with the conditions and the cautions regarding them, you will find yourself to be far better off than you were before. In short, you won't be so readily and willingly deceived by them.

Truly, those rational, thinking individuals who gave their best for ten, twenty, or more years to the Exoteric System—and who are now reading this book because of the failure of that system to deliver what it promises—probably made a leap of faith. I prefer to think of it as the Fire and Brimstone leap. These individuals no doubt went on by offering themselves over to some religious belief. More than likely they were as diligent in this practice as they were following the precepts of the Exoteric System.

Yet the results never came. Indeed, the Fire and Brimstone leap had them believing and eventually accepting the inevitable. Their reward would come in the next life, while the priest, minister, reverend, and rabbi barkers of those spiritual con games told them what to do, and controlled their lives in the here and now. It lasted, for awhile.

But the blissful state of ignorance and blind trust in the Halls of Hallelujah eventually faded, leaving the determined individual seeking other tools for making their own heaven on earth a reality. Such people are completely justified in having crossed over to the occult, or to the Esoteric System as it can also be termed, which I defined earlier as that which is considered strange or mysterious by a given people or society.

As with the Exoteric System, the Esoteric System will now be explored at some length, in order to insure the reader's own state of subjective synthesis is being properly built up as they go along. Vague thoughts, incomplete concepts, and half-formed ideas as to any of these methods of the Esoteric System are more lethal than those of the Exoteric System. This is because each of the methods that come under the umbrella of this system are effective to some extent. That is the danger. They work partially, but never completely, or they work in specific instances and require much preparation, and thus are not available for immediate use.

They are also not capable of independent verification. Any two people using any given method never get the same results. Some methods lack predictability and repeatability, which eventually causes the individual to run around in confused circles of doubt, desperately trying to force a given method or methods to work with at least some degree of regularity. Usually, because the individual has found the Exoteric System to fail completely, and the Religion Trap to be empty, they remain with the Esoteric System, darting and flashing from one method to another, in order to gain some measure of control, and thereby achieve some degree of certainty in their lives. Keeping these factors in mind, let us turn our attention to the components of the Esoteric System.

 • **Astrology**. In his splendid reference book, *The New Encyclopedia of the Occult*,[18] John Michael Greer essentially summed up the classical definition of this branch of Esotericism as, "The art and science of divination according to the position of sun, moon, planets, and stars relative to a position on the surface of the Earth." I would add to that definition, in an attempt to understand one's own nature, and to predict trends and potentials in the occurrence of future events.

The fact is, however, that while this well-meant, millennium-old human practice does indeed have an operational base and a genuine usefulness in occult activities, it is useless as a means of establishing any degree of certainty in one's daily life. I say this because astrology is—properly speaking—neither a science nor an art, although it does require artful interpretation in order render any use from it. Nevertheless, its chief usefulness throughout the centuries has been to forecast major events for royalty.

On a more practical level, it has been used to determine the times of important religious holidays and national celebrations. As the forerunner of modern astronomy, it was also used to predict the most favorable times for planting food, for harvesting, and for assuring the most auspicious times for the private practice of magical rituals and ceremonies by the priesthood of various cultures. It was only much later that the study and application-proper of the tenets of astrology taken up by practicing medieval, Western European magicians, was directed toward more personal ends.

But the various astrological systems upon which these uses hinged—along with their rigorous methods of calculations, the calendars upon which those calculations were based, and the theoretical base of the interpretations themselves—have become buried among the miasma of pop-culture astrology publications found in any bookstore today. One has only to meticulously study Henry Cornelius Agrippa's, *Three Books of Occult Philosophy*,[19] to see how convenient extractions have been made from that work, and applied to the so-called New Age Astrology.

Always, the excuse given by these purveyors of the modern day astrological hard-sell is, "Well, you know, everything changes! And of course, that includes astrology, its base of understanding, and of course the new interpretations needed so we can apply it to our new-spangled, teckie era of bigger, faster, cheaper, more of the same! After all, everything evolves! Everyone knows that!" I don't, and I'll wager that neither do you.

In fact, the principles of any science or art do not change, in and of themselves. Newton's Laws of Motion—despite our fascination with Quantum Mechanics—are still used to run the macroscopic world you and I live in everyday, in addition to being the sole physical laws employed to get our space probes from this planet to any other. Only human purposes and designs for their use changes, and these, according to the unstable, light-speed fluctuations of the times. But the Laws themselves, and their straightforward interpretation? No. These do *not* change!

Yet other almost unknown approaches to this stellar study, such as *Mazzaroth—The Constellations, Parts I–IV, including Mizraim: Astronomy of Egypt,*[20] by Frances Rolleston, reveals a completely different approach to the underlying theory of the practice of this art, and serves to further illustrate the fragmented, personal, teckie systems of astrology that have arisen over the past forty-or-so-odd years.

Nevertheless, regardless of these problems in functional differences, astrology is founded on the idea that for any given moment in time, the placement of the stars and planets in the constellations, the angles made between the planets (their aspects), the placement of the zodiacal signs in the Houses, and a vast myriad of other conditions or components, all lend themselves to interpretation. In theory, the state of the heavens can be used to: gain insight into one's inner or psychic nature, personality, or spiritual makeup; predict the outcome of some event in the material world; or provide the best time for one to begin an important action.

Any and all uses to which astrology is to be put however, are always to be referenced back to the individual's natal chart. In the case of such a chart, its individual components—along with the blended overall meaning of those components and their effects on one another—are fashioned into a type of map of the occult forces that were in motion at the moment the individual took his or her first breath of life. This event—and the forces in operation at

the time—were, or will be contained in the heavens and
reflected in the chart, which can be interpreted and understood by an astrologer.

This same idea applies to any other event as well. For
example: The individual wanting to find the best time to
start a business, would have an astrologer erect his or her
natal chart, interpret it, and either reference it to a chart of
the time the business is to be started, or find the best time
for the venture to begin. A progressed chart would also
have to be constructed, and it—along with the natal chart
and chart of the forces in effect at the time of beginning the
enterprise—are closely compared, analyzed, and interpreted by the astrologer.

An additional chart, referred to as a horary chart, cast
for the exact moment the question was asked, could also
be constructed and used in the overall analysis. But even
here, there are no guarantees, owing once again to the state
of subjective synthesis of the astrologer. As in all matters
occult, the subconscious belief system of the individual
directly effects the result produced: in this case, the accuracy of the chart, and the interpretation produced from it.

The crux of astrology—its central thesis—is that the
universe is seen to be an expression of a matrix of complex,
occult forces that pervade all matter, all time, all space, and
all events. These same forces and their energy content
which flow through stars and planets are, by the theory of
correspondence, believed to also influence the mental,
emotional, psychic and physical nature of individual
human beings. This is in keeping with the occult maxim,
that which is above, is like that which is below, and that
which is below, is like that which is above.

The movements of the heavens are also reflected in
events occurring on the earth. In turn, these forces effect all
manifestation: from the birth of the individual; to the ideal
time of conceiving a child; to starting a business; to making
any major decision, or indeed, beginning any important
action. Perhaps the reader can now see why the current
trend of reading one's daily horoscope in a newspaper,
monthly magazine, or any of the readily available pocket

books designed to give guidance for all individuals who come under any one of the twelve signs of the zodiac, is an exercise in futility and absolute ignorance. Responsibly, the serious use of astrology in daily life requires it be limited to major events in the life of the individual, and that a reliable, exact, and thorough natal chart be erected for the person, based upon his or her exact time and place of birth, along with the appropriate progressed chart, a chart for any specific event, and even a horary chart if so desired. The initiated practice of astrology is an important and powerful tool when confined to Ceremonial, Ritual, Talismanic Magic, or any of the major events that will surely arise in life. Its contemporary use in finding the best time to go out to dinner, make a hair salon appointment, or ask your boss for a raise, are absurd. For all of these reasons then, it is virtually impossible to apply astrology to the concerns of daily life. This is especially true for many of those concerns that come upon the individual spontaneously, since the exercise of this discipline requires so much advanced preparation.

• **Rosicrucian Daily Cycles**. It usually comes as quite a surprise to most present day hardcore occultists when they hear that this system is in widespread use today. In his book, *Self Mastery and Fate with the Cycles of Life*,[21] H. Spencer Lewis, the former Imperator of the Rosicrucian Order (AMORC) for North and South America, deals with what he terms Daily Cycles, along with other cycles in human life. The testament to the popularity of this book is made plain by the fact it has gone through over thirty editions since it first appeared in October 1929.

In his chapters on the daily cycles, Lewis divides each of the seven days of the week into seven periods, each period ruled by one of the original 'Seven Planets of the Ancients,' as they are termed in occult literature. These would be the Sun, Mercury, the Moon, Venus, Mars, Saturn, and Jupiter. Each period is then divided into three hours and twenty-five minutes, and labeled period number 1 through 7 inclusive. But Lewis does not admit that his daily cyclic system is actually based upon classical astrological lines. Instead of stating the planets that rule each of the periods, he assigns the letters 'A' through 'G' to them, unnecessarily confusing the issue. In actuality, his schema corresponds to:

• Period A = Sun
• Period B = Venus
• Period C = Mercury
• Period D = Moon
• Period E = Saturn
• Period F = Jupiter
• Period G = Mars

He also employs the convention of beginning each day at midnight. That is, he assigns midnight as 'Period No. 1' to the hours midnight to 3:25 AM. The astute student however, will quickly see that it is Period No. 2 which is actually assigned the planet ruling the day and that in fact, this second period, from 3:25 to 6:51 AM encompasses the time of sunrise for nearly any day of the year; a property of his attempted *a priori* system which again reveals the astrological basis of the Daily Cycles structure.

For example: On Sunday, the letter 'G' or Mars, is assigned to Period 1. Yet during Period 2, the letter assigned is 'A', which of course is the Sun, and the classical ruler of the day of Sunday. Lewis also provides a description of each of the letter designations, which again are exact corollaries of the attributes and influences the Seven Planets of the Ancients. While his descriptions of the planetary influences are good, there is—in my opinion—too much frequent overlap of the attributions between planets, as well as over generalized explanations of what can and cannot be done during a given planet's influence.

Nevertheless, the system is workable, and has its devotees. Having tested this system consistently over a twenty-year period, however, I have never found it to yield very dependable results over prolonged periods of time. This is another way of saying that the results achieved using this schema have always been just a little better than what could have been attributed to the laws of chance. In my opinion, while this system is simple to use, it is not very dependable. Additionally, other occult colleagues have also received the same results over extended periods of testing.

Since the basis of this system is a greatly watered-down type of astrology, I cannot in all honesty recommend it as something for the reader to hang his or her hat on. (As an aside, I do, however, recommend that the interested reader obtain further information on the Rosicrucian Order, AMORC, from the Order itself. Despite the New Age 'spiritual giants' that decry all of the Order's mystical teachings, I for one have found them to be extremely practical and very effective for incorporating into one's personal eclectic philosophical system, and quite frankly, second to none in content, breadth, and depth of coverage. As with any system, mystical order, or metaphysical society, there are always difficulties, and such is the case with their Self Mastery and Fate Cycles System. Nevertheless, their overall program is very effective, and I heartily recommend readers so moved to investigate the Order further.)

• *I Ching.* As the Richard Wilhelm translation of the *I Ching*[22] explains, "The Book of Changes" is a Chinese divinatory system whose roots extend backward into the remote, legendary past. Throughout its three millennium history, the most profound philosophical and theological thought of these people has been hammered out and presented in this book of wisdom.

In its more pragmatic aspects, "The Book of Oracles" was a collection of straight lines that were quite literally used as oracles. 'Yes' was indicated by a single unbroken line, [—] while a 'No' response was suggested by a simple broken line, [– –]. No doubt, as time went on, and the questions posed by the querent became more complex, the lines were combined into pairs. To each of these pairs, a third line was added. Eight trigrams, each consisting of a combination of three solid, broken, or solid and broken line combinations, thus became generated. These trigrams came to represent all phenomena that occurs both in heaven and upon earth. Each of these eight geometric figures were also imbued with a name, attribute, image, and family relationship.

For example: In the trigram, K'un, the name is 'The Receptive,' the attribute is 'Devoted, yielding,' the image is 'Earth,' and the family relationship is 'Mother.' At some later point in time however, these eight trigrams were combined to produce a total of sixty-four figures, each of which consists of six lines, thus producing a total of sixty-four hexagrams which form the basis of the I Ching system of divination. The study of this amazing system of wisdom and divination is well worth the interested reader's attention, although as with any other system, a great deal of effort will have to be expended in order to grasp its fundamental concepts.

As in astrology, where ever-changing aspects between planets are understood to mirror the continual changes going on in the heavens and upon the earth in the lives of people, the 'I' (abbreviated form of the I Ching used in conversation and pronounced 'Ye'), also mirrors these states of continual transition, one state or phenomenon changing into another, as occurs moment-by-moment in our physical universe.

Also like astrology, the 'I' does not focus on things or events as they are, but rather upon their movements through change, thus giving the querent a potential-to-kinetic view into the event. Hence, the eight trigrams do not represent things or events as being fixed, but rather, their tendencies or the potential for manifestation that they contain in those movements. The same is true of course, for the final resulting hexagrams. The reader can see—as with astrology—the theory behind the I Ching becomes complex, as do the interpretations of the hexagrams: a matter that is as completely dependent upon the state of subjective synthesis of the diviner, as it is in astrology.

As to the method of the divination. While the generation of the hexagrams was originally based upon casting 49 yarrow stalks, once again, New Age prophets have devised 'simpler' methods for obtaining 'quick' hexagrams, along with ready-reference books that are supposed to provide instant interpretations. There are even computer programs available, based upon an internal random number generator program, that will produce hexagrams in response to your questions, and then interpret them for you! And there are other methods of casting the 'I' as well, such as the coin-toss and roll-of-the dice methods.

Naturally, when you get your results, you have only to look up the meanings in your handy, dandy $3.95 reference book. You see my point. At the risk of being redundant through repetition, I will say it again. *There are no easy ways to learn and effectively use any divinatory system, that is, if you are fortunate enough to find one that works consistently, immediately, ever-available to you at a moment's notice, and something you can hang your hat on.*

Divination takes study. It requires you to build a strong, precise state of subjective synthesis. It requires energy. It takes work. This Kabbalistic System provided herein will take care of the first set of conditions just stated. You will have to supply the second set. But if you do, I guarantee you, you will be able to chart your course through life with an effectiveness and efficiency second to none. As you will soon see, the results you get will convince you of this within a single day.

• **Crystal Pendulum Divination.** Although it is quite obvious that the sudden onset of an important or critical situation that requires immediate action makes this type of divination a near-impossibility, its widespread use demands that it be reviewed here.

An entire cult-type mentality has arisen within the past twenty-or-so odd years around the use of crystals. Today's New Age market is overflowing with crystals of different mineral-type compositions, sizes, shapes, clarities, and densities, each 'designed' to 'insure' the attainment of some end. From wealth and health to love; from the constructive to the destructive; from the ethereal to the practical, these treasures of nature have found their way into the dust bins of many, if not most of today's homes. And their use in divination has not been overlooked. The mechanical use of a crystal for divinatory purposes is rather simple and straightforward. The crystal is suspended—usually by some expensive gold or silver chain which supposedly helps the crystal to 'work better'—over a circular or rectangular cardboard template or pattern. The template contains the letters 'A' through 'Z,' the numbers '1' through '10,' 'Yes' and 'No', and can even be individually styled to include planetary symbols and zodiacal signs.

While resting their elbow on a table surface, the inquirer drops their hand at the wrist to form a right angle to their arm, with the pendant chain being held between their thumb and index finger. The crystal at the end of the chain then hangs suspended above the template. A question is asked, and without any apparent or observable movement of the arm or fingers, the crystal begins to move in the space above the template in straight lines, circles, or both, spelling out, giving a numerical answer or indicating a Yes or No response to the question, or providing some other indication that will satisfy the demand made upon it.

Whether the querent holds to the underlying theory that it is micro-muscular movements in the arm and fingers, used by the subconscious mind to communicate the answer via the responses given by the crystal/board combination, or that some spiritual entity is providing the energy to move the crystal pendulum, matters little. Once again, it is the state of the subjective synthesis of the individual that is the operational factor here: that set of unified, mutually-supporting, structured beliefs that are held as 'truth' by the inquirer's deeper mind that makes all of the difference as to the accuracy and repeatability of this method of divination.

While I have experimented extensively with this procedure, and (perhaps) spent more time than I should have on building my own state of subjective synthesis as to the underlying theory of this phenomenon that I favor, I have not found its results to be either consistently reliable or reproducible. They were much better than those achieved with the Rosicrucian Daily Cycles, but again, were nothing I could 'hang my hat on' in the majority of important or critical situations.

And as with the method of the astrology and the I Ching, unless one intends to carry around the equipment needed to employ this form of divination, make excuses to sneak away somewhere and use it before making a decision or acting to resolve some situation, I would not recommend this as a method by which the individual charts his or her life, or to make important daily decisions.

• **The Tarot.** As in the case of the I Ching, this form of divine wisdom has been butchered beyond recognition by the New Age prophets. But, as with the I Ching, it does have a self-declared practical side. That is, it can most certainly and legitimately be used as a system of divination. This type of divination, *depending upon the precision and completeness of the subjective state of the individual,* **can** be used to provide effective, efficient, and to a significant degree, repeatable *guidance* in daily life matters.

I use the term *guidance* as opposed to *answers*, because, as with the I Ching—and with correctly executed astrology for that matter—the Tarot *can* provide penetrating and startling insight into the ever-changing occult flux of forces that underlie and influence human life. This subject is so important that I have chosen to give a more complete rendition of it further on in this book. But for now, the reader may find the following to be of immediate use and merit in making plans.

Please remember, however, that as in the case of astrology and the I Ching, the Tarot requires some set up time. The Tarot does not provide any reaction time for many, if not most of the human conditions and crises that must be dealt with immediately, or with decisions which must be made on the spot.

Either you confine its use exclusively to the more important questions of life that can be divined in advance or use it to plan a course of action in some upcoming matter, or else be prepared to carry the items needed around with you, and somehow try to sneak off, cast a spread as it is called, and quickly try to interpret it. In this case, you are still up against it, because the added pressure of this routine will destroy the quiet, meditative and reflective state of mind needed to make an accurate reading. With that said, realize that this method of divination is powerful, and can yield dependable results over long periods of time.

The Tarot is a pictorial symbol system believed by some to portray the Mysteries of God, the deepest secrets underlying the nature of mankind and the universe, and the relation and interactions between the three. It is my contention that there are no absolute meanings behind the symbolism of the cards. Rather, according to the state of subjective synthesis achieved by the occultist, the cards do become imbued with the complex, ever-changing flux of ideas and psychic energy of the individual, which then serve not only as an accurate divinatory system, but which enable one to develop their psychic faculties and mystical natures to an exceptionally high degree.

The most popular version of the Tarot in use over the past ninety-or-so years has been the Rider-Waite deck, produced by Arthur Edward Waite and Pamela Colman Smith, both of whom were members of the Victorian magical society, the Golden Dawn. Since its release in 1910, it quickly became the preferred deck of occultists; not simply for its clean yet complex renditions of the mystical ideas expressed by Waite and others of that magical society, but because the deck's publication was accompanied by the book, *The Pictorial Key to the Tarot*,[23] written by Waite himself, which explains clearly how to use the cards.

As an idea sourcebook, there is no other like it, and it is highly recommended to the interested reader. This book not only explains how to use the deck, but presents the deeper metaphysical meanings behind the images, which were then stepped down or stylized into the more pragmatic meanings used in the divination of more mundane matters, and which are discussed in the book in Part Three, "The Outer Method of the Oracles".

The deck itself contains two Arcana or sets of Mysteries. The Greater Arcana or Trumps Major, consists of twenty-two cards, and the Lesser Arcana or Trumps Minor, has fifty-six cards divided into four suits: Wands, Cups, Swords, and Pentacles, each suit of which contains fourteen cards. For detailed readings, all seventy-eight cards, that is both the Major and Minor Arcana are utilized, although many other methods have been devised over the past century that apply only the twenty-two cards of the Greater Arcana, many of which produce quite good results.

Other decks have surfaced over the past fifty-odd years as well. Such decks as the BOTA—"Builders of the Adytum"—the deck designed by Paul Foster Case, the Golden Dawn deck, along with numerous Wiccan, Pagan, and Egyptian decks, to name just a few. Some are based on the seventy-eight card format of the Rider-Waite deck, others have as few as thirty cards, or as many as one-hundred and forty! To be sure, all have their devotees, who insist in one way or another that theirs is the true or correct deck, and offer 'proof' through their own a priori system of assuming what they are trying to prove.

The greatest offender in this regard, in my opinion, are those that herald the Golden Dawn deck as the beginning and end of all true wisdom. Enough said. Suffice it to say that I have found the Rider-Waite deck, and the methods of the spreads advocated by Waite in his book, to constitute a legitimate, accurate, and repeatable system of divination.

• **Cheap Magic**. You've seen them. You may even have spent your hard earned money on more of them than you care to admit, especially to yourself. Those 'magic made easy' books that are so proudly featured as full page advertisements in the occult equivalent of a supermarket sex-and-scandal tabloid: the New Age Journals. These are poorly disguised catalogs of the latest Magic and Wiccan fads that denigrate the legitimate practice of these forms of Divine Worship and human Becoming.

Usually they occupy the last several pages of such journals, right next to the classified ads section whose wares promise you the sun, the moon, and all of the stars on the golden platter of your choice. These magical grimoires and wiccan spellbooks usually sell for ten to twenty dollars each, with page after page guaranteeing you utter and absolute success from the systems they are pushing in this month's issue.

Whether its advertisers are in Europe or in America, the process is so simple, they will have you wondering why you didn't think of that before you get to the end of their hard sell. But after you finish reading the high-pressured sell, you suddenly realize, well, kind of suspect because of what it *seems* to imply, that this book is something special. You could try to do yourself what it's telling you it will do for you, but there's just something about it that makes you reach into your wallet and all but beg them to take your money so you can have your heart's desire.

You may even go out late that night, and mail your cash, check, or money order to 'the address given below,' anxious to start your new life. Oh. Just to be sure, you opted for airmail delivery, which was a mere fifty-percent or more of the book price itself. But hey! What the heck! The sooner it comes in, the sooner your dreams can be fulfilled. Never mind all that nonsense and hard work, building states of subjective synthesis and testing other systems in order to gain insight into who you are, and map your way through life on a daily basis! Every fool knows it can't be that hard!

Lo and behold, your book arrives. You notice the shipping only cost four dollars but they charged you ten. Hmmm. Then you wonder why it looks a little skimpy for twenty bucks, but maybe that's because the book isn't as big as you *thought* the advertisement said it was! Geeze. Seventy pages, stapled inside a thin cardboard cover that has a hand drawn picture on it. Oh well. You have your magic key now, and that's all that matters!

So off you go, doing what you now realize you could not have done on your own after all, because the ritual is so secret. Heck, you couldn't have known all this! So maybe the ritual in your secret grimoire tells you to find a small creek out in the woods, and at sunset—or sunrise— sit next to it, and read, uh, powerfully 'command' the water elves to bring you this or that (never mind that these living, intelligent, incredibly powerful beings are actually elemental, water Undines, not 'elves,' and 'commanding' them is certainly not the way to go about interacting with them.) You know all of this of course, because you are not exactly a neophyte when it comes to such matters. But hey! Maybe this is something new! You are so right. It is.

Now you are beginning to wonder as the first doubts sneak across the screen of your mind, but no, never mind. After all, you don't want to get the water elves mad at you. So you wait a day, and then three, which stretches into a week, and then into two weeks. Nothing has happened. That is, nothing except—*maybe*—your hot water heater burst for no apparent reason, your washing machine leaked gallons of soapy water all over the laundry room but only once, because it's alright now, and come to think of it, there were a few other problems, all of a water nature.

Could you have done something wrong in the 'ritual?' Did you get the water elves mad at you? Put simply, play with fire in an ignorant way, and yes, you will get burned. As you did. You're out another three hundred for the hot water heater, another seventy-five bucks for the plumber, and you don't want to even think of adding up the rest of the money the other water-related incidents cost you. Two weeks later, you look back on it all, wiser, wondering if anyone was fool enough to dig your copy of that 'amazing grimoire' out of your trash where you placed it. In truth, there are no short-cuts to living a happy, structured, confident life. That type of instant magic doesn't exist, and I'll wager it never will.

If the above scenario sounds all too true for you, please know that I am not making fun of you. The you in the previous example is a generic one which applies to *all* of us who have been desperately trying to find a way to add certainty and control to our lives. All of us have done the kind of things portrayed in the above example, including myself, many years ago. And yes, there are those of us who have done such stupid things many, many times over, always trying to find the Magic Key for our lives. All were born out of states of despair and crisis, out of times of utter desperation. But we did learn—in time. That is the reason you are reading this book now.

You want something that will work, and it will be given to you here, soon, in the pages to follow. So forget all of the cheap magic. It doesn't exist. Not in this world, or in any other. But mind you, it does work in making people rich—the charlatans who write the books. And always from the never-ending stream of fools who buy them, looking for a quick fix for their desperate lives.

• **Other Divinatory Methods.** There are probably as many different methods of divination as there are desires among humankind. No doubt many have been lost in the dark walkways of the past, while others enjoy popularity in the present. Such systems as divination by Celtic and Germanic Runes, crystal gazing, scrying in anything from a magic mirror to a bowl of clear or colored water, to the sophisticated and complex methods of Geomantic Divination and an advanced form of astrology known as Astro-Cyclic Pulsations. All are interesting, intriguing, and have their role to play in the field of occult literature, and in the life of the individual practitioner who undertakes the *serious* study and experimentation of one or more such forms of inquiry.

However, as with most of the others discussed in this chapter, all require advanced planning, or make it necessary for the individual to carry around the equipment needed to work the system. For example, dice, Tarot Cards, Yarrow Stalks, Runes, or boards and the particular devices each of those approaches require for working. All in all then, the general esoteric systems in popular use today present more mechanical difficulty in their immediate use than at first appears, while still requiring an effective synthesis be achieved by the inquirer before they will work with any degree of effectiveness, efficiency, and repeatability. And as we have seen, each system also poses its own limits.

For example, the extreme complexity of astrology mandates that it be used almost exclusively for gaining insight into the Self, and for determining the potentials that do or will exist, primarily in major life events. Another example can be found in the daily use of the I Ching. This system's deep philosophical base, coupled to an exceedingly intricate symbol-interpretation system, can literally lead the less knowledgeable querent into flights of sheer fantasy, rather than provide reliable quick answers to daily life situations. Finally, the spreads of the Tarot require time, planning, and extensive study, if the guidance obtained from the spreads are to be of any value.

It is important for the reader to understand that it was not and is not my intention to run down any of the legitimate systems of divinatory inquiry covered here, nor to cast aspersions upon practitioners who are adamant about adopting or using any of these systems. Far from it. My caustic remarks—as those readers who have been reading with an open mind have no doubt guessed—are directed completely to the tawdry *use* to which these systems have been put by those instant gratification demanding individuals who think they have a divine right to have an easy life, and who believe that control and certainty just must be for them, no matter what.

To this type of individual—who through some stroke of endurance may have made it thus far into this book— my advice is that you put it on your bookshelf, along with all of your other dreams of an easy out. But to those of you who are prepared to *make* your life what you *will* it to be, I invite you to continue on. You will not be disappointed!

In closing this chapter, there are a few details that should be cleared up. As you have noticed, with the exception of the Esoteric Method of Cheap Magic, all of the models discussed here have been placed into the Divination category. Such a classification might be obvious for such systems as the I Ching and the Tarot, while this label may not be so apparent when applied to, for example, Astrology. Nevertheless, when each technique is used in an attempt to forecast or extract information about some future event, the individual is indeed attempting to divine (gain foreknowledge) of circumstances or trends prior to their advent in the empirical world. This is the act of divination.

All too often, however, the concept of divination is confused with the act of fortune-telling, which is an attempt to gain foreknowledge about a future event which *will* take place. Notice I said *will* take place. There's the rub. There is a vast difference between fortune-telling and legitimate divination. Fortune-telling seeks to *guarantee* some future outcome or the occurrence of some yet-to-be event. Divination, on the other hand, seeks to provide insight into the *possibilities* and *probabilities* of future occurrences, if the conditions that exist at the moment the question is asked are maintained 'as is.'

That is, divination recognizes the ever-shifting and changing mundane and occult forces contained within a specific question, and will even address these matters depending upon the spread used. Thus, it asserts the Free Will of the individual, and his or her ability to change the forces operating in the question. Fortune-telling does not.

Fortune-telling assumes the future is secure, or already exists out there, just waiting for the individual to enter it. It is based upon the concept of Predestination, which denies the existence of the individual's Free Will. Hence, divination can be though of as fluid, fortune-telling as fixed.

As to the Kabbalistic Cycles System, as with divination, it recognizes the Free Will of the individual at all times, while taking into consideration the fluidic nature of all mundane and occult phenomena that enter into any life situation. Unlike divination however, it allows for very rapid planning, both of short-term as well as long-term goals, while providing an instantaneous method by which one can successfully react to those eventualities of life that spring up out of nowhere. It is also unlike divination in that it is not designed to offer depth insight into the operations of the Self, nor to be used as a meditative system whereby one can enter into contact with other intelligences. Instead, the Kabbalistic Cycles System was designed as a practical tool to help the individual navigate and map his or her way through life on a daily basis. This is its strength, and its sole purpose.

CHAPTER FIVE

A Kabbalistic Primer for the Attainment of Control and Certainty

I t is not simply the reader's state of subjective synthesis that will determine how accurately the Kabbalistic Cycles System will work, as important as this state is. The conscious knowledge of the Kabbalah, which includes its history, structure, the operational characteristics of its practical components, i.e., the Sephiroth, Paths, and their attributions, will likewise have an equal and direct bearing upon the accuracy of the interpretations the individual derives from the will-full use of the Kabbalistic Cycles System.

In this latter regard, put simply, the more the reader knows of these matters, the more stable and complete his or her subjective state will be, and the more practical knowledge he or she will have to consciously draw upon in order to make an immediate and accurate interpretation of the occult influences operating in any life condition. In order to provide the reader with a comprehensive overview of the Kabbalah (also spelled Kabalah, Qabalah, and Cabala, depending upon the occult subject in which it is discussed), this chapter will be devoted to presenting an extensive discussion of what I consider to be *Classical Kabbalah*.

Owing to my feelings regarding the New Age and its schizophrenic, quick-fix, instant gratification mentality toward occult subjects, I will have nothing to do with a patchwork approach to the subject. My other reason for doing this is that throughout my past forty years in the occult in general and magic in particular, I have found that nearly all of my students became attuned, if you will, to the more rigorous approach to the Kabbalah, provided they started with the classical presentation of the subject immediately.

Other students who already had somewhat of a background in the Qabalah, as the New Age denotes the subject, found they preferred the classical approach, as they were more capable of integrating the disconnected bits and pieces of Kabbalistic thought than when they studied New Age Qabalistic doctrine which treated the subject incompletely or mistreated it altogether.

Since it is my intent to get the reader started now on building their state of subjective synthesis, while also laying a solid, conscious foundation of knowledge, I strongly suggest studying this chapter carefully. If you do, you will be well on your way to achieving these ends. You may even come to realize that the Kabbalah is not as confusing, boring, or impossibly nebulous as many bemoan it to be. The few books mentioned along the way are highly recommended.

Regardless of the connectivity and depth of the Kabbalistic issues covered in this chapter, it is not possible to completely cover the Kabbalah in a book not exclusively devoted to the subject. Even one book devoted to the matter is well nigh impossible. It will take an assiduous study of several of the recommended books, over time, for the individual to ferret out the priceless gems of knowledge that are contained within the Heart of Kabbalah.

As such, these recommendations are provided as resource musts. Hence, by studying and contemplating them, the individual will continue to deepen his or her understanding of this incredibly important subject. In turn, these further explorations of Kabbalah will expand the reader's conscious understanding and subconscious comprehension of this subject, giving rise to one of the most powerful, practical life tools imaginable.

THE CLASSICAL KABBALAH—AN OVERVIEW

As to the word Kabbalah itself, it specifically refers to a collection of religious writings, meaning, doctrines received through tradition. However, it was not until around circa 1200 C.E. that the term Kabbalah designated this complete, self-contained system of theosophy. In my opinion, the Kabbalah can be called a doctrine of Jewish Occultism, the bedrock of which is founded upon Hebrew Mysticism. There is a difference here, and it would do the reader well to further contemplate this subtlety.

From a historical perspective, the main canons employed to create the Kabbalah were the *Zohar,* or the *Book of Splendor,* a large tomb of books dealing with mysticism, and the *Sepher Yetzirah,* or the *Book of Formation,* which is actually a synthesis of medieval mysticism and scientific thought. The date of origin of this latter work has been contested for millennium, but from all historical accounts, it seems to have originated before 800 C.E.

More legendary views hold that one rabbi by the name of Simeon bar Yochai, along with his son, hid from the Romans in a cave for thirteen years. Being highly learned in the mysticism of their people, the rabbi and his son produced both the *Zohar* and the *Sepher Yetzirah* during that thirteen-year period of seclusion. It is said the books were written by them around circa 100 C.E., and that the content of the *Zohar* is actually a written account of the dialogues that took place between God and Adam, while Adam was still in paradise.

Most modern authorities however, hold to the view that the *Zohar,* which was popularized around 1200 C.E. by one Moses de Leon, was actually authored by him. Even so, it contains an enormous number of important and ancient mystical insights, speculations, and wisdom traditions of the Hebrew people. The *Zohar,* a rather substantial collection of writing, is actually a set of commentaries on another important Hebrew text, the *Pentateuch.*

The *Zohar* includes eleven dissertations on the *Pentateuch,* of which the *Secret of Secrets,* the *Book of Secrets,* the *Mysteries of the Pentateuch,* and the *Hidden Interpretation* are believed by many to be the most important of those writings.

As a system of theosophy, the Kabbalah deals with the nature of God, the ten 'spheres of divine emanations' radiating from God (which are referred to as Sephiroth in a plural sense, and as Sephirah when speaking of a single sphere or divine emanation), along with the natures of angelic beings, man, and the worlds or aspects of the Intelligible and the Sensible, as these latter relate to the Sephirothal concepts. (While the concepts of Intelligible and Sensible are considered by some to be advanced Kabbalistic concepts, I view them as properly belonging to the more rigorous *Classical Kabbalah*).

I have presented them here and have tried to integrate them in such a way as to lend a more rounded, extensive explanation of the subject. While most of the discussion that follows in this section has been drawn from Classical Kabbalah directly, other parts were derived from my own mystical and meditative introspections, and from personal experimental work in the fields of Kabbalah, Magic, and the Occult in general.

By creating a synthesis of these intellectual, mystical, and occult experiences, it is my intention to help the reader further their own understanding of this fascinating and practical theosophy in a more holistic manner, yet not compromise the essential tenets of the Kabbalah. You will discover sufficient repetition, both in different ways and in different places as a learning aid.

The ten divine emanations, *through* their Intelligible and Sensible manifestations in both concept and form respectively, are represented by a geometrical figure of ten circles or spheres, connected to each other in a precise pattern of twenty-two lines or Paths, as Figure 1 illustrates.

These paths represent the specific relation that any two or more spheres so connected bear to each other. They represent the particular interconnectedness that exists between the attributes, correspondences, and concepts that those spheres or Sephiroth represent in both the Intelligible and Sensible worlds.

The Intelligible world can be thought of as the realm of pure abstraction of a specific attribute manifested by God, or a particular behavior in which God involves Itself. The very idea of the pure abstraction of a concept or behavior enables the higher aspect of that attribute or behavior to become comprehensible to the limited mentality of the human mind. Put another way, by understanding that some abstraction exists behind the normal or casual meaning of a concept, the individual realizes there is some ethereal aspect of that attribute or behavior implied, beyond which the concept is taken to mean in the everyday world of humankind. Hence the meaning behind the term Intelligible.

The manifestations of attributes or properties of God are ten in number, and exist as Intelligible, pure abstractions of particular aspects of God, which are brought down into conceptual form for mankind's understanding through Divine Revelation and the Mystical Experience of Union with the Divine. These abstractions are rendered more comprehensible and actually manifest in Creation *through* the Sensible nature of each Sephirah, and through the twenty-two interconnecting Paths.

In the Kabbalistic context, the idea of Sensible refers to the manifestations and laws of Nature, and the methods by which Nature brings about form in the physical world. But also in Kabbalistic terms, the idea of Sensible moves beyond this. It also designates those ideas, perceptions, mental constructs, activities, and actions, by which we as humankind, superficially react, act, and interact with Nature.

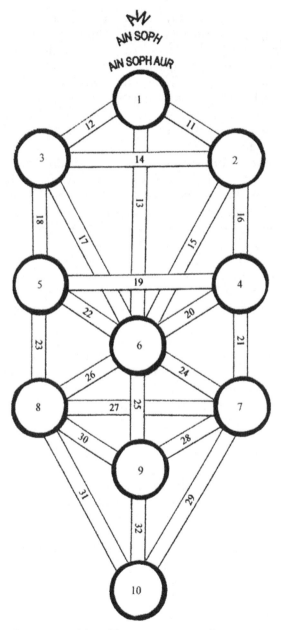

FIGURE 1. THE TREE OF LIFE. GLYPH 1.

It can be Nature out there, as, for instance, in our passing appreciation of a breathtaking sunset, or within our own minds, when we struggle to understand something about the workings of Nature out there or of our own human nature. In a way, the Sensible can be thought of as a kind of Divine superficiality brought down to earth. It forms our universe, all aspects of Nature, along with the laws of Nature as they operate—both *within* and *without* our bodies and *everyday* minds.

By contrast, our divine inheritance as Creations of God, enables us to reach up through our daily nature and through mystical, meditative, or magical techniques, extend ourselves upward, and share some aspect of the Intelligible by comprehending, understanding, and finally apprehending something that cannot be formed into words, but only experienced in the silence of experience.

As an example. The causal appreciation of that magnificent sunset can be transformed from a Sensible *event* into a transcendent Intelligible *experience* if—through some technique—the beauty and grandeur of that sunset effects us at all levels of our complex existence, and produces something more within us. This would be something we *experience*, but cannot express in words. While this may appear to be doubletalk or confusing at first, if the reader will take a line at a time and think through these perhaps unfamiliar terms and ideas, he or she will readily grasp the basics.

Remember. When attempting to put that which is transcendent into words, difficulties must, by definition, arise. Why? Because when the reader contemplates these words of explanation, a transition is being attempted to move from the Sensible to the Intelligible itself. But once achieved, it becomes a matter of course for the reader to continue the process, building or adding to his or her Kabbalistic knowledge foundation, depending upon previous familiarity with the subject. In the process, the individual's state of subjective synthesis becomes so enhanced that their results from the use of the System of Kabbalistic Cycles will be assured.

In Classical Kabbalah, three fundamental ideas are considered first. They are referred to as the **Three Veils of the Unmanifest**, namely, the **Ain**, the **Ain Soph**, and the **Ain Soph Aur**. The Ain—the Nothingness—is the Causeless Cause of all causes. It simply was and is. It is not a being. It is not even a Nothing, but rather, it is *No-Thing*. As the *Zohar* explains, "Before having created any shape in the world, before having produced any form, HE was alone, without form, resembling nothing. Who could comprehend HIM, as HE then was, before creation, since HE had no form?" HE is that which is incomprehensible and unknowable, and as such, HE does not exist.

But this Unknowable, conceived of IT-SELF as the **AIN Soph**—Infinity—in order to be comprehensible to ITSELF. It then became the **Ain Soph Aur**—or Absolute Boundless Light—a limitless Existence-Ideation. (Here, the concept of Ideation is taken to mean something that is imagined in the mind. A mind-construct with or without plan, according to the impulses of the Ideationist.) It contains the entire universe, while yet pervading every part of it.

This Existence-Ideation also includes all that is manifest and unmanifest, including all forms of light, energy, matter, space, time, mind, being, etc. IT is so boundless, and ITS nature so unknown, that the mind of man cannot conceive of IT, any more than it can of the **Ain Soph,** which is Infinity itself. Because IT not only contains all of that which has been made manifest, and in principle also contains that which at any moment is as yet unmanifest, in a certain mystical sense, this IT is also nonexistent.

In the process of apprehending ITS Own Existence-Ideation, (here, to apprehend means to become conscious of; to understand through a profundity not within normal perceptual definition and experience), this IT—this Ain Soph Aur—became alive and creative in order to give meaning to, and to project that meaning of ITS existence. IT did this is in a dynamic sense, by projecting the ten Sephiroth—also referred to as Intelligences in Kabbalistic literature—through which IT could express its dynamism into the world of the unmanifest (non-form) and the manifest (the world of form).

From the root No-Thing, the Ain, the Nothingness, and through its progressions, the Glyph of the Tree of Life sprang into form, a symbolic model of the forms, forces, life, and ideation of the One Existence-Ideation. The Glyph became the medium through which God *as* the Existence-Ideation, or the IT, was able to become active, reactive, and create within its own Creation. The IT could only produce and project that which was and is of its own nature.

ITS first manifestation was as the Kether, the primal root source from which all issues and from which all will issue in the Intelligible and Sensible worlds. All must spring from it. It is indivisible and without dimension, yet it gives rise to all. It is the essential point of generation of all physical things, as well as the point of origin of all consciousness.

Kether, in all of its correspondences and concepts, represents and is itself all unification, and all indivisibility. It is ever in motion. It is the core of all life, and the metaphysical focus of all spiritual energy and beings. Mankind's Sensible perception of this first Sephirah has been made into the concept of the God of the physical universe, or the representation of that desire the IT had to become manifest. As ITS Nature was apprehended completely unto itself both before, during, and after assuming the form of the Crown, it contained within it the other nine Sephiroth or Intelligences of the Tree of Life, each of which emanates from the previous one.

In other words, the second Sephirah proceeded from the first, the third from the second, the fourth from the third and so on, throughout the entire number sequence until the final expression was achieved in the tenth sphere, Malkuth. The Kabbalistic names of each, beginning at the top of the Glyph and following down in descending order are: Kether (the Crown; The Father), Chokmah (Wisdom; The Son), Binah (Understanding; The Mother), Chesed (Mercy), Geburah (Severity), Tiphareth (Beauty), Netzach

(Victory), Hod (Glory), Yesod (Foundation), and Malkuth (Kingdom; the world of matter, the world of form).

It must be remembered that these are the pure abstractions or Intelligible concepts. They are the purest forms of attributes which flow from God. The more mundane forms, the Sensible qualities that mankind can understand, are the stepped-down qualities that have their roots in each of these pure abstractions.

Another fundamental attribute assigned to the Sephiroth of the basic Tree of Life glyph are numerical correspondences. That is, Kether = One (1), Chokmah = Two (2), Binah = Three (3), Chesed = Four (4), Geburah = Five (5), Tiphareth = Six (6), Netzach = Seven (7), Hod = Eight (8), Yesod = Nine (9), and Malkuth = Ten (10). Beyond Kether, in emptiness or beyond or above—as the student may wish to imagine them in order to comprehend in human terms the structural arrangement of the Tree and its point of origin—exists the lowest of the Three Veils of the Unmanifest that were mentioned earlier.

That is, the Ain Soph Aur, the first of the Three Veils, followed by the Ain Soph, which is the second of the Three Veils and which can be thought of as being behind or above the Ain Soph Aur, and finally at some remote, non-conceptual point beyond or above the Ain Soph, the third and highest of the Three Veils, the Ain. In the case of Ain, its numerical correspondence is zero (0). Please refer to Figure 1 for a graphical representation of the these Three Veils of the Unmanifest.

Owing to the individual Intelligible and Sensible natures of the ten Sephiroth, the Kabbalah postulates them as existing within four planes or Four Worlds of being. Atziluth is the highest of the Worlds, and through its Intelligible nature, it corresponds to the realm of Divine Being. As that abstraction of the Intelligible which mankind can comprehend, it is said to correspond with the ideas of Jung's Archetypal World.

The next lower world is Briah, or the World of Creation, followed by Yetzirah, the World of Formation. The Worlds are said to end in Assiah, the World of Matter.

There are two methods by which Kabbalists schematically represent the placement of the Four Worlds on the Tree of Life. I refer to them as the overt method of placement and the occult method of placement.

In the occult method of placement, the *Zohar* assigns an entire tree of ten Sephiroth to each of the Four Worlds of the Kabbalah. This placement is extremely important from a theoretical and theosophical point of view, but becomes rather complex, at least as far as working out the preliminary pattern is concerned. As such, it is beyond the scope of this present book. The overt method of placement is much simpler, and may serve better for a graphical comprehension of the Four Worlds.

In this method, Kether is the sole Sephirah that occupies the World of Atziluth. It is the root of all, and projects the other nine Sephiroth from itself, with Atziluth being the divine or archetypal realm of being in which Kether exists. The next World, Briah, the Creative World, is occupied by Chokmah and Binah. In Briah, we have the realm of pure idea and universal potency or force, energizing all. As Atziluth is the realm of pure being or divinity, Briah is the plane of the archangelic beings, into whose hands the ceaseless ordering of the patterns underlying Creation have been entrusted.

Yetzirah—the World of Formation—consists of the Sephiroth: Chesed, Geburah, Tiphareth, Netzach, Hod, and Yesod. That is, Sephiroth numbers Four (4) through Nine (9). It is the World of rarefied matter and energy, of force and form, electric, manifesting in various subtle levels; it is the region in which the tenuous states of rarefied energy and matter constantly transition back and forth between one another. This is the angelic world of existence, whose governance is always in accord with the laws operating at this plane of Creation. All are coalesced in the lowest of the Four Worlds, the World of Assiah, the world of physical form, and the energy that underlies the gross expression of this three-dimensional form. In short, Assiah is the material world within which we live and move on a daily basis, and in which we have our normal sensory or conscious awareness.

It within this fold of the Kabbalistic Tree of Life, with its Four Worlds and the Three Veils of the Unmanifest that the practical Kabbalist or Mystic or Magician works. But for our more intensely practical application—while realizing that a theoretical knowledge of these features of the Kabbalah are also strictly necessary and must be obtained by the student over time—our concern will now focus on the more mundane characteristics of the Tree: the Sensible characteristics, forces, and attributions of the ten Sephiroth and the Twenty-Two Paths that interconnect them.

First, however, as promised, the list of musts that will help the reader attain this necessary theoretical knowledge of the Kabbalah. Remember, these readings will neither be fully understood nor comprehended by you in a conscious sense during a single reading, or even after many years of assiduous study. But as the root of all extends into Kether, so too will your labors and growing, conscious, understanding extend into the deepest recesses of your subjective mind.

There, they will rapidly form a coherent, potent, energy-center of inner light and form that will influence you daily, permitting you to effectively work the Kabbalistic Cycles System, and do so much more in your life. Yet even all of this will only be the beginning of the many blessings this inner comprehension will bestow upon you and the affairs of your daily life.

(While complete publication details of each of the following can be found in the Reference List at the end of this book, I have added a commentary to each one here, in order to help the reader through the seeming maze of available Kabbalistic literature. It would also be a good idea to begin to acquire these books at this juncture.)

A Garden of Pomegranates,[24] by Israel Regardie, offers a comprehensive view of the Kabbalah. It cites correspondences, attributes, and meanings of the components of the Tree from many different perspectives, thereby lending the new student insight into the importance and application of the Kabbalah. For the seasoned student, it will serve as an excellent refresher, while perhaps throwing new light on old concepts.

The Essential Kabbalah—The Heart of Jewish Mysticism,[25] by Daniel C. Matt, is an extraordinary book, giving an accurate and precise overview of the main tenets of Kabbalah. It should be studied in concert with Regardie's book.

Following this, Dion Fortune's *The Mystical Qabalah,*[26] should be carefully read and compared with Regardie's text. Despite New Age claims as to it being a dated approach, all of the material it presents is accurate—with but one issue I take strong exception to, and which is discussed later on. Her work is clear, and thoroughly presented within a well-designed framework.

Sepher Yetzirah, The Book of Creation,[27] by Aryeh Kaplan could be studied with profit. It sheds a great deal of light on the mystical as well as magical aspects of Kabbalah, and suggests that the text can be used to develop the individual's powers of concentration, telekinesis, and telepathy (notice these are psychic faculties, not the oft touted spiritual powers.) It is unusual to say the least. But in my opinion, it too is an extraordinarily valuable book.

Zohar, The Book of Splendor—Basic Readings from the Kabbalah,[28] edited by Gershom Scholem, is important for its peculiar insights into this ancient text. It could be studied after Regardie's, Matt's, Kaplan's, and Fortune's books.

De Arte Cabalistica—On the Art of the Kabbalah,[29] by Johann Reuchlin, is one of the most important texts on the subject that has ever been penned. Dating back to the 16th century, its knowledge is available today in a reprint edition. This text should be studied by itself, after the sequence of the former books has been gone through.

In the 19th century, the great Occultist, Eliphas Levi, wrote a three volume discourse on the mysteries of occultism. Of those three volumes, the first two are important for our purposes. Levi's first volume, *The Book of Splendours,*[30] and his second volume in the trilogy, *The Mysteries of the*

Qabalah,[31] could be studied one at a time after completing Reuchlin's work.

Finally, there is the magnificent production, *The Holy Kabbalah,*[32] by Arthur Edward Waite. Despite the ranting of his intellectually deficient New Age detractors, the complexity of Waite's work—as opposed to his verbosity as his critics so love to label that complexity—is worth every bit of effort. His compound, shaded meanings within a single sentence; the structure of his rigor in presentation; his syntactical maneuvering—all leave no stone unturned in any of the occult subjects of which he wrote, and all make this the final text the diligent reader should study.

Throughout these readings, I strongly recommend Greer's *The New Encyclopedia of the Occult.*[18, (Chpt 4)] Its 2003 copyright does not betray its content, as so many of the current books in this genre do. It is extremely well structured, very complete, exceptionally accurate, and allows for ease of cross-referencing. Consider it your road map through the vast expanse of Kabbalistic literature. It will take time and hard mental effort, to be sure. But then, that's what Kabbalah—as with the rest of life—is all about.

THE SEPHIROTH

In this section, we will lay the groundwork for those aspects of the Kabbalah—as contained in the Tree of Life proper—that will be built up into the Kabbalistic Cycles System throughout the remaining chapters of this book. Each of the ten Sephiroth will be explored. Both Intellectual and Sensible qualities and correspondences of each Sephirah will be given. As we progress throughout our derivation of the Kabbalistic Cycles System, the qualities and correspondences will be narrowed down into the Sensible characteristics and aspects exclusively. Where appropriate, a Commentary has been added to elucidate points that might be confusing, or which can pose later problems when studying Kabbalah.

In the next chapter, we will add *the* fundamental correspondence traditionally assigned to the Paths, after which the reader's newly acquired knowledge of the Tree of Life will then be used to build the Kabbalistic Cycles System itself, step-by-step. As in advanced mathematics, when we begin with postulates and proceed through a logical formalism, we eventually arrive at a specific method of solution for a *set* of problems being analyzed. In like manner, this approach applied to the Tree will illustrate the obvious nature of the Kabbalistic Cycles System. This system will then become apparent to the reader, never to be forgotten, lending itself to a direct and accurate application in daily life.

Only a very limited number of attributions and qualities of the Sephiroth are given below. The reader's study of the recommended texts will expand this list, along with a comprehension of the concepts. As the study of those other texts continues, your understanding and apprehension will increase exponentially. Please remember I did not invent the attributions of the Sephiroth given below. They are general characteristics of the spheres, cited and distributed in one form or another throughout occult, magical, mystical, and metaphysical literature.

KETHER

Number on the Tree: One (1). *Primary Title*: Crown. *Other Titles*: the Inscrutable Monad; the Macroprosopus which, according to the *Zohar*, is The Great Countenance; in terms of the Christian trinity-theology and Neoplatonic cosmology from which the Christian idea of the Trinity was derived, Kether is the Father, or the First Existence; also The Ancient of Ancient; The Ancient of Days; The Head which is not; according to the *Sepher Yetzirah*, the Admirable of Hidden Intelligence; the Primordial Point. *Astrological Attribution*: the Primum Mobile, or that which is called the Beginnings of Turnings. *Intelligible Quality*: The First Cause; the Root of all things; the Initial Unity that was, is, and will be, and from which all else proceeds. *Peak Human Experience of this Sephirah*: Union with God. *Sensible Qualities*: As assigned by humankind for magical purposes, the God of the physical universe; the divine component, or the spark of divinity within the individual; the spiritual essence of the individual. *Color on the Tree*: white. *Color Scale*: In Atziluth, pure brilliance. In Briah, its color appears as a brilliant white. In Yetzirah, the pure brilliant white remains. In Assiah, the brilliant white becomes flecked with bright gold. *Elemental Attribution*: Air. *Polarity*: None. *Tarot Card Correspondence*: the Four Aces of the Lesser Arcana, being one from each of the Four Suits.

Commentary: The idea of polarity on the Tree can cause no small amount of confusion. First off, it must be remembered that the Sephiroth are states of existence, not physical points, positions, or stations. Neither do they occupy some portion of space 'out there' in the universe. Yet this 'polarity' is interpreted in human terms to be something with which the mind can identify. In this case, positive or negative, masculine or feminine, force or form.

Since Kether is the "I AM" state of existence, it contains all potential, yet, as Dion Fortune states in her book, "The Mystical Qabalah": Kether...is pure being, all-potential, but not active... Wherever there is a state of pure, unconditioned being, without parts or activities, it is referred to Kether. But earlier I mentioned that Kether is ever in motion, so how can this be? In theological and theosophical fact, neither Fortune's comments nor mine contradict each other, owing to the state that Kether is in at any given moment, to use the human construct of time. In its pure state of potential, Kether is non-active. When its potential changes to a kinetic state, it becomes ever in motion.

In fact, the definitions that the science of physics gives to these two states is highly applicable here: potential, meaning the energy of position, that is, a placement or state without motion; and kinetic, meaning the energy of motion. In brief, while this Sephirah lacks polarity, yet it gives rise to the polarities of positive and negative, masculine and feminine, male and female, through its projections of the other nine Sephiroth. Such is a characteristic of its Intelligible and incomprehensible nature.

CHOKMAH

Number on the Tree: Two (2). *Primary Title*: Wisdom. *Other Titles*: In Christian trinity-theology and Neoplatonic cosmology, Chokmah is the Son. In Kabbalistic theosophy, the title of Father is assigned to this Sephirah; the Supernal Father; the Second Supernal. *Astrological Attribution*: the Zodiac. Chokmah is also assigned the planet Uranus as an attribution, but this is not typically used in Occult and Magical work. *Intelligible Quality*: that Divine Wisdom which is beyond human comprehension; the Illuminating Intelligence; that energetic, dynamic, all-conscious force underlying existence. *Peak Human Experience of this Sephirah*: the Vision of God. *Sensible Qualities*: Wisdom of the most subtle, profound type, of which humankind is capable of comprehending; the essential *impulse* behind the very essence of intellectualism; the Will that exists beyond one's personal, individual will, and which is the Divine Will within the individual. Magically, it is the 'True Will' of the aspirant: that part of the Will of God seeking to express itself in the world through the individual. It is also the Chiah, the energy of the eternal part of the Self. *Color on the Tree*: gray. *Color Scale*: In the World of Atziluth, Chokmah is an unadulterated, soft blue. In Briah, gray. In Yetzirah, a pearl gray that exhibits rainbow-like reflections. In Assiah, the color is a soft white, flecked with red, blue, and yellow. *Elemental Attribution*: Fire. *Polarity*: Chokmah is the primary positive, masculine, and active power of the Tree. It sits at the summit of what is called The Pillar of Mercy on the right side of the glyph of the Tree of Life. As such, it is the active dynamism of the Tree (but with the understanding given in the Commentary below.) *Tarot Card Correspondence*: The Four Twos of the Lesser Arcana, being one from each of the Four Suits.

Commentary: The Four Twos of the Tarot's Lesser Arcana representing Chokmah, can indeed represent a dynamic force, positive and masculine in nature. But according to the Kabbalists, this is only true for Chokmah on the subtle planes of existence, owing to its being the second Sephirah of the three Supernals of the Supernal Triad of the Tree: Kether being the first Supernal, and Binah the third. When the Chokmah influence appears on the less subtle planes of form however, its force is negative. That is, it lends equilibrium to the world of form through its dual polarity-aspect.

BINAH

Number on the Tree: Three (3). *Primary Title*: Understanding. *Other Titles*: The Great Mother; The Great Sea; The Universal Root Substance which our senses are in contact with, yet which is so rarefied we cannot perceive; the Sanctifying Intelligence. *Astrological Attribution*: The planet Saturn. *Intelligible Quality*: Divine Understanding, cognition of which mankind cannot perceive. *Peak Human Experience of this Sephirah*: the Summit of Sorrow, perceived as a universal experience. *Sensible Qualities*: The individualized, divine comprehending faculty within man, or the spiritual understanding of the Neshamah—one of the higher, spiritualized forces within the human soul; stability. On the more mundane level, owing to its planetary attribution of Saturn, issues relating to financial debts; the repayment of these debts; the acquisition of real estate; death; crops and agriculture; lassitude; inertia; lack of individual will; activities that require intensive thought followed by a period of consistent action; an influence that is good for legal matters in which justice is sought, and which involves the authorities: such as government offices, both state and federal, as well as police, judges, courts; also a good influence for bringing issues to the attention of those who have the power to decide an outcome favorable to the petitioner; excellent for literary work requiring deep insight; a positive period for attempting sales and the advancement of products through advertising by means of printed media; beginning or advancing any scientific pursuit; an excellent influence under which to engage in deep thought regarding any issue. This Saturanean influence however, is extremely adverse for seeking favors or recognition from those who can grant them. It is also adverse for: making investments, whether in the stock market or in any kind of business; beginning agricultural projects such as planting or seeding. It is also a very ill time for making new acquaintances, and is extremely adverse for beginning a marriage, the use of any medical remedy for body or mind, or attempting any cures of the body or mind by any metaphysical system. Additionally, it is very adverse for surgery of any kind, and a very unfortunate hourly influence under which to enter into a contract of any kind (see Commentary 1 below.) *Color on the Tree*: black. *Color Scale*: In the World of Atziluth, a brooding crimson red. In Briah, a flat, all engulfing black. In Yetzirah, a dark, flat brown. In Assiah, a flat, cool gray, flecked with pink. *Elemental Attribution*: Water. *Polarity*: Binah is negative, feminine and passive, the essential feminine power of the Tree, just as Chokmah embodies the principle masculine power. Binah is situated at the summit of the Pillar of Severity on the glyph (see Commentary 2, below). *Tarot Card Correspondence*: The Four Queens of the Lesser Arcana, being one from each of the Four Suits.

Commentary 1: From Binah onward, the Sensible attributions of each Sephirah take on mundane qualities, in addition to their more aesthetic, humanly comprehensible characteristics. This is due to the nature of the planetary concepts themselves, of which the physical planets of the same name are simply projections in our physical universe. More will be said on this matter in the section dealing with the Paths of the Tree.

Commentary 2: On the subtle planes of existence, Binah is feminine, passive, and negative in polarity. Below these planes — in the world of form — she is positive, dynamic, and active. Why? Because 'she' is actually projected from Chokmah, and as such, represents 'his' masculine, positive, dynamic nature below the subtle planes — that is, in the world of form. It is through her dynamic aspect that the positive polarity of Chokmah is projected into the world of form, while the two together — both Chokmah and Binah — maintain equilibrium throughout the subtle planes and the planes of form. But Binah does not act simply as a mirror, projecting Chokmah's positive force below the Supernal Triad. In her feminine, passive nature, she provides equilibrium within the Chokmah-Binah dualism of the Supernal Triad in the World of Briah. Below this Triad, she projects the Chokmah, the positive principle in order to maintain equilibrium in the world of the other seven Sephiroth. As one cannot exist without the other, neither can one understand either of these two Sephiroth without considering its counterpart.

CHESED

Number on the Tree: Four (4). *Primary Title*: Mercy. *Other Titles*: Love; Majesty; Gedulah. According to the *Sepher Yetzirah*, also the "Receptacular Intelligence." Also, the Cohesive or Receptive Intelligence. *Astrological Attribution*: the planet Jupiter. *Intelligible Quality*: The Perfect Mercy and Love of God. *Peak Human Experience of this Sephirah*: the Vision of Love; the Experience of Supreme Mercy or Compassion stemming from that Vision of Love. *Sensible Qualities*: human love as a devotional force as it is applied to another person, an action, or objective; dedication stemming from love. On the mundane level, issues relating to or involving abundance; plenty; money; all aspects and types of growth and expansion; visions; dreams; spirituality as a way of life. This Jupiteranean influence is very good for beginning a new venture, a new plan, or a new idea of any kind, for working out the details of new plans and ideas, and for making contracts or agreements, regardless of their nature. It is an excellent influence under which to study and gain new knowledge, as it is for involving oneself in educational matters of any kind. It is a very fortunate influence under which to marry, and is a very beneficent period for making new acquaintances, borrowing money, and dealing with powerful or prominent people who can be of genuine benefit to your plans, ideas, and desires. It is likewise an excellent influence for purchasing or selling real estate, asking for favors from virtually anyone directly, and for indulging in all forms of speculation for profit. This influence also has a spontaneous, instinctive, and involuntary characteristic that must be guarded against, lest the individual becomes careless in weighing and analyzing situations. Yet even so, the outcome of most activities that take place under this Jupiteranean power are benefic and positive. *Color on the Tree*: blue. *Color Scale*: In Atziluth, a deep violet. In Briah, blue. In Yetzirah, a deep purple. In Assiah, a deep azure flecked with yellow. *Elemental Attribution*: Water. *Polarity*: as Chokmah is positive in Briah, on the subtle planes, Chesed—also on the Pillar of Mercy—is positive, masculine, and dynamic on the less subtle or less rarefied planes below the Kether-Chokmah-Binah Supernal Triad. Yet, due to the equilibrium it brings to the Tree, it possesses feminine characteristics on the less subtle and material planes of existence, as exemplified by the Water correspondence of its Elemental Attribution. *Tarot Correspondence*: The Four Fours from the Lesser Arcana.

Commentary: *Again, notice how the dynamic, positive, masculine nature of Chesed is attributed to this Sephirah, despite the negative, passive, feminine characteristic of the element Water assigned to it. By doing so, the Kabbalists worked out the dual aspects of Divine manifestation below Kether: both polarities are needed for existence and expression throughout Creation, through the attainment and maintenance of equilibrium.*

GEBURAH

Number on the Tree: Five (5). *Primary Title*: Severity. *Other Titles*: Strength; Power; Force. According to the *Sepher Yetzirah*, Geburah is called "The Radical Intelligence." *Astrological Attribution*: the planet Mars. *Intelligible Quality*: Divine Power beyond mortal comprehension. *Peak Human Experience*: the Summit of Power, perceived as a universal experience. *Sensible Qualities*: determination; perseverance; vigor; aggression; construction or destruction according to purpose; vitality; endurance. This martial planetary influence is excellent for dealing with material pursuits and matters requiring physical—as opposed to mental—energy; it is also a fortuitous time for dealing with sensual affairs of every type, problems of a mechanical nature, or working out the intellectual details of new ideas that will lead to new, mechanical inventions. Athletes, bodybuilders, and weightlifters will find this an excellent period in which to develop and shape their physical form, while effectively and safely exerting the maximum amount of energy in that physical development. The influence also provides for experimental scientific activities as opposed to purely theoretical investigations. It exerts a very adverse effect in asking for favors, or for dealing with any beneficent matters of a personal nature whatsoever. It is also a very adverse influence under which to seek or make new acquaintances with the intention of seeking favors from them at the time, or at some point in the future. It is also a very unfortunate time in which to deal with any and all legal matters, including those involving judges, courts, or attorneys in any way, as well as for gambling, speculation of any type, entering into marriage, or having surgery—whether outpatient or that requiring even the briefest period of hospitalization. The emotions are extremely volatile under this influence, particularly those of an aggressive, hostile, or violent nature. It is a time best spent alone, dealing exclusively with matters that the influence favors. *Color on the Tree*: red. *Color Scale*: In Atziluth, orange. In Briah, red. In Yetzirah, a bright, scarlet red. In Assiah, red, flecked with black. *Elemental Attribution*: Fire. *Polarity*: Negative; feminine, passive. *Tarot Correspondence*: the Four Fives of the Lesser Arcana of the deck.

Commentary: Once more, notice that Geburah (see Figures 1 & 2) is on the left hand column of the Tree, and has a feminine nature, as do all of the Sephiroth in that column which is headed by Binah. Yet, her attributes are decidedly male, masculine, dynamic, positive, and active, for the reason previously discussed. As such, the equilibrium of the Tree is maintained. This dynamic, masculine nature is expressed through the elemental attribution of this Sephirah, namely, Fire.

TIPHARETH

Number on the Tree: Six (6). *Primary Title*: Beauty. *Other Titles*: the Mediating Intelligence; the Microprosopus or the Lesser Countenance; the Son; the Man; the Son of Man, referring to the Christ-Consciousness. *Astrological Attribution*: the Sun. *Intelligible Quality*: Perfect Beauty; Perfect Harmony; the Ideal; the sum total of all that is Good. *Peak Human Experience of the Sephirah*: the Vision of the Harmony of all things, and through this Vision, the apprehension of or direct experience of the essence of Beauty itself. *Sensible Qualities*: the imaginative faculty of the individual; the realm of the HGA, the Holy Guardian Angel in magi-

cal literature; the point of arrival of the Abramelin Operation: an intensive, six-month magical working for attaining
the K&C—Knowledge and Conversation of the Holy
Guardian Angel. In the more mundane sense, owing to its
Astrological Attribution, the Sun, the attributions include:
power and success in life; Life itself; illumination; mental
power and ability; as with Jupiter under Chesed, also
money; robust physical, emotional, and mental health;
growth at the personality, character, and psychic levels;
dealing with superiors of all kinds, and in any situation;
asking for favors from people in authority; seeking the
approval, recommendation, or help from others in any
proposal whatsoever, be it of a business or personal
nature; composing important letters that produce in the
mind of the intended recipient a picture of the writer as a
confident, balanced individual whose request for aid,
introductions, or favors should be immediately granted.
This is also an excellent influence under which one can act
in noble and high-minded ways that will build up his or
her public esteem and prestige. This influence however is
adverse for involving oneself in illegal plans, actions, or
activities of any kind whatsoever. Curiously, it also provides a negative influence for beginning or launching a
new business, a new plan, or a new idea, owing to its
underlying Elemental Attribution which is always shifting,
changing in force and form, as the Sun itself, the most
Sensible of this Sephirothal influence that has further
descended into the realm of matter. By the same rationale,
it is likewise adverse for signing contracts of any kind, and
for entering into any partnerships, mutually beneficial
arrangements or agreement—whether of a social, business,
professional, or personal nature—or for entering into any
kind of relationship in which there is a political element of
any kind. Additionally, this planetary influence is also
quite adverse for marriage, for making any new investments of any kind, for purchasing or liquidating real estate
holdings, and for all forms of surgery. *Color on the Tree*:
bright yellow. *Color Scale*: In the world of Atziluth, a clear,
rose pink. In Briah, a golden yellow. In Yetzirah, a rich,

salmon pink. In Assiah, a golden amber. *Elemental Attribution*: Air. *Polarity*: None, as Tiphareth is the product of the positive, masculine polarity of Chesed, and the negative, feminine polarity of Geburah, acting in equilibrium and unison to project this central point of the Tree. *Tarot Correspondence*: the Four Sixes of the Lesser Arcana of the deck.

NETZACH

Number on the Tree: Seven (7). *Primary Title*: Victory. *Other Titles*: the *Sepher Yetzirah* gives this Sephirah the title of "The Occult Intelligence." Also, Eternity; Triumph; Firmness. *Astrological Attribution*: the planet Venus. *Intelligible Quality*: the Vision of Beauty Triumphant. *Peak Human Experience of this Sephirah*: the Experience of Beauty Triumphant. *Sensible Qualities*: Unselfishness; Love, but of a sexual nature; beauty of form, and the appreciation of that beauty; the emotions of the conscious level of our being; women; music; self-indulgence; extravagance. Also on the mundane level, this influence governs all material and sensual affairs; music; art; the theater; any form of behavior or expression that supports sensuality. It is also a very fortuitous influence under which to begin any new enterprise or project, whether sensual or business in nature. It is also an excellent influence in which to make new acquaintances, but only those that are met through spontaneous social contact. It is also a very favorable influence for entering into marriage, to borrow or loan money, and to host social gatherings and parties, but only those affairs that are meant for pure enjoyment. It is very positive for speculating in stocks, bonds, or in any new business proposition. It is important to note here that due to the Venusian planetary influence of this Sephirah, almost any activity or action that is begun or ended while this influence is in operation, will bear very significant, desirable, or fortunate results. It is an influence that, in effect, blesses and magnifies activities of almost any kind, but especially those of a sensual and material nature. There are a few very adverse aspects of this influence, such as dealing with social underlings or subordinates; beginning

long trips to remote locations; using social means to harm
enemies or competitors, or to attempt using social
functions as a means of gaining a business or personal
advantage at the expense of a collaborator or fellow
worker. *Color on the Tree*: green. *Color Scale*: In Atziluth,
amber. In Briah, emerald. In Yetzirah, bright yellow-green.
In Assiah, olive, flecked with gold. *Elemental Attribution*:
Fire. *Polarity*: Masculine, positive. *Tarot Correspondence*: the
Four Sevens of the Lesser Arcana of the deck.

HOD

Number on the Tree: Eight (8). *Primary Title*: Splendor.
Other Titles: Glory; the **Yetziratic** Text calls Hod the
"Absolute or Perfect Intelligence." *Astrological Attribution*:
the planet Mercury. *Intelligible Quality*: the Vision of
Splendor. *Peak Human Experience*: once again, according to
the **Yetziratic** Text, Hod is called the Perfect Intelligence,
because it is power in a state of equilibrium. For the individual to experience this state is to attain the peak experience of this Sephirah. *Sensible Qualities*: On the higher
levels, Truthfulness and Honesty are two of the blessings
of this Sephirah, along with the philosophic and laboratory
pursuit of Alchemy. On the more mundane levels, this
Mercurial influence is very positive for dealing with intellectual discernments; scientific thought; mathematics;
writing of all kinds; logic; reason; using and accelerating
the analytical faculty of the conscious self; thinking;
speaking, whether in public or private. Additionally, as
with Netzach and Venus, the Mercurial influence of Hod is
very beneficial for art, music, and the theater; for literary
work of any kind; to design or begin new advertising
efforts; to plan new projects or involvements; to launch
new business plans; to make new acquaintances in business or academic circles, and to begin new business relationships. It is an excellent influence under which one can
successfully initiate contracts, but short-term ones only. It
is also an excellent time for reading or buying new books
that can be of great help to the individual in an intellectual,
life-sustaining, or life-enhancing way; also for dealing with

business or academic journals, papers, or researching documents, such as land and property Title and Deed searches. This influence also favors educational matters of every type, as well as the buying and selling of printed material. It imparts a very benefic influence for taking any medicine or beginning any system of mental cure. It is an excellent influence for mystical, metaphysical, or magical study, under which profound insight into occult, esoteric, mystical, or magical concepts can be achieved, the essence of which can be then used for intellectual growth, the attainment of considerable material benefit, or both. It is also a positive influence for speculating and taking chances in a business or proposition that at other times may appear unsound or chancy. This is also an excellent influence under which important letters can be written. This Mercurial influence has some serious negative aspects as well, such as dealing with enemies in any legal manner; entering into marriage, or seeking favors from people in authority. It is equally adverse for either purchasing or selling real estate holdings, and is a period in which the individual can become the target of fraudulent or even illegal schemes. In general, it is an influence under which the truthfulness of all statements coming from anyone must be carefully evaluated, despite the overall positive aspects this influence exerts. *Color on the Tree*: orange. *Color Scale*: In Atziluth, a violet-purple. In Briah, orange. In Yetzirah, a russet-red. In Assiah, a yellowish-black or brown flecked with white. *Elemental Attribution*: Water (feminine, creative, passive, negative.) *Polarity*: Negative (feminine.) *Tarot Correspondence*: the Four Eights of the Lesser Arcana of the deck.

YESOD

Number on the Tree: Nine (9). *Primary Title*: the Foundation. *Other Titles*: the Anima Mundi, or the Soul of the World; also the "Pure Intelligence or Clear Intelligence." *Astrological Attribution*: the Moon (Luna). *Intelligible Quality*: the Divine Cognition of the working of the universe. *Peak Human Experience of this Sephirah*: the Vision or Experience of the working of the universe. *Sensible Qualities*: according to the **Yetziratic** Text, Yesod purifies the emanations received from the other Sephiroth, as it is the receptacle of all of the emanations from the other eight spheres above it. Additionally, since Yesod is the sole focus of the other Sephiroth emanations, it is the sole projector of those forces into the world of matter: the physical plane of Malkuth. It is also the Astral Plane of occultism, and the realm of the Astral Light. It is the sphere of Magic as well, as all operations of a magical nature that are intended to produce an effect in Malkuth, have their foundations in this Sephirah. On the daily, more pragmatic level, the planetary attribution of Yesod, the Moon, takes the correspondences of, and produces its influence upon: women; the personality; modifications; rapid changes; fluid conditions, ever cycling between extremes. As with Hod's projection, Mercury, educational efforts of all kinds are also ruled by the Moon, it being the projection of Yesod into our universe. Additionally, this lunar influence provides a positive impulse for the planting of seeds, beginning journeys by water, or making new acquaintances in a social, business, or academic setting. It is also an excellent influence for all literary work, for entering into the sacrament of marriage, for taking any medicine, or to begin any mystical or metaphysical system of body or mind treatment in which a direct, complete cure is sought. This Lunar influence of Yesod is also very positive for surgery of all types, and for dealing with metaphysical, mystical, and magical studies. This fluid, creative, Lunar influence provides an energy dynamic backdrop against which most activities and aspirations indulged in during the time of its reign will prove both prolific and productive. *Color on the Tree*: purple. *Color Scale*: In Atziluth, indigo. In Briah, violet. In Yetzirah, a very dark purple. In Assiah, a citrine flecked with azure. *Elemental Attribution*: as with Tiphareth, the elemental attribution of Yesod is Air, owing to its position on the Middle Pillar of the Tree. *Polarity*: Neutral. *Tarot Correspondence*: the Four Nines of the Lesser Arcana of the deck.

Commentary: Notice, that as with Yesod and the other Sephirah on the Middle Pillar, Kether also takes the elemental attribution of Air as well. This is thought to be due to the impulsive, ever-changing, fluid, potential-to-kinetic and back again dynamics of this Air element, but in its most pure, rarefied, and complete form in the case of Kether. In Yesod however, these transitional properties of the Air Element can be seen as being reflected directly into Malkuth, where they become more stable by virtue of their appearance in the densest, most material form of matter—the physical matter which is found in Malkuth.

MALKUTH

Number on the Tree: Ten (10). *Primary Title:* the Kingdom. *Other Titles:* the World of the Four Elements—Air, Earth, Water, and Fire; the "Resplendent Intelligence," because as Fortune has reflected, it is exalted above every head and sits upon the Throne of Binah. Also, The Gate of Justice; the Gate of the Daughter of the Mighty One; the Gate of Prayer; the Gate of the Shadow of Death and of Death itself; the Gate of the Garden of Eden; the Queen; the Bride; the Inferior Mother. *Astrological Attribution:* the Element, Earth, but divided into four quadrants, representing the World of the Four Elements: Air, Earth, Water, and Fire. That is, matter in its entirety, yet not simply the gross form that composes matter as we perceive it with our five senses. The other subtle psychic qualities of the Four Elements are also included in this attribution, namely, the subtle, psychic aspects of Air, Earth, Water, and Fire. These too are encompassed by Malkuth. *Intelligible Quality:* the Existence and Projection of the Psychic and Mundane Essences of Four Elements into the realm of Malkuth. *Peak Human Experience of this Sephirah:* the Vision of the Holy Guardian Angel. *Sensible Qualities:* discernment; astuteness; acute sensory perception of ordinary matter. The physical performance of the Abramelin Operation, leading to the Vision of the HGA, and the Attainment of the Knowledge and Conversation of the HGA while the individual is yet in human form (see Commentary below). *Color on the Tree:* the tenth Sephirah is divided by an 'X' into four equal sections in order to bisect the sphere. The colors olive, russet, citrine, and black are then assigned, one color to each of the four equal sections. *Color Scale*: In the Atziluthic World, a clear yellow. In Briatic World, olive, russet, citrine, and black. In the Yetziratic World, olive, russet, citrine, and black, flecked with gold. In the Assiatic World, black, rayed with yellow. *Elemental Attribution*: Earth (as described above.) *Polarity*: Neutral. The grounding-point of the purified emanations from all of the other Sephiroth, radiating from Yesod into Malkuth. *Tarot Attribution*: the Four Tens of the Lesser Arcana of the deck.

Commentary: *There is a difficult point here regarding the mystical relationship between Tiphareth and Malkuth of the Middle Pillar, which some readers may need to understand clearly for their Kabbalistic studies and beyond. Specifically, it involves the concept of the 'True Will,' the Holy Guardian Angel (HGA), and the Attainment of the Knowledge and Conversation (K&C) of the HGA through the magical working of the Abramelin Operation.*

The True Will of the individual; that is, the Will of God for the individual, is identified with the Chiah. In turn, the Chiah is the essential energy of that part of the self which is eternal. But the realm of the HGA who delivers the True Will to the individual, is that of Tiphareth. Here, the HGA is considered by some to be the Higher Self: a type of pure consciousness so exalted as to be above the everyday reach of the individual. Fortune said of it, "...it is an intensification of awareness..." and from it "...comes a peculiar power of insight and penetration which is of the nature of hyper-developed intuition."[33]

Thus, in some occult circles and magical societies, it is conceived of as the elevation of the individual's highest qualities, raised to the nth level, yet partaking of divine qualities by its very definition. While the Experience of the HGA most certainly does exhibit this divine state that does lie beyond ecstasy—which quickly transforms into an Experience of Divine Love and Beauty beyond description—it is my opinion that Fortune's viewpoint is far, far, from the sum total of the experience of Attaining to the Knowledge and Conversation of the HGA.

*In point of fact, the HGA is an individual being with its own universe, holding an utterly profound and nebulous personal consciousness of its own, yet with a conscious awareness of the individual human being over which it presides. Hence, it is through the Abramelin Operation, conducted physically in Malkuth according to the Abramelin text, that the individual does attain to the actual, physical Vision of the HGA, which is then immediately followed by the Attainment to the **full** K&C of this being.*

In other words, both Fortune's view of the HGA's nature and the individual's experience of it as I have laid down herein, are valid in my opinion. That is, through the classical perform-ance of the Abramelin Operation, the individual calls down the True Will from Chokmah into Malkuth, as that True Will has manifested in the centralized focus of Tiphareth, and through the being of the HGA. Through this act, the Godhead of Chokmah— as projected from Kether—is brought down into Manhood—into Malkuth—through the intervention of the Holy Guardian Angel in Tiphareth.

At the same time, Manhood, existing in Malkuth, is elevated into Godhead, through the agency of the HGA, in Tiphareth. And so the ancient admonition, "Bring Godhead down into manhood, and elevate manhood into Godhead," is fulfilled. It is a fundamental error to think however, as Dion Fortune herself so unfortunately states later on in her classic book on Kabbalah, that the HGA "...consists neither in voices nor visions, but is pure consciousness..."[33]

*Why is this error so dangerous? Because the state of the individual's subjective synthesis is effected thereby, precluding the actual Vision of the HGA. This occurs through the very acceptance of her point of view: an attitude engendered, pro-jected, and maintained by mainstream New Age Magick. As a result of accepting this limiting viewpoint, the individual can only attain to a partial experience of the HGA; a partial result that ends more often than not in hallucinations regarding the experience, and confusion as to the individual's **full** True Will.*

In more applicable terms, this error in understanding can cause difficulties in the diligent individual's formation of his or

*her subjective state; one that can produce subconscious errors in
the use of the Kabbalistic Cycles System.*

*There is no need for an either-or scenario as so many magical
schools, occult circles, want-to-bees, self-professed magicians,
and occultists insist, all as a result of never having attempted the
Abramelin Operation, let alone having Attained to the **full** K&C
of the HGA. But then, it is only through the direct Experience of
Attaining to the **full** K&C of the HGA, and this by attaining to
the Vision of this being in Malkuth, that this simple understanding can become known.*

THE PATHS

In order to literally derive the Kabbalistic Cycles
System, all components of that system must be made
known. Not simply to build and strengthen your state of
subjective synthesis (as important as that is), but to provide you with necessary tools to apply this system
correctly in your daily life. If you use it correctly, it will
work for you one hundred percent of the time. Have I
make a typing—or worse yet—an error of the ego by
making such a claim? Something that will work one
hundred percent of the time?

There is no error. It is as simple as this. Derive the
system along with me here. Learn the Kabbalah as presented in this book, for the time being, before moving on to
a further study of it. Learn the Sensible Qualities of each
Sephirah and those of the Paths that will follow below, and
you will find my statement to be one hundred percent
accurate. Period. People will argue the point that nothing
is ever one hundred percent! My response to that is
twofold.

First, it's not that 'things' are not 'one hundred percent.' If you look even casually at any situation, you will
find it is *people* that are not one hundred percent. Why?
Because most individuals truly expect something for nothing. Or more usually, they expect something to work one
hundred percent of the time after learning it in a slipshod
fashion, and then applying it in a casual, shoddy way.
Then of course they complain, "Well, I tried it, and as

usual with these things, it doesn't work the way I wanted it to!" The key word in that statement of course, is 'as usual,' because their learning, effort in application, and habit patterns are slipshod and shabby, as usual.

Secondly, it has always been my position that anything in the occult or magical worlds should and must work with regularity and precision, as surely as do the Laws of Nature I study and experiment with as a physicist. If they do not—if it seems that there are too many variables as the New Agers so love to proffer as an excuse, or equally, that the occult and magic are Arts and not a Science as that tepid group also loves to use as a rationale for their lack of results—then it would be madness for anyone to devote a significant portion of their life to the study and practice of such flippant, *causally unconnected* 'disciplines.'

The truth is that the occult in general, and magic in particular, are the same as any of the hard or soft sciences. They have as much of an artful twist as they do a rigorous, logical, repeatable, scientific base. Understanding this, you can exercise your natural flare and variations in the use of any occult or magical technique—that artful twist—all the while assured of the outcome of that technique from the scientifically applied logical, rigorous, repeatable base.

There you have it. Use your artful flare, but only through your scientific application; an application/technique that can only come by understanding and rigorously applying the underlying principles of whatever occult or magical work you are involved in. I further guarantee you that there truly are *principles* underlying *any and all* occult and magical work. If you heed this counsel, I promise you will succeed one hundred percent of the time. So please pay close attention, and let's proceed.

Now, as both the Intellectual and Sensible qualities and correspondences of each Sephirah were given, we will concern ourselves with the Intelligible and Sensible qualities and attributes of the Paths. Since you will be using the Kabbalistic Cycles System in your daily life, the Sensible characteristics of the Paths—as with the Sephiroth—will eventually become your prime focus.

For now, however, it is important that you understand, or at least are made aware of both their Intelligible and Sensible attributions. And as promised, after you have been exposed to the mystical basis of the Paths, we will add *the fundamental correspondence* traditionally assigned to them in the next chapter, which is used in the Kabbalistic Cycles System. After which, your newly acquired knowledge of the Tree of Life will be used to build up the Kabbalistic Cycles System itself in your mind, step-by-step.

In point of fact, you have probably realized that you have been building up this system while studying this book so far, and indeed you have. After Chapter Six gives you the *fundamental correspondence* to the Paths and discusses their importance, Chapter Seven will launch you into the actual derivation of the Kabbalistic Cycles System. Chapter Eight will then take you deeply into this new system of attaining certainty and control over your life; and it will be in that chapter that *you* will be able to complete the derivation of the entire system for yourself, using this book as your guide. With these promises now made to you at this point, let us proceed to our investigation of the Paths of the Tree of Life.

There are a number of factors I ask the reader to keep in mind as we explore the Paths and their attributions. First of all, as with the Sephiroth, please remember that only a very limited number of attributions and qualities of the Paths are given here. The reader's study of the previously recommended texts will greatly increase this list of attributions. As that list grows, so will your comprehension of the concepts. In turn, as your comprehension increases, so will your understanding and apprehension.

Secondly, and again as with the Sephiroth attributions and correspondences, kindly remember that I did not formulate or derive the attributions of the Paths that will follow. They are general characteristics of these interconnections between the Sephiroth that are distributed or cited in one form or another throughout the voluminous tomes of occult, magical, mystical, and metaphysical literature.

Third, be warned if you are new to Kabbalah, that you will find the Paths to have a plethora of attributions and characteristics that may sound redundant. For example, with Path Number Eleven, you will find it corresponding to the Element Air, while for Path 12, you will find its attribution to be Mercury, which has already been assigned to the Sephirah Hod. This is not some Kabbalistic slight-of-hand, but rather, an assigned characteristic based upon the natures of the Sephiroth connected by these Paths.

Additionally, these seeming repeated correspondences have higher meanings when applied to the Paths, owing to the exalted natures of the Sephiroth connected by them. In other words, these higher octaves of the correspondences are actually referring to the *Intelligible Quality* of each Sephirah being connected by a specific Path. But all of this will be discovered by you as you wade through all the books.

Please also be aware that even though the Intelligible Quality must be firmly rooted in your mind, we will be paying special attention to the *fundamental correspondence.* After all, we eventually need to become *practical,* and we will do so because this *fundamental correspondence* applies to the *Sensible Qualities* of the *Paths only,* which are *the* attributions you will be using to work the Kabbalistic Cycles System. It would be a wise move on the part of the reader to pause at this point, and reread and contemplate what has just been stated. It will pay big dividends as you proceed through the Paths.

Previously, I mentioned that there are twenty-two paths on the Tree, and that the connecting Paths indicate and explain the relationship that any given two or more Sephiroth bear to each other. But in fact, there are *thirty-two* paths. How can this be? *Because each Sephirah is considered to be a Path as well.* Why is this so? To be sure, there are several explanations for this, all of which are interesting and theoretically sound, as a review of any of the recommended texts will reveal.

In terms of a *daily working model* however, I prefer my own concept. *I prefer to think of each Sephirah as a Path, due to its Sensible qualities, which are those more mundane or earthy correspondences, attributes, and governances that are ascribed to each Sephirah.* Put another way, if the reader will accept this working model and definition, then it is not difficult to understand that the Path characteristic of each Sephirah is simply due to the modus operandi which enables a Sephirah to have an effect in the World of Malkuth.

In this case, it is the *planetary projections* of each Sephirah, referred to as the Astrological Attribution in the section on the Sephiroth. If the reader reviews the *Sensible Qualities* of the Sephiroth given earlier, he or she will see that in the case of Binah through Yesod, the planetary projections of these Sephiroth are classically and historically assigned as the influences that project the lower qualities of these Sephiroth into the everyday world in which we live, move, and have our being—the World of Malkuth.

Thus, for Binah, Saturn is the planetary force that projects the attributions of the more mundane aspects of this planet into our world. For Chesed, Jupiter is assigned, and so on, until we finally end in Malkuth (Earth). In the cases of Kether and Chokmah, where there are no planetary attributions given, it nevertheless becomes easy for us to understand the Sensible Qualities given, owing to the extrapolations made from the nature of these higher Sephiroth. In the case of Malkuth, our understanding that it is the focal point of all the previous Sephirothal projections, including the planetary projections that came before it, that provides us insight into its Sensible state.

If this is the case and all of the Seven Planets of the Ancients—as the planetary projections Saturn, Jupiter, Mars, the Sun, Venus, Mercury and the Moon are termed in occult literature—have already been assigned to Binah through Yesod, then where are the projectors of the remaining twenty-two Paths that provide their projections into the lower or more mundane World of Malkuth, as did the Sephiroth? To answer this question, a few other salient facts must be addressed.

First off, we must consider the attributable characteristics or correspondences spoken of above which are assigned to the Paths by the Classical Kabbalah. The manner of such assignment is accomplished by designating one of the twenty-two letters of the Hebrew alphabet to each Path. This can be a type of convention for naming a Path, if you will, and for building a foundation upon which one can gain an understanding of the multiple meanings and ideas of a given Path, along with the spiritual or psychic forces that Path is said to represent.

These letters have five basic characteristics, or additional attributions assigned to them. I am also assigning the classical Kabbalistic quality of a Basal Attribute as another correspondence of each Path: be this attribution planetary, elemental, or zodiacal. Along with this, the reader will find an Occult Concept that lends a feeling for the meaning of the Symbolic Meaning of the Path. Lastly, by stating the obvious, I refer to each Path by a Path Name, derived by simply naming each Path according to the name of the Hebrew letter assigned to it.

Taken together, these eight characteristics will embody a view of the individual and collective concepts of a Path, in addition to establishing a procedure for us to add to those meanings based upon our own individual mystical, magical, metaphysical, and daily life experiences.

The five characteristics of each of the twenty-two Hebrew letters are:

- Path Number on the Tree.
- A specific position in the alphabet. For example, first letter of the alphabet, fourth letter of the alphabet, and so on.
- A numerical value of letter.
- A symbolical meaning applied to the Path.
- A Tarot card attribution of the Path.

A discussion of each of these five characteristics relative to each Path, along with the Path Name, Basal Attribute and Occult Concept, now follows. As the reader will come to understand by the end of this section, however, there is *one and only one* of these eight correspondences that will be used in the Kabbalistic Cycles System. Nevertheless, for the sake of subjective synthesis, all will be presented and briefly reviewed.

Since there are thirty-two Paths on the Tree, and since each Sephirah is also considered to be a Path in its own right, the convention of listing the Paths begins with Path Number Eleven (11) and follows sequentially down the Tree. In addition, by assigning a Hebrew letter to each Path, it becomes easy for us to learn the Paths by simply calling or referring to each Path by its Hebrew letter. Using this mental code, you will be amazed at how quickly this schema will enable you to master the Occult Meaning behind the Tree, along with its multitude of correspondences.

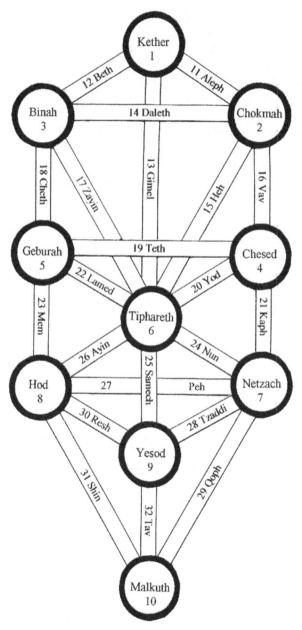

FIGURE 2. THE TREE OF LIFE. GLYPH 2.

Lastly, remember that the Tarot Attribution of each Path applies to the twenty-two cards of the Greater Arcana or the Trumps Major, and not the cards of the Four Suits (the Lesser Arcana.) In terms of the five characteristics of the twenty-two Hebrew letters, the Path Names, Basal Attributions and the Occult Concepts, we can now begin the study of the Paths.

• *Path Number on the Tree*: Eleven (**11**), connecting Kether and Chokmah.

Path Name: Aleph (Hebrew letter, 'A'), meaning, the head of an Ox. *Position of Hebrew letter in alphabet*: First, or One (1). *Numerical Value of Hebrew letter*: 1 (One). *Symbolic Meaning of Path*: "The Scintillating Intelligence." *Occult Concept of Path*: the primeval movement of the Great, Creative Breath, spinning the chaos from the moment of Creation into a creative core. *Basal Attribute of the Path*: the Element, Air. *Tarot Attribution of Path*: Tarot Trump, Zero (O)—The Fool.

• *Path Number on the Tree*: Twelve (**12**), connecting Kether and Binah.

Path Name: Beth (Hebrew letter, 'B'), meaning, House. *Position of Hebrew letter in alphabet*: Second, or Two (2). *Numerical Value of Hebrew letter*: 2 (Two). *Symbolic Meaning of Path*: "The Transparent Intelligence." *Occult Concept of Path*: the combined natures of the Sephiroth Chokmah and Hod are reflected by this Path. Their properties are Mercurial, here, in an alchemical sense of Universal Mercury, as hinted at in the section on Hod. That is, due to the higher octave of this Path, the Mercurial nature expressed here is more in line with the Intelligible Quality found in the Mercury of the Philosophers, which can be reached through the higher aspects of the Sensible Qualities of Hod: Initiated working in the realms of Philosophic *and* Laboratory Alchemy. This Mercurial Principle is therefore that living, ever-changing Principle of cohesive force that holds all of Creation together, from the subtlest of matter to its most material of form. *Basal Attribute of Path*: the planet, Mercury, but with the understanding given above. *Tarot Attribution of Path*: Tarot Trump, One (I)—The Magician.

• *Path Number on the Tree*: Thirteen (**13**), connecting Kether and Tiphareth.

Path Name: Gimel (Hebrew letter, 'G'), meaning Camel. *Position of Hebrew letter in alphabet*: Third, or Three (3). *Numerical Value of Hebrew letter*: 3 (Three). *Symbolic Meaning of Path*: "The Uniting Intelligence." *Occult Concept of Path*: The portal of entry into an Inner Magical Sanctum or College of the Masters, as understood by advanced practitioners of Magic. *Basal Attribute of the Path*: the 'planet' Moon. *Tarot Attribution of Path*: Tarot Trump, Two (II)— The High Priestess.

• *Path Number on the Tree*: Fourteen (**14**), connecting Chokmah and Binah.

Path Name: Daleth (Hebrew letter 'D'), meaning, Door. *Position of Hebrew letter in alphabet*: Fourth, or Four (4). *Numerical Value of Hebrew letter*: 4 (Four). *Symbolic Meaning of Path*: "The Luminous Intelligence." *Occult Concept of Path*: The force by which opposites are attracted to each other. Due to the Basal Attribute assigned to this Path, the implication is one of Love, although in a higher aspect. In this instance, a Love whose end result of uniting the opposites, produces a mystical creation and experience through the act of union. *Basal Attribute of the Path*: the planet, Venus. *Tarot Attribution of Path*: Tarot Trump, Three (III)— The Empress.

• *Path Number on the Tree*: Fifteen (**15**), connecting Chokmah and Tiphareth.

Path Name: Heh (Hebrew letter 'H'), meaning, Window. *Position of Hebrew letter in alphabet*: Fifth, or Five (5). *Numerical Value of Hebrew letter*: 5 (Five). *Symbolic Meaning of Path*: "The Constituting Intelligence." *Occult Concept of Path*: Although many martial characteristics are applied to this Path due to its Basal Attribution, the higher aspect of this Path is of more interest and use to us here. This Path is associated with the alchemical Principle of the Sulphur, itself a fire related concept exhibiting energy, and the penetrative dynamics of the mind, the mental dynamics being equally fiery when used properly. Why this latter correspondence? Because to those initiated into Alchemy, the alchemical Sulphur possesses a physical vehicle, the exact nature of which depends upon which of the Three Kingdoms of Nature from which it is extracted. It is this vehicle which embodies and actually contains the *consciousness* of the substance being worked upon alchemically. *Basal Attribute of the Path*: the Zodiacal Sign of Aries. *Tarot Attribution of Path*: Tarot Trump, Four (IV)—The Emperor.

• **Path Number on the Tree**: Sixteen (**16**), connecting Chokmah and Chesed.

Path Name: Vav (Hebrew letter 'V'), meaning, a Nail. *Position of Hebrew letter in alphabet*: Sixth, or Six (6). *Numerical Value of Hebrew letter*: 6 (Six). *Symbolic Meaning of Path*: "The Son of Tetragrammaton." *Occult Concept of Path*: In its higher aspects, this Path is symbolic of the act of Redemption, and the Joy that issues from that redemption. *Basal Attribute of the Path*: the Zodiacal Sign of Taurus. *Tarot Attribution of Path*: Tarot Trump, Five (V)—The Hierophant.

• **Path Number on the Tree**: Seventeen (**17**), connecting Binah and Tiphareth.

Path Name: Zayin (Hebrew letter 'Z'), meaning, Sword. *Position of Hebrew letter in alphabet*: Seventh, or Seven (7). *Numerical Value of Hebrew letter*: 7 (Seven). *Symbolic Meaning of Path*: "The Disposing Intelligence." *Occult Concept of Path*: Again, in its higher aspects, this Path is symbolic of the Primal Force behind all of the fabricating and forging forces within Nature, and is symbolic of the depths of the consciousness of Nature itself. *Basal Attribute of the Path*: The Zodiacal Sign of Gemini. *Tarot Attribution of Path*: Tarot Trump Six (VI)—The Lovers.

• **Path Number on the Tree**: Eighteen (**18**), connecting Binah and Geburah.

Path Name: Cheth, pronounced using the guttural 'Ck' sound made in pronouncing the word 'rock' (Hebrew letter 'CH'), meaning, Fence. *Position of Hebrew letter in alphabet*: Eighth, or Eight (8). *Numerical Value of Hebrew letter*: 8 (Eight). *Symbolic Meaning of Path*: "The House of Influence." The process by which accomplishing the Great

Work itself. Also the Work, Devotion, Dedication, Comprehension and Understanding, by which one comes to grasp the reality of Kether, through the Accomplishment of the Great Work. *Occult Concept of Path*: the first step of the process in the Attainment of the Great Work, which is the Attainment of the Knowledge and Conversation (K&C) of the Holy Guardian Angel (HGA). *Basal Attribute of the Path*: the Zodiacal Sign of Cancer. *Tarot Attribution of Path*: Tarot Trump Seven (VII)—The Chariot.

• *Path Number on the Tree*: Nineteen (**19**), connecting Chesed and Geburah.

Path Name: Teth (Hebrew letter 'T'), meaning, Serpent. *Position of Hebrew letter in alphabet*: Ninth, or Nine (9). *Numerical Value of Hebrew letter*: 9 (Nine). *Symbolic Meaning of Path*: I refer to this Path as "The Alternate Path," uniting the opposites of the male potency of Chesed, with the female potency of Geburah; the Path joining the opposites of Mercy and Severity, as shown by the Chesedian-placement on the Pillar of Mercy, and the Geburahian-situated Sephirah on the Pillar of Severity. *Occult Concept of Path*: Although the Serpent is assigned to this Path due to its association with Teth, the Lion is also a corollary of this connecting pathway between Chesed and Geburah. In the higher aspects of this Path's meaning, it is the Lion which is of interest here, having a very special meaning in Alchemy: the production of—at first a menstrum—termed the "Green Lion," from which the Stone of the Wise is eventually produced. By allegory, it also has implication for that psycho-spiritual process of self-transformation through which the 'lead' of Man's lower nature is transmuted and united with the Higher Nature that dwells within the deepest recesses of the Self. *Basal Attribute of the Path*: the Zodiacal Sign of Leo. *Tarot Attribution of Path*: Tarot Trump, Eight (VIII)—Strength.

• *Path Number on the Tree*: Twenty (**20**), connecting Chesed and Tiphareth.

Path Name: Yod (Hebrew letters 'I', 'Y'), meaning, a Hand, but with the index finger pointing, and the other fingers closed, forming a Fist, which is also the meaning of this Path. *Position of Hebrew letter in alphabet*: Tenth, or Ten (10). *Numerical Value of Hebrew letter*: 10 (Ten). *Symbolic Meaning of Path*: "The Forceful Intelligence," as I term this Path, owing to the nature of its higher meaning, as given in the Occult Concept. *Occult Concept of Path*: The movement of the One Consciousness through which the forces of the universe have been set in motion. *Basal Attribute of the Path*: the Zodiacal Sign of Virgo. *Tarot Attribution of Path*: Tarot Trump, Nine (IX)—The Hermit.

• **Path Number on the Tree**: Twenty-One (**21**), connecting Chesed and Netzach.

Path Name: Kaph (Hebrew letter 'K'), meaning, a cupped hand, or spoon. *Position of Hebrew letter in alphabet*: Eleventh, or Eleven (11). *Numerical Value of Hebrew letter*: 20 (Twenty). *Symbolic Meaning of Path*: "The Conciliatory Intelligence." *Occult Concept of Path*: With its higher aspects through its Intelligible Quality of the pure, expansive, open nature of Chesed to its Sensible Jupiteranean influence which is eventually united or conciliated with the Intelligible Quality of Netzach, being the Vision of Beauty, it is then expressed in the World of Malkuth through the Venusian Sensible Quality of Love. In effect, a conciliation occurs between the Sensible Qualities projected by the planetary attributions of these two Sephiroth into the lower worlds. Yet, this same act of conciliation also occurs between the higher aspects of these two Sephiroth. What we have as a result of this conciliatory act is a balance between the Intelligible and Sensible Qualities of these spheres, each on their own plane, yet complementing each other on their respective planes of existence through the nature of this Path. *Basal Attribute of the Path*: the planet, Jupiter. *Tarot Attribution of Path*: Tarot Trump, Ten (X)—The Wheel of Fortune.

• **Path Number on the Tree**: Twenty-Two (**22**), connecting Geburah and Tiphareth.

Path Name: Lamed (Hebrew letter 'L'), meaning, a Whip. *Position of Hebrew letter in alphabet*: Twelfth, or Twelve (12). *Numerical Value of Hebrew letter*: 30 (Thirty). *Symbolic Meaning of Path*: "The Faithful Intelligence."

Occult Concept of Path: This Path has a combined meaning, much as did Kaph. Here we find the higher aspects of balance, justice, equity, and law, but ruling not only in the higher realms, but dispensing its lawful decrees in the world of Men through action/reaction. In this way, the Path exerts a leveling influence on the actions of mankind through a cause/effect relationship. The results stemming directly from those actions are thus brought about without regard to emotional appeal, social convention, or excuse. *Basal Attribute of the Path*: the Zodiacal Sign of Libra. *Tarot Attribution of Path*: Tarot Trump, Eleven (XI)—Justice.

• *Path Number on the Tree*: Twenty-Three (**23**), connecting Geburah and Hod.

Path Name: Mem (Hebrew letter 'M'), meaning, Water. *Position of Hebrew letter in alphabet*: Thirteenth of Thirteen (13). *Numerical Value of Hebrew letter*: 40 (Forty). *Symbolic Meaning of Path*: "The Stable Intelligence." *Occult Concept of Path*: The higher aspects of this Path refers to Mankind in a state of sin, unredeemed, but possessing that spiritual nature which will lead him to his ultimate Salvation. *Basal Attribute of the Path*: the Element, Water. *Tarot Attribution of Path*: Tarot Trump, Twelve (XII)—The Hanged Man.

• *Path Number on the Tree*: Twenty-Four (**24**), connecting Tiphareth and Netzach.

Path Name: Nun (Hebrew letter 'N'), meaning, Fish. *Position of Hebrew letter in alphabet*: Fourteenth, or Fourteen (14). *Numerical Value of Hebrew letter*: 50 (Fifty). *Symbolic Meaning of Path*: "The Imaginative Intelligence." *Occult Concept of Path*: The higher aspects of this Path have a two-fold attribution. The first is reflective of the alchemical process of Putrefaction that leads to the stage of Regeneration. In this case, reference is made to the Work on the Stone of the Wise. Through this process, the former *physical*, putrefied base material is exalted through a spiritual unfoldment and psychic development on the part of the alchemist, eventually leading to *the* physical manifestation of the Philosophic Substance in the laboratory. This is a highly elevated activity of the Sensible Qualities of this Path. It is this laboratory operation that combines the unfoldment of the alchemist with the 'first part' of the laboratory alchemical act—using the "First Trinity Process" as I term it—of Maceration, Digestion, and Cohobation, to produce the Black Dragon. This seemingly dead substance is then used to produce the Philosophic Substance through the "Second Trinity Process" of Separation, Purification, and Cohobation. The second meaning of this Path is its reference to the spiritual process which mirrors the laboratory process exactly: The Dark Night of the Soul, a time in which the individual undergoes the stages of Separation, Purification, and Cohobation, but within his or her own nature, so that the Light of the Spirit within them becomes manifest throughout their entire nature: physical, psychic, and spiritual. *Basal Attribute of the Path:* the Zodiacal Sign of Scorpio. *Tarot Attribution of Path:* Tarot Trump, Thirteen (XIII)—Death.

• **Path Number on the Tree**: Twenty-Five (**25**), connecting Tiphareth and Yesod.

Path Name: Samech (Hebrew letter 'S'), meaning, Prop. *Position of Hebrew letter in alphabet*: Fifteenth, or Fifteen (15). *Numerical Value of Hebrew letter*: 60 (Sixty). *Symbolic Meaning of Path*: "The Tentative Intelligence." *Occult Concept of Path*: Once again, in its higher aspect, the individual's ascent to the Holy Guardian Angel is implied by this Path. Notice the 'upward' movement from Yesod into Tiphareth: the latter being the realm of the HGA. The ascent is thereby through the world of Yesod, the foundation for all magic that is to have an effect in the world of Malkuth (See entry under Yesod in the section on the Sephiroth.) Yesod also takes the correspondence of the unconscious mind, that gateway leading to the realm of ritual and ceremonial magic, and through them, upward toward the HGA. *Basal Attribute of the Path*: the Zodiacal Sign of Sagittarius. *Tarot Attribution of Path*: Tarot Trump, Fourteen (XIV)—Temperance.

• **Path Number on the Tree**: Twenty-Six (**26**), connecting Tiphareth and Hod.

Path Name: Ayin (Hebrew letter, 'O' (nasal), meaning, an Eye. *Position of Hebrew letter in alphabet*: Sixteenth, or

Sixteen (16). *Numerical Value of Hebrew letter*: 70 (Seventy). *Symbolic Meaning of Path*: "The Renovating Intelligence." *Occult Concept of Path*: The higher aspect of this Path is indicative of that creative, innate spiritual power of God existing within the individual. If this God-power actually manifests itself within the individual, that person becomes as a semi-divine being, partaking of both the nature of a man and a God. He or she knows their True Will, is exalted thereby, and begins the arduous process of liberating the world through the exercise of that True Will in the world of mankind. *Basal Attribute of the Path*: the Zodiacal Sign of Capricorn. *Tarot Attribution of Path*: Tarot Trump, Fifteen (XV)—The Devil.

• *Path Number on the Tree*: Twenty-Seven (**27**), connecting Netzach and Hod.

Path Name: Peh (Hebrew letter 'P'), meaning, Mouth. *Position of Hebrew letter in alphabet*: Seventeenth, or Seventeen (17). *Numerical Value of Hebrew letter*: 80 (Eighty). *Symbolic Meaning of Path*: "The Exciting Intelligence." *Occult Concept of Path*: This Path exhibits the correspondence of Mars by virtue of its Basal Attribute, and consequently of the Sephirah Geburah in general, but in a more mundane manner. That is, it represents raw force, which although destructive in nature, yet has an implication in terms of a higher aspect in that it leads to a position of exalted spiritual, psychic and magical power, by he or she who survives the test of its raw, destructive force. Additionally, in a purely mystical sense, it endows every being in existence with spirit and movement, thereby giving motion to all life. *Basal Attribute of the Path*: The planet Mars. *Tarot Attribution of Path*: Tarot Trump, Sixteen (XVI)—The Tower.

• *Path Number on the Tree*: Twenty-Eight (**28**), connecting Netzach and Yesod.

Path Name: Tzaddi (Hebrew letters 'Ts' or 'Tz'), meaning, a Hook, or a Fish Hook. *Position of Hebrew letter in alphabet*: Eighteenth, or Eighteen (18). *Numerical Value of Hebrew letter*: 90 (Ninety). *Symbolic Meaning of Path*: "The Natural Intelligence." *Occult Concept of Path*: The feminine aspects of both the Moon and Venus which correspond to the two Sephiroth so joined by this Path, indicate the feminine nature of this Path as well. Through its creative impulses of this Path, Creation throughout the natural world is perfected and made whole. *Basal Attribute of the Path*: the Zodiacal Sign of Aquarius, though an Air Sign, is attributed to this Path, owing to its Water-Bearer symbology. *Tarot Attribution of Path*: Tarot Trump, Seventeen (XVII)—The Star.

• *Path Number on the Tree*: Twenty-Nine (**29**), connecting Netzach and Malkuth.

Path Name: Qoph (Hebrew letter 'Q'), meaning, the Back of the Head. *Position of Hebrew letter in alphabet*: Nineteenth, or Nineteen (19). *Numerical Value of Hebrew letter*: 100 (One hundred). *Symbolic Meaning of Path*: "The Corporeal Intelligence." *Occult Concept of Path*: While there are a host of attributions and correspondences assigned to this Path, none of them truly explain its nature. My own metaphysical and magical investigations of this Path have shown it to be a type of channel in the Astral Light through which those spiritual, psychic, and material desires and wants of the individual are made manifest. Specifically, I am referring to those magical acts that are intended to produce an effect in the physical world. It does not matter what Sephirah the magician may be working with—the role of Yesod as the foundation for all manifestations of metaphysical, mystical, and magical work being taken into account, of course—it nevertheless appears that this Path is invoked automatically in translating those manifestations into physical form. It is a very powerful Path in this regard, and one that is all too often overlooked in magical work in particular, and in occult work in general. The meanings of the two Sephiroth involved, and this Path's effects, should be carefully studied by the modern occult and magical practitioner. *Basal Attribute of the Path*: the negative, or feminine, polarity: watery, Zodiacal Sign Pisces. *Tarot Attribution of Path*: Tarot Trump, Eighteen (XVIII)—The Moon. (Notice the watery, female, creative aspects of the card in reference to the *Occult Concept of the Path*. Also, the reader would do well to consider the Lunar nature of this card as being the Planetary Attribution of Yesod, and the characteristic of this Path as a channel for material manifestation, as explained above.)

• *Path Number on the Tree*: Thirty (**30**), connecting Hod and Yesod.

Path Name: Resh (Hebrew letter 'R'), meaning, a Head. *Position of Hebrew letter in alphabet*: Twentieth, or Twenty (20). *Numerical Value of Hebrew letter*: 200 (Two hundred). *Symbolic Meaning of Path*: "The Collecting Intelligence." *Occult Concept of Path*: All of the attributions of this Path are strictly solar. As such, they refer to the attributes and correspondences assigned to the Sephirah Tiphareth, and to its Sensible Qualities produced and governed by the Sun. It is therefore a Path that 'collects' the attributes of the Sun such as Light, Life, Love, and Growth of every type, as well as the attributes of Hod, and combines them with foundational characteristics of Yesod discussed earlier in preparation for bringing them down into Malkuth through the Thirty-Second Path. This part of the process of manifestation in Malkuth—here, through Path 30—occurs in a masculine, fiery, and dynamic way, owing to the solar forces involved, as contrasted to the watery, passive, feminine process used by the Path 28, Tzaddi (the Feminine, Passive nature of the Pillar of Severity of which Hod is a part notwithstanding.) *Basal Attribute of the Path*: the First Planet of the Ancients, the Sun. *Tarot Attribution of Path*: Tarot Trump, Nineteen (XIX)—The Sun.

• *Path Number on the Tree*: Thirty-One (**31**), connecting Hod and Malkuth.

Path Name: Shin (Hebrew letter 'Sh'), meaning a Tooth. *Position of Hebrew letter in alphabet*: Twenty-First, or Twenty-One (21). *Numerical Value of Hebrew letter*: 300 (Three hundred). *Symbolic Meaning of Path*: "The Perpetual Intelligence." *Occult Concept of Path*: The fiery descent of Divine Wisdom and the dedication to live that state in the world of mankind. An example which conveys the principles behind such an awakening is found in the descent of the Holy Ghost upon the Apostles, enlightening them, and bringing about the resolve within each of them necessary to take the teachings of the Divine Christ to the people of the world, amidst the hostile Roman and Pagan forces that pressed upon them from every side. Recall also the *Occult Concept* of Path 30 as well, and its implication in this Hod-to-Yesod and Hod-to-Malkuth connection. *Basal Attribute of the Path*: the Element, Fire. *Tarot Attribution of Path*: Tarot Trump, Twenty (XX)—The Last Judgment.

• **Path Number on the Tree**: Thirty-Two (**32**), connecting Yesod and Malkuth.

Path Name: Tav (Hebrew letter 'T'), meaning, a Cross, and specifically a three-armed cross. That is, a cross shaped as the letter 'T.' *Position of Hebrew letter in alphabet*: Twenty-Second, or Twenty-Two (22). *Numerical Value of Hebrew letter*: 400 (Four hundred.) *Symbolic Meaning of Path*: "The Administrative Intelligence." *Occult Concept of Path*: Besides the implication of the purpose of this 32nd Path given in the discussion for Path 30, Path 32 possesses a bittersweet characteristic, but only owing to the 'higher-minded' of the Kabbalists who translated such a bitter-sweet necessity as 'evil.' This 32nd Path is that portal or channel which allows the coarsest matter of the Astral Plane to enter the world of Malkuth, while also representing all existing intelligences throughout Creation at the same time. My personal experience of this Path has shown it to be, in reality, the Path that governs the mechanics of physical existence, which can be pointedly summed up as providing a common plane for the existence and expression of both good and evil, all at the same time. Thus, it is a stage wherein the drama of daily material, psychic, and spiritual life unfolds, grows, expands, interacts, and develops, with each of these facets of Creation set up according to its own rules and laws. *Basal Attribute of the Path*: The planet, Saturn. *Tarot Attribution of Path*: Tarot Trump, Twenty-One (XXI)—The World.

If the reader has paid careful attention to the Sephiroth and Path material, and has spent a reasonable length of time contemplating it, he or she now has an adequate base of knowledge. Up to this point I have focused on the Intelligible Qualities of the Sephiroth and Paths, by providing the higher aspects of the Symbolic Meanings, always extrapolating the more practical or Sensible Qualities as if they were of secondary importance. But now we will finally focus exclusively on what underlies the Kabbalistic Cycles System, which is the *Sensible Qualities of both the Sephiroth and the Paths.*

If you will recall, I stated earlier that since each of the Sephiroth are Paths themselves, they possess a Sensible Quality by virtue of their Astrological Attribution, their planetary correspondence. The Sensible Qualities of the Sephiroth are projected into the world of Malkuth through the projections radiating from their planetary correspondences. I also posed the question that if this is the case, and all of the Seven Planets of the Ancients have already been assigned to Binah through Yesod, then where are the projectors of the remaining twenty-two Paths which project into the lower or more mundane World of Malkuth, as the Sephiroth did?

I had further stated that there was only one important, fundamental correspondence to the *Sensible Qualities of the Paths*, and that fundamental correspondence is *the* attribution of the Paths that you will be using to work the Kabbalistic Cycles System. As you may have guessed, *the fundamental attribution that projects the Sensible Qualities of the Paths into the World of Malkuth is the Tarot.*

Neither the feminine or male polarities of the Paths, their Basal Elements, the numerical values of the Hebrew letters, their placements in the Hebrew alphabet, nor their Symbolic Meanings, have anything to do with the use of the Kabbalistic Cycles System in *daily life*. I caution here however, to take note of the term *daily life*, because these other attributions do most certainly have a great deal of importance in understanding, comprehending, and apprehending the Kabbalah proper.

In reality, all parts not only support the whole, but go into making it up as well. It is simply that we use the Tarot and the planetary projections of the Sephiroth to apply the Kabbalistic Cycles System to our daily, worldly, affairs. Since you now know the planetary attributions of the

Sephiroth, we will turn to an exposition of the Paths' Tarot correspondences.

CHAPTER SIX

The Tarot and Its Path
Assignments

A t this point you may be asking, "What! What are
you talking about? The Tarot can be used in this
'Cycles System' business you're harping about? I
thought you said the Tarot was not convenient as a divinatory tool, because there are too many possible sources of
error involved, and because of this subjective synthesis
stuff you're so fond of mouthing!

"And now you tell me it's the sole projector of the
Sensible Qualities of the Paths, and that I am to use this
along with that planetary projection business of the planets
to gain control and achieve certainty in my life? What's
going on here?!" Whew. Some readers can certainly ask
compound questions in the same breath! Be that as it may,
allow me to explain, and in so doing, answer your percep-
tive and well-stated questions.

To begin with, the Tarot cannot be used conveniently
in daily life. In fact, it cannot be used at all in the great
majority of cases, simply because life has a way of throwing problems at you so fast, you are lucky if you can catch
your breath in between them, let alone sneak off somewhere with your trusty deck to cast a spread.

Secondly, this is most certainly true. The Tarot—as
with any other divinatory system—will only work for you
as accurately and effectively as your state of subjective
synthesis allows. But this is also due primarily to the complex types and natures of the methods-of-spreads themselves, as well as the depth of your familiarity, memory,
and understanding of the symbolism and meanings of *all*

the cards. In many spread-methods this would mean all 78 cards, which is no easy task, I can assure you! So while we cannot use the Tarot as a divinatory tool in daily life by casting a spread, we can use it in the Kabbalistic Cycles System by doing two relatively simple things:

- Develop a relatively quick understanding and comprehension of Sensible Qualities *only*, that the cards are said to 'project' or stand for according to tradition, and—
- Confine ourselves to using only the twenty-two cards of the Greater Arcana or the Trumps Major, as opposed to the additional fifty-six cards of the Lesser Arcana. That is, the four Suits or fourteen cards, each.

"But how do you 'legitimize' such a procedure? Isn't this some contrivance of yours to 'make' this 'System' of yours work?" I can hear some of my readers saying. Well, to prove to you this is not some contrivance on my part, but rather a discovery I made throughout the decades of deriving this Kabbalistic Cycles System, let me explain.

First of all, with the Sephiroth and Paths, it was necessary for you to gain a foundational understanding of their attributes and correspondences, so you could begin to use this system. Remember also that I cautioned the state of your subjective synthesis, which is the extent of the superstructure you erect on this foundational knowledge, will determine how effectively and efficiently this system will work for you.

But as I promised, the information I gave you on the Sephiroth and Paths is more than sufficient for you to start using the system quite effectively and efficiently, starting almost immediately. Of course, if you are serious about the Tarot, you will take my advice to heart, and study the book I recommended in Chapter Four—*The Pictorial Key to the Tarot*, written by Arthur Edward Waite.[34] It explains clearly how to use the cards.

Even though Waite's work is complete, I also strongly recommend the following, but only for those who wish to penetrate further into the study of this fascinating divinatory device. They are: *The Tarot, Its Occult Significance, Use in Fortune-Telling, and Method of Play*, by S.L. MacGregor Mathers,[35] and *The Magical Ritual of the Sanctum Regnum, Interpreted by the Tarot Trumps*, by Eliphas Levi, and translated by W. Wynn Westcott.[36]

Using Waite as your primary text, contemplate the Intelligible and Sensible meanings he assigns to the cards, along with a contemplation of their symbolism. You will eventually reach that same state of apprehension of the Tarot as in your mastery of the Kabbalah. Then you possess it all. But for now, to enable you to begin using the system as soon as you finish this book, only the mastery of the Sensible Qualities of the cards is necessary. *That is, those that you will find in this chapter.*

Secondly, *I* did not assign the twenty-two cards of the Greater Arcana to the twenty-two Paths of the Tree of Life. These were assigned to the Paths by the creators of the Kabbalah. Thus, you can legitimately concern yourself with this limited Arcana only.

Since the reader and I are deriving this system together, it is necessary to build upon what has gone before, and with each further level, add yet another. That procedure necessitates the format that follows for us to explore the Sensible Qualities of the twenty-two cards of the Greater Arcana in a comprehensive and logical manner.

Please be certain to refer to Figure 3 throughout the discussion to follow. It will help you to understand, and enable you to quickly become acquainted with the position of the Tarot Trumps on the Paths. Of course, you should also have in your possession the Rider-Waite Tarot deck, and view each card as they are discussed herein. Remember too, that these mundane or Sensible Qualities, as I term them, are just that. They are brief, mundane characteristics that I and many, many others have found to hold true for these cards: both in casting a spread, and most importantly, for use in this system.

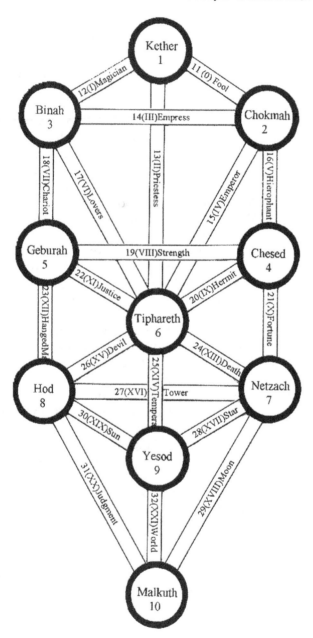

FIGURE 3. THE TREE OF LIFE. GLYPH 3.

Lastly, you will see meanings given for each card in both its 'upright' position and its 'reversed' or 'upside down' position. That is, in the upright position, the figures on the card are in a normal position, and the card number—for example, the card, The Fool (0)—points outward and away from you. In the reversed or upside down position, the picture literally appears upside down or reversed, and the card number—as with the example of The Fool—points inward and toward you.

The meanings of the two positions of each card must first be memorized and then studied and contemplated. You will understand why all of this is necessary when we study the 'Flow' on the Tree.

THE FOOL (0)

Corresponding Path on the Tree: Number 11 (Eleven)—Aleph—Connecting Kether and Chokmah. *Sensible Meaning in Malkuth.* In the **upright** position: Foolhardiness in action; foolishness in thought and deed; wildly excessive behavior; extravagant behavior, thoughts, and propositions. A greatly exaggerated sense of one's own importance and position in life; fantastic ideas and speculations. In the **reversed** position: trouble stemming from the extravagances listed above. Also difficulties from indecision, vacillation, and irresolution.

THE MAGICIAN (1)

Corresponding Path on the Tree: Number 12 (Twelve)—Beth—Connecting Kether and Binah. *Sensible Meaning in Malkuth.* In the **upright** position: power of the individual's resolve; appropriate skills to meet the task at hand; power of the will to effect the change desired; confidence in one's own ideas, abilities, and the determination to carry them through to completion. In the **reversed** position: conceit; lack of appropriate skills for the task at hand; lack of self confidence; lack of will to effect the change(s) sought; lack of individual power and resolve to effect the ends desired.

THE HIGH PRIESTESS (II)

Corresponding Path on the Tree: Number 13 (Thirteen)—
Gimel—Connecting Kether and Tiphareth. *Sensible Meaning in Malkuth.* In the **upright** position: knowledge; deep thought; scientific thought, ideas, and all matters pertaining to scientific education. Also, educational matters in general. Logical thought; rational thinking and cogent argument style; cognitive skills. In the **reversed** position: illiteracy; ignorance; shallowness of thought and idea; surface knowledge; a lack of structure of the knowledge one is seeking.

THE EMPRESS (III)

Corresponding Path on the Tree: Number 14 (Fourteen)—
Daleth—Connecting Chokmah and Binah. *Sensible Meaning in Malkuth.* In the **upright** position: fecundity in all matters, prolific results; accomplishment; the act of doing, fruitfulness in all things; earthiness; creativity. In the **reversed** position: dissipation of one's energy; loss of power in general; incomplete results due to hesitancy, indecision, or irresolution in acting.

THE EMPEROR (IV)

Corresponding Path on the Tree: Number 15 (Fifteen)—
Heh—Connecting Chokmah and Tiphareth. *Sensible Meaning in Malkuth.* In the **upright** position: one's right or prerogative to rule or to determine for one's self; authority; command; control; domination; effective action; mastery; might; the power of reason; justification; the making of rationalizations that are right and just. In the **reversed** position: juvenile, childish emotions and their display; loss of authority, control, and command. Blocked plans and schemes.

THE HIEROPHANT (V)

Corresponding Path on the Tree: Number 16 (Sixteen)—
Vav—Connecting Chokmah and Chesed. *Sensible Meaning in Malkuth.* In the **upright** position: kindness; mercy; righteousness; morality; virtue; the quality of goodness; a person who exhibits these high human qualities. In the

reversed position: excessive kindness; excessive mercy; weakness resulting from such excess; the inability to discern such excess, due to a lack of emotional control.

THE LOVERS (VI)

Corresponding Path on the Tree: Number 17 (Seventeen) —Zayin—Connecting Binah and Tiphareth. *Sensible Meaning in Malkuth.* In the **upright** position: a trial in life or an experiment of a personal nature that you will successfully conclude; the emergence of a new affection or object of devotion, whether it be a person or new interest of some type. In the **reversed** position: a failed life-trial or experiment; the loss of affection for a person or interest.

THE CHARIOT (VII)

Corresponding Path on the Tree: Number 18 (Eighteen)— Cheth—Connecting Binah and Geburah. *Sensible Meaning in Malkuth.* In the **upright** position: victory, conquest, overcoming odds and obstructions, but only after battle. In the **reversed** position: defeat after battle; obstructions to plans and actions; plans and actions defeated by either internal or external obstructions and obstacles, but once again, only after battle. *Commentary*: this card, and card XVI—The Tower, Path 27, Peh—are the most difficult cards of the Greater Arcana. With either card, the plans made, the opportunities that arise, and the actions taken under their influence, have an extremely grim, major component to them. Of the two cards however, this card (VII) The Chariot, is perhaps surprisingly the hardest of the two to work with, even in its upright position, for it bespeaks of a long, arduous struggle which will take a heavy toll on the individual, even though he or she will become victorious (when it is in the upright position).

STRENGTH (VIII)

Corresponding Path on the Tree: Number 19 (Nineteen)— Teth—Connecting Chesed and Geburah. *Sensible Meaning in Malkuth.* In the **upright** position: metaphysical or spiritual force and strength; inner strength which overcomes danger and adversity. The strength through which the

Holy warrior battles against overwhelming odds, and victoriously subdues and overcomes a great threat. Subjugation of opposition through spiritual power. In the **reversed** position: power and strength, but physical in nature. Endurance and determination in matters requiring physical strength, and the physical prowess through which these qualities are sustained.

THE HERMIT (IX)

Corresponding Path on the Tree: Number 20 (Twenty)— Yod—Connecting Chesed and Tiphareth. *Sensible Meaning in Malkuth.* In the **upright** position: deliberation, due to watchful attention, or a feeling of caution; a warning, things are not as they seem. Also, the furthering of psychic growth. In the **reversed** position: excessive self-admonition or over-cautiousness in important matters; imprudent actions; ill-advised activities; indiscreet behavior.

THE WHEEL OF FORTUNE (X)

Corresponding Path on the Tree: Number 21 (Twenty-one)—Kaph—Connecting Chesed and Netzach. *Sensible Meaning in Malkuth.* In the **upright** position: beneficence; expansiveness; growth; money; good luck; good fortune; success. In the **reversed** position: ill fortune; the reversal of dame fortune; hardship; loss; contraction; struggle; failure.

JUSTICE (XI)

Corresponding Path on the Tree: Number 22 (Twenty-two)—Lamed—Connecting Geburah and Tiphareth. *Sensible Meaning in Malkuth.* In the **upright** position: harmony, justice, stability; poise; equilibrium; balance. In the **reversed** position: conflict, injustice; instability; imbalance, intolerance.

THE HANGED MAN (XII)

Corresponding Path on the Tree: Number 23 (Twenty-three)—Mem—Connecting Geburah and Hod. *Sensible Meaning in Malkuth.* In the **upright** position: the acquisition of knowledge which eventually matures into wisdom. The process is slow however, and as with life in general, requires sacrifices on the part of the individual for that knowledge to ripen into wisdom. In the **reversed** position: self-centeredness; concern for one's self exclusively at the obvious expense of others; sly, deceptive behavior designed to have one accepted by the group or masses.

DEATH (XIII)

Corresponding Path on the Tree: Number 24 (Twenty-four)—Nun—Connecting Tiphareth and Netzach. *Sensible Meaning in Malkuth.* In the **upright** position: physical death; an end; a massive, nebulous change or transformation in the individual, comparable to the end of a part of the self as occurs—for example—in the Attainment of the K&C of the HGA. In the **reversed** position: corruption; disintegration; decomposition through putrefaction; stasis. *Commentary:* this Path is not as difficult as it sounds. In reality, its meanings usually refer to the evolution and development of the Self through the process of self-growth, the means used to achieve this state notwithstanding. It is a hard path in terms of process, but its end results are stunning and utterly glorious.

TEMPERANCE (XIV)

Corresponding Path on the Tree: Number 25 (Twenty-five)—Samech—Connecting Tiphareth and Yesod. *Sensible Meaning in Malkuth.* In the **upright** position: to unite or wed seemingly disparate concepts, ideas, or actions in a positive and beneficial way; the use of temperate or measurable means and ways in thoughts and actions; a balanced approach to a problem, and the judicious implementation of its solution. In the **reversed** position: disparate concepts, ideas, or actions which cannot be conjoined or united; disagreement; loggerheads; an extreme approach to a problem and its unbalanced implementation, which not only does not resolve the original problem, but which creates additional problems as a result of the extreme measures employed.

THE DEVIL (XV)

Corresponding Path on the Tree: Number 26 (Twenty-six)—Ayin—Connecting Tiphareth and Hod. *Sensible*

Meaning in Malkuth. In the **upright** position: an eventual beneficial or favorable result arises from a seemingly deleterious event or situation. In the **reversed** position: that same situation produces a unfavorable or very unsatisfactory result, or is concluded in some negative and possibly harmful manner.

THE TOWER (XVI)

Corresponding Path on the Tree: Number 27 (Twenty-seven)—Peh—Connecting Netzach and Hod. *Sensible Meaning in Malkuth.* In the **upright** position: devolution; downfall; degeneration; decadence; disaster; calamity; tragedy; woes; catastrophe, disruption. In the **reversed** position: the same, but to a lesser degree. *Commentary*: this card, and card VII—The Chariot—along with their Paths, are by far the most difficult and dangerous Paths on the Tree. As you will see when working the Cycles System, their influence is to be watched for carefully at all times, and avoided if at all possible.

THE STAR (XVII)

Corresponding Path on the Tree: Number 28 (Twenty-eight)—Tzaddi—Connecting Netzach and Yesod. *Sensible Meaning in Malkuth.* In the **upright** position: happy expectation; joyful expectancy; happy prospects; an exciting future filled with many possibilities. In the **reversed** position: happy expectations and joyful expectancies are disappointed or thwarted; emptiness; effeteness.

THE MOON (XVIII)

Corresponding Path on the Tree: Number 29 (Twenty-nine)—Qoph—Connecting Netzach and Malkuth. *Sensible Meaning in Malkuth.* In the **upright** position: secret enemies; cunning on the part of others for their own ends; deceit; duplicity; concealed forces in operation; hidden enemies; conspiracies against the individual innocently involved in a matter or situation. In the **reversed** position: the same, but to a lesser extent.

THE SUN (XIX)

Corresponding Path on the Tree: Number 30 (Thirty)—Resh—Connecting Hod and Yesod. *Sensible Meaning in Malkuth*. In the **upright** position: bliss; happiness; contentment; joy; desires and goals achieved; wants satisfied; appeasement in general. In the **reversed** position: the same, but to a lesser extent.

THE LAST JUDGMENT (XX)

Corresponding Path on the Tree: Number 31 (Thirty-one)—Shin—Connecting Hod and Malkuth. *Sensible Meaning in Malkuth*. In the **upright** position: rejuvenation; renewals of all types; outcomes reached; new beginnings; fresh starts. In the **reversed** position: problems causing efforts to bog down; delays; reversals; cowardly behavior.

THE WORLD (XXI)

Corresponding Path on the Tree: Number 32 (Thirty-two)—Tav—Connecting Yesod and Malkuth. *Sensible Meaning in Malkuth*. In the **upright** position: completion; assured success; compensation; remuneration; repayment; recompense; a prosperous or thriving conclusion. In the **reversed** position: stagnation, inertia; stasis; failed project or attempt; failure as a force, in general.

At this point, I would like to call the reader's attention to one very important point. Please keep it in mind as you proceed through the next chapters. As you will see, we will be using a simple mnemonic device to place the planets in the Kabbalistic Cycles Chart. (Chapter Seven) And as usual, the reason for doing so will be explained.

In like manner, there is a consideration here with the twenty-two Tarot cards of the Greater Arcana, of which you need to be aware. That is, cards Zero (0) through Five (V), and cards XVIII, XX, and XXI, are not used in the Kabbalistic Cycles System.

Of course, you have probably deduced the reason for this yourself, having diligently studied the Sephiroth and Paths. But just in case, let's take an initiated look as to why these eight particular cards are not used.

Specifically, cards Zero (0) through Five (V) are assigned to Paths that connect the highest three Sephiroth on the Tree in such a way that at least one of the first two Supernals—Kether or Chokmah—are always involved. Being involved, they do not enter into the stream of daily, mundane life. Neither do those mundane planetary attributions of the other Sephiroth that are so connected by them in this schema. Why is this? Look at Figure 3.

There you can see that the Path, Aleph—which is assigned the card, Zero (0) The Fool—connects Kether and Chokmah. From your study of these two Sephiroth, by now you can understand that their nature is beyond even the most exalted areas of human concern. In like manner, there is the Path Beth—connecting Kether and Binah— which takes card One (I) The Magician, also beyond everyday interaction, due to its partaking directly of the exalted nature of Kether.

In like fashion, Gimel, being the Path connecting Kether and Tiphareth—and taking card Two (II) The High Priestess—is a unique Path and card attribution that is actually reserved as a means of special ascent for those who have Attained the K&C of the HGA. In the overall then, its principles and properties though which this ascent is made are too rarefied to have a corresponding influence in the mundane world of humans. It has other uses to be sure, but they too are beyond the play of material life, and as such do not enter into use. The Path Daleth acts as the bridge between Chokmah and Binah, and from the dynamism we know to exist as a result of this jointure, it is clear that card Three (III) The Empress can have no play in our daily use either.

Then we come to Heh, card Four (IV) The Emperor. Obviously Chokmah, being *the* Reflection by which the One, Kether—'reflected upon itself to become Two' as the Kabbalists teach—allows only for its majestic influence in Tiphareth in higher Alchemical pursuits and genuine spiritual growth, as explained in the section on the Paths. Thus it too is unavailable for mundane application. And finally, Vav—the Path uniting Chokmah and Chesed—which

takes card Five (V) The Hierophant, is also above the normal spire of daily human life, due to the very nature of
Chokmah as the First Creative Impulse from Kether.

In the case of card Eighteen (XVIII) The Moon, its
assignment to Path 29 which connects Netzach and
Malkuth, does not allow its effects to flow directly into the
dense plane of Malkuth. This can only occur through
Yesod and the Moon which—if you remember from the
discussion of Yesod—means this Sephirah and its lunar
correspondence projects all of the previous forces from the
Tree into Malkuth directly.

*In other words, in the Kabbalistic Cycles System, the other
forces of the Tree **are** focused into the human life-stream in
Malkuth, but **only** through the Moon, via the subconscious
(unconscious) mind of the individual. They do not enter
Malkuth directly to influence the individual's life, except though
the subconscious portal.* **Perhaps now you can see why your
state of subjective synthesis is so very important.** This is a
very important discovery, and it would do the reader well
to consider and reflect upon it carefully.

For the same reason, card XX The Final Judgment and
card XXI The World, cannot enter into the individual's life-
stream in Malkuth directly. *They too must do so through
Yesod and the Moon*: hence the importance of Path 28—
Tzaddi, connecting Netzach and Yesod—and Path 30—
Resh, connecting Hod and Yesod. Pay special attention
and look closely at their respective associations and card
imagery.

For instance, attend to card XVIII The Moon, and card
XVII The Star, and you will come to understand the occult
significance behind this seemingly odd situation. You may
even come to understand that cards XVII and XIX are
actually higher harmonics of XVIII and XX, and in this
way, bring the Sensible Qualities of the Sephiroth involved—through the planetary projections of their planetary attributions—down into Malkuth, after attenuating
them for use by humankind.

Lastly, there is card XXI The World, flowing from
Yesod to Malkuth through Path 32, Tav. Since all flow

from Yesod into Malkuth is considered to be good and beneficial, card XXI The World acts as a symbolic completion of the process of the Tree, bringing its fruits down into this, the densest of the worlds of matter. It is a given, if you will, and as such, has no bearing on the Kabbalistic Cycles System whatsoever.

It could very well be argued that I am attempting to fit a rationalization to a system that I favor. I tell the reader this. After working with the Cycles System for even a brief period of time, you will come to understand that this is not the case. The thirty-two years it took to uncover the laws behind these phenomena, provided more than ample time for such self-deception to inevitably reveal itself to me. And the plain fact of the matter is, in the system presented to you in this book, there simply was none. It works. Period. Further, as your study of the Kabbalah continues, you will come to realize that these are not *my* arguments or conventions, but are ones stated or inferred in one way or another and in greater depth throughout Kabbalistic literature.

With the information given in this chapter and Chapter Five, the reader now has sufficient background to proceed with the final parts of the derivation. You might have also noticed that Figures 1, 2, and 3 are evolutionary in structure. That is, in Figure 1, I gave a simple glyph of the Tree of Life with as few labels as possible. This was done to familiarize those readers who have little or no background in Kabbalah with the basics of the Tree.

In Figure 2, more labels were added, further expanding the reader's scope of awareness of the Tree and its correspondences and attributions, thereby adding to his or her new or existing knowledge base. Finally, in Figure 3, all pertinent and applicable features of the Tree that we will be using in the Kabbalistic Cycles System were added, expanding the individual's foundational knowledge and awareness still further.

You see, your developed state of subjective synthesis is so incredibly important in occult matters in general and magical matters in particular, and in understanding and using the Kabbalistic Cycles System, that I wanted to be sure your study of the material would pay you the dividends you deserve and expect. By the use of such simple devices, along with rephrasing and repetition as methods of presentation, I am confident your operational intellectual base and state of subjective synthesis will be nothing short of excellent.

There will be more of this 'evolutionary' approach as we continue on to the end of this book, so please be aware of this and be patient! You are learning something entirely new; something which has never been previously introduced to the public at large. As a result, your thought patterns must be adjusted to a multitude of old concepts, but employed in a new way. This takes work, energy, and of course, time. These facts are all important. Remember, I simply want you to have the finest base which will enable you to gain that which you so desperately need, desire, and deserve in your life—*Certainty and Control.*

CHAPTER SEVEN

The Agrippa System of Planetary Hours of the Day and Night

I f the reader is at all familiar with the Occult, he or she is no doubt aware of some system of plotting the hours of the day and night. To be sure, there are many such systems in the literature of the field, the most commonly known and used today being the Rosicrucian Order (AMORC) system presented by H. Spencer Lewis in his book, *Self Mastery and Fate with the Cycles of Life*,[37] as was discussed in Chapter Four.

In magical literature, there are even more such astrologically based systems, with different Grimoires or Grammars of Magic requiring their own particular method to successfully work that grimoire. So what astrological system, if any, do we use in order to work this system? Fortunately, there is a remarkable easy solution to this problem.

In 1533, the *Three Books of Occult Philosophy*,[38] attributed to the scholar and magician, Henry Cornelius Agrippa von Nettesheim, first appeared in print as a complete set in Cologne, Germany. In this massive, all important sourcebook of Magic and Occultism, the author discusses a system of hours of the day and night—along with their planetary rulers—that serves as the basis of today's so called Western Magic. Although it is accurate to call it Western Magic, I feel it has become wedded to New Age Fad magic.

Nevertheless, the contents of Chapter XXXIV, "Of the True Motion of the Heavenly Bodies to be Observed in the Eighth Sphere, and of the Ground of Planetary Hours" in the Three Books, are accurate and precise in both their theory and application, as laid down by their author. This two-page chapter *effectively* explains that the astrologers of his time were committing a fundamental error by dividing the day (sunrise to sunset) into twelve equal periods. Agrippa (if he was indeed the author), refers to such an invention as an "artificial hour." Additionally, the hours of the night (sunset to sunrise) were obtained with the same method. (Note also, how a much more grievous, inaccurate variation of this erroneous system is in use throughout the world today in determining what 'time' it is.

In a difficult fashion, his text argues that these twelve equal segments of day and night hours are not to be divided into twelve equal parts, but rather, "...so also in planetary hours the ascensions of fifteen degrees in the ecliptic constituteth an unequal or planetary hour, whose measure we ought to inquire and find out by the tables of oblique ascensions of every region."[39] This is suggested as a more favorable division of the hours of the day and night into sections of unequal lengths, depending on the astronomical requirement stated in the quotation!

This is in answer to the equal hour division which the author acknowledges but does not favor as he states, "...for as in artificial hours, which are always equal to themselves, the ascensions of fifteen degrees in the equinoctial constituteth an artificial hour;..."[39] You can see the problem. If we use the more favorable division we would have to be profound astrologers in the nth degree, continuously calculating and recalculating every time any contingency of any kind arose!

In effect, adopting *any* system for achieving control and certainty in our lives would be utterly impossible. In such a case we would literally have to resort to sneaking off with our trusty deck of Tarot cards, attempt to cast a spread, and muddle through life as best we could, which most people unfortunately do. No. What the author of the Three Books was really suggesting was that such astronomical observances are to be confined to ritual and ceremonial magical practices of a major type, which is the same practical use of the cards.

In my opinion, it was his understanding of both sides of the coin that eventually gave rise to the system of artificial hours as they are applied in Occult and Magical work today, and which we indeed use in the Kabbalistic Cycles System. These artificial hours are truly magical hours and are astronomical in nature, as is indirectly argued for and defended in the Three Books. These hours are not based on the progressive movements of the hands on any watch or clock, whose accepted convention of marking time is a complete fabrication of social expediency in the first place.

Instead, these magical hours are not sixty-minutes in length. Rather, they are based upon the time between sunrise and sunset, and sunset and sunrise, which of course changes on a daily basis. Now, I can hear you asking just how are these hourly periods calculated and why is it even necessary to do so? Is all this instruction absolutely essential and imperative to use?!

The answer to your last question is yes. It is absolutely necessary, essential, and imperative, for reasons you will come to understand. The calculations are simple, and require no more mathematics than addition, subtraction, multiplication, and division. A simple handheld calculator will suffice, as long as it has at least a single memory cell to store one piece of data, and no more. Now, onto answering some of your other silent concerns.

THE REASON FOR CALCULATING THE HOURS OF THE DAY AND NIGHT

Cycles appear as frequencies, or patterns of repetition everywhere in Nature: from the change of seasons to a change in your sleep pattern; from the frequency of the electricity coming through your electrical wall outlet, to the beat of your heart. Cycles and an innumerable number of other rhythms are *the* fundamental *basis* of Nature, not simply just some part of it. From Babylon to Egypt to Greece, the early astrologers hammered out and synthesized an eclectic system not just of charts and maps, but a system to understand and employ the heavenly bodies.

They observed events in Nature-at-large and within their personal lives, and correlated those events, changes, and circumstances that seemed to flow from or be influenced by the arrangement and placement of the heavens. They studied the cyclic nature of the heavenly progressions and the periodicity of the movements of the wanderers, the Greek word from which the term planet arises. These early scientists' philosophy of the Natural Sciences was applied in one way or another in universities throughout the Mediterranean and Western European countries until at least the beginning of the 18th century.

As they formed and fashioned their astronomical knowledge, their philosophical inclinations were added to it, producing—among a vast number of other philosophical or occult and magical characteristics—an assignment of the planets to different hours or parts of the day and night, but in a certain order. Their occult and magical motivations were sparked not only from their observations of Nature and their own lives, but from their deeper philosophical apprehensions of the planets and the influences they produced upon all life. As a result, we have the planetary assignments to the hours of the day and night but in the special sequence mentioned.

These assignments were later commented upon and used by the author of the Three Books, and are still in use in today's magical systems. In our case, we calculate the times of sunrise and sunset as the beginning of that process by which the planets are then assigned to both twelve-hour periods of any given day. According to the sequence of these planets derived by the ancient astrologers and used by (later) magicians, we in turn ascribe them to these hours of the day and night. This is therefore the first step in the mechanical part of deriving the Kabbalistic Cycles System. Now that you are aware of what we will be doing and why, the rest will flow easily.

CALCULATION OF THE HOURS OF THE DAY AND NIGHT USING THE 'AGRIPPA SYSTEM'

The first information you need for calculating the hours of the day and night are the exact times of sunrise and sunset for the geographical position where you live. You will need to learn the exact longitude and latitude of your town or city, as that is where you no doubt spend the great majority of your time and consequently, the place where you will be applying the daily system.

While there are many astrological books, magazines, and guides out there, ready to provide this information for six dollars or so, I have never found them to be very precise. They wind up leaving it up to the individual to complete some tedious calculations which although very simple from a mathematical point of view, are messy to work with, and which inevitably encourages calculation errors. You can save your money, and obtain the most mathematically precise sunrise and sunset times by accessing any computer, logging onto the World Wide Web, and going to the following web address:

http://aa.usno.navy.mil/data/docs/RS_OneDay.html

When this address is placed into the URL Field (Universal Resource Locator field) of the web browser, it will take you to the United States Naval Observatory's web page of "Astronomical Applications Department—Complete Sun and Moon Data for One Day." On that page you will be able to enter the state or territory where you live, along with the actual city or town. After pressing the enter button on the web page, you will receive a display of the times of sunrise and sunset for your exact location for any day of the year. And surprise! It will also give you the exact latitude and longitude of your location, so you need not worry about obtaining this data from those six-dollar books to figure it out by yourself!

Save yourself a lot of bother however, and simply scroll down the web page to the Notes section, and in the third paragraph you will find an option for printing out all of the times of sunrise and sunset for your location for the entire year on one notebook size piece of paper. Do this, and you are all set for an entire year of using the Cycles System.

Now, to find the length of each of the twelve hours of the day for any day of the year, simply calculate the number of minutes between sunrise and sunset. Divide this number by twelve, and the quotient is the number of minutes in each of the twelve hours of that day. Next, subtract this number from 120—the number of minutes in two hours—which will give you the number of minutes in each of the twelve hours of the night, that is, in each of the hours from sunset to sunrise. The rest of the Kabbalistic Cycles System Chart construction is very simple and mechanical (see the tables of Figure 4 and Figure 5 at the end of this chapter), but as with anything new, can cause problems until you are familiar with it. To eliminate this possibility, let's take an example to make the point clear.

I am writing this from my specific location on Wednesday, August 25, 2004. According to my latitude and longitude, the times of sunrise and sunset are 5:28 AM Standard Time and 6:51 PM Standard Time. When obtaining the sunrise and sunset data from the web page, be certain to *always* specify that you want your chart in Standard Time for your location. Daylight Savings Time is not acceptable, since we need the true time to determine each period of the planetary influences.

Simple addition shows that there are a total of eight-hundred and three (803) minutes between sunrise and sunset for my position in this country. Now let's proceed in a stepwise fashion, to make it easy to follow this simple procedure.

1. Divide the total time of the hours between sunrise and sunset by twelve. That is, [803 ÷ 12]. When you do, you will find this yields 66.9167 minutes for each of the twelve hours of the day. Do not round off just yet. You need to carry this accuracy of the calculation through so your hours of the day and night end when they should. This extreme accuracy is not some weird penchant of mine for precision. The process of rounding off is an very serious matter in higher mathematics, as it *will* effect the

results obtained in the final answer. The same applies here. An error made at this point will grow in magnitude, because the error of this initial value will become compounded as further calculations are carried out.

2. Now refer to Figure 5—the **Kabbalistic Cycles System Chart for the Planetary Hours Ruling the Day(s) Specified**—and record the data you have so far. (Figure 4 is a blank chart that you can enlarge and photocopy so you won't have to make a new one each time. The actual example we are plotting out will be found in Figure 5, so please refer to it throughout this example.) On your chart, record the Name of the Day, the Date, the time of sunrise and sunset, and the division process that gave you the number of minutes in each of the twelve hours of the day. For me, in this example, today is Wednesday, August 25, 2004, 5:28 AM Standard Time, 6:51 PM Standard Time, $[803 \div 12 = 66.9167]$ (day).

3. Next, subtract the number of minutes in each day hour from one-hundred and twenty to get the number of minutes for each hour of the night, and enter it into your chart. For me, this would be: $[120 - 66.9167 = 53.0833]$ minutes for each night hour.

4. Label your chart for no more than three days at a time. In the example, you will see Wednesday through Friday, but we will follow through our example for Wednesday's calculation only, to be explained later. Now for the Key, which is a handy mnemonic device for remembering the order of the planets for those of you who are new to this idea. The Key is *"The first hour of the day of every day, takes the planet that rules that day."* The rulers of the days of the week are classically assigned as—

Monday = ruled by the Moon = 9
Tuesday = ruled by Mars = 5
Wednesday = ruled by Mercury = 8
Thursday = ruled by Jupiter = 4
Friday = ruled by Venus = 7
Saturday = ruled by Saturn = 3
Sunday = ruled by Sun = 6

The first hour of today in this example is ruled by Mercury, the planetary projection being projected into the World of Malkuth by the planet attributed to the eighth Sephirah on the Tree: Hod. Remember the Planetary Attribution of Hod in Chapter Five, under the section on The Sephiroth? Remember that since it is the eighth Sephirah on the Tree, it takes the number 8? This is how we begin to use that knowledge to work the Kabbalistic Cycles System.

Thus, Mercury and its attributions and the matters it rules as we discussed in Chapter Five, is the governing planet of this first hour of the day. As such, it provides for the effects and the matters it rules, during this hour. For practice, you can do as I have done and enter "Mer" in column one, row one—or cell 1—on a sample chart of your own.

And what is the mnemonic device for remembering the order of the planets? Easy! It's just "3, 4, 5, 6, 7, 8, 9, and back again!" You will see this applied in the next step. (Notice we only use the numbers and hence the planets of the Sephiroth 3 through 9. Please make note of this, as it will be an important point discussed a bit later in the appropriate part of your derivation.)

5. Please look at the chart again. You will see that the left hand division, labeled "Hours of the Day" is divided into three columns for Wednesday through Friday in this example, and that each column is divided into twelve rows, making twelve cells, one for each of the twelve hours of the days, for Wednesday through Friday. The same holds true for the right hand division of the chart. There are three columns, each divided into twelve rows labeled "Hours of the Night," producing twelve cells, one for each of the twelve hours of the night for each of the three days listed on the chart.

So the question now becomes, "What do I put in the remaining eleven cells of the Hours of the Day, and what gets put into the twelve cells of the Hours of the Night for Wednesday, in this example?" Here is where the mnemonic comes into play. It's just, "3, 4, 5, 6, 7, 8, 9 and back again!" You have 'Mer' in the first row, first column (cell 1). And what number does Mercury take? 8, of course. So what happens now? Use the mnemonic! "3, 4, 5, 6, 7, 8, 9 and back again!" What comes after 8? As we know, it is Nine (9). So place a small 9 off to the side in the next cell directly beneath Mer (cell 2). Now you have the first two cells filled.

To fill in the rest of the cells for the Hours of the Day, just, "3, 4, 5, 6, 7, 8, 9, and back again!" That is, start again at the number three (3), place it in the next or the third cell, and proceed to do the same with numbers 4, 5, 6, 7, 8, and 9. Now you will have nine of the twelve cells for the Hours of the Day for Wednesday filled in. That is, from the first hour of the day through the ninth. To fill in the final three cells and thus completing the twelve Hours of the Day of Wednesday, you simply "...and back again!" Start at number three (3), place this in the tenth cell, and the numbers four (4) and five (5) into the eleventh and twelfth cells, respectively. You're almost done.

Now look at the list above of the planets to which these numbers are assigned. See what I mean? Next to each number in each cell, you now simply write the names of the corresponding planets. In this case, all twelve cells will be filled in with—

Cell 1	Mer(cury) = 8
Cell 2	(the) Moon = 9
Cell 3	Sat(urn) = 3
Cell 4	Jup(iter) = 4
Cell 5	Mars = 5
Cell 6	(the) Sun = 6
Cell 7	Venus = 7
Cell 8	Mer(cury) = 8 (again, as the planets' sequence repeats.)
Cell 9	(the) Moon = 9
Cell 10	Sat(urn) = 3
Cell 11	Jup(iter) = 4
Cell 12	Mars = 5

And there you are. All of the planetary attributions for the twelve Hours of the Day for Wednesday are completely and accurately filled in. What's next? Let's take care of the twelve Hours of the Night.

6. Look at the second division on the Kabbalistic Cycles Chart. It is labeled "Hours of the Night." Under the column labeled Wednesday, you have twelve empty cells. How do you fill them in? "3, 4, 5, 6, 7, 8, 9 and back again!" With what number did you end the twelfth hour of Wednesday? The number five (5) which is equal to the planet Mars. So, in the first cell of the Hours of the Night of Wednesday, you start again at the number six (6), and continue, 7, 8, 9. The first four cells are filled. As to the remaining eight cells? "...and back again!" The fifth cell will take the number three (3). In succession after that we have, 4, 5, 6, 7, 8, 9, the last number of which will occupy the eleventh cell of the column. The twelfth cell is, of course, three (3) again.

By looking at the list of planets assigned to these numbers, you can write in their names or the abbreviations just as you did for the Hours of the Day. Take a look at the list again to see the Planet-Number designations. You now have the entire chart for all twelve Hours of the Day and Night for this particular Wednesday, filled in almost completely. Note the twelve larger empty spaces (periods column) next to each of the cells in both divisions of the chart. Of course, you know the *times of the planetary rulers must be placed in them.* Otherwise, you would only know which planet rules each of the twelve Hours of the Day and each of the twelve Hours of the Night, but you would not know *when* those times of rule begin and end! That's the next and final part of this particular process.

7. Now is the time to break out your trusty, humdinger of a calculator. You will need it from here on in! In Step 1 you calculated there were 66.9167 minutes for each hour of the day in this particular example. Enter this number into your calculator's memory cell. (In Step 2, your calculation showed there were 53.0833 minutes for each hour of the night. Don't worry about this latter number right now.)

(This seems like a good time to say something which may be bothering the more advanced readers who are familiar with this or other astrologically-based hourly systems. I am not being condescending in the slightest in this chapter—or in any of the other chapters for that matter— either in my approach to the subject matter or in the details given, however seemingly picayune this approach and details may seem. Nor am I trying to drag this out to make the book longer. God knows, writing is hard enough without mudding up your own waters for some tacky, greedy, unprofessional reason. This book is a broad-spectrum publication, meant to be read by every and any type of reader—those who are adept in such matters, as well as those who are new to them—as all of us were at some time in the past. If the advanced readers among you remember your own early days, maybe you will understand why I am being as detailed as I am!)

Now, to fill in the times during which each of the planets rule, begin with the Hours of the Day division, and start with the first hour of the day in cell 1, ruled by Mer(cury.) From the sunrise/sunset data you obtained from the United States Naval Observatory web page, you know the day begins at 5:28 AM Standard Time. Hence the planet Mercury begins its rule at that time. But when does it end, and the next hour ruled by the Moon begin? The minutes part of the hour is where we begin our calculation.

Since there are sixty (60) minutes in an hour, subtract *from* the 28 in your calculator window, 60, which will give you, [-32 minutes]. That's *minus* 32 minutes. This is only by the calculator's convention, since you actually use a negative sixty (60) to add to your plus twenty-eight (28). It's of no consequence mathematically, I assure you. It is simply the technique employed here, and it is perfectly correct mathematically.

Of course, we can't do anything with a set of negative integers here, so we add the stored number in the memory cell to it. That is, [-32 + 66.9167 = 34.9167] minutes. Obviously, since [-32] took you to 6:00 AM, the remaining 34.9167 minutes is that part of the next hour—the hour of 6:00 AM—in which Mercury is still ruling. Hence, the time in which Mercury has its effect is from 5:28 AM ST–

6:35 AM ST. Notice here—and only here—you can round off.

The rule of thumb to use in all rounding off procedures in this Cycles System is to look at the first number to the right of the decimal place: the "tenths" position. If it is five (5) or higher, round up to the next minute, as was done here. If this number is five (5) or less, round down. Let me make this point clear. For the sake of argument, say the final number was, "34.2167" In that case, the hour would have ranged from 5:28 AM ST to 6: 34 AM ST.

These small differences do make a significant difference, not simply in the calculations, but in using the system in daily life. Why? I wish I had a penny for each time something happened within the last minute or two of a given hour. If I did, I'd be a rich man right now! The moral is, don't introduce any more error into your life than is absolutely necessary. In this matter, it certainly isn't necessary at all.

Thus, in the space to the left of the first cell occupied by Mer(cury), you record, "5:28 AM ST–6:35 AM ST," the way I have illustrated in Figure 5.

Owing to some slight mathematical manipulations that you will run into when calculating your daily charts—and which could cause some confusion for you at first—it seems best if we finish the twelve Hours of the Day here, together, calculating the times when each planet is 'in effect' as it is referred to in occult and magical literature.

So let's move on to cell 2 directly beneath Mer(cury). Since Mercury's effect ends at 6:35 AM, that will be the exact minute the Moon's effect in cell 2 will begin. So please enter that into your chart so you can follow along in this example. The calculation for this is then: 34.9167—*the original number received from the finished Mercury hour calculation, and not the rounded off number*—minus 60 = -25.0833 (minutes.) Add the number 66.9167 in the memory cell of your calculator to it, to yield 41.8333 (minutes.) By the same reasoning we used for the first hour of the day where we subtracted sixty (60) minutes from 34.9167, and which took us up to the sixth hour of the morning, that same process here takes us up to the second hour, in which there are 41.8333 minutes remaining in that hour for the lunar effect to hold. Rounding off we get 41.8333 = 42 minutes. The length of the lunar hour is then from 6:35 to 7:42 AM ST.

For the third hour of the day, ruled by Sat(urn) on the chart: we begin with the *precise* final number received for the ending of the lunar hour, which was 41.8333. Now: [41.8333 - 60 = -18.1667 + 66.9167 = 48.7500], or 8:49 AM. So record 7:42 to 8:49 AM in your sample chart.

The fourth cell, occupied by Jupiter is calculated in exactly the same way as the first three. That is: [48.7500 - 60 = -11.2500 + 66.9167 = 55.6667] minutes or, rounded off, 56. Thus the time in which the Jupiter influence rules is from 8:49 to 9:56 AM ST.

Using the same procedure for the fifth period: [55.6667 - 60 = -4.3333]. But when we add + 66.9167 to it, we receive 62.5834, clearly, over the sixty-minutes in any given hour. Why? Because we are working with a fixed limit of a sixty-minute period in an hour, true for calculations of the planetary hours for the day and night of *any* system. To offset this problem, you simply pay attention to the number that results when you subtract sixty (60). If that number—when added to the negative figure received from the subtraction—yields a number over sixty, you must subtract another sixty (60) minutes from the time-figure received, to bring the final result under the sixty-minute limit.

It is not hard at all. Just by inspection, you will be able to determine if the number received from the subtraction will give a new number greater than sixty, that is, when the number in your memory cell is added to it. It works like this: to find the time of the fifth hour of the day in the example, proceed as follows: [55.6667 - 60 = -4.3333]. Subtract another 60 as instructed: [-4.3333 (-60) = -64.333]. To this figure, add the number in your calculator's memory cell—the length of each hour of the day, 66.9167 (minutes). This now yields: [-64.333 + 66.9167 = 2.5834] which is rounded off to 3. Since you began this fifth hour at 9:56 AM ST, and passed through one complete sixty (60) minute period through your calculations, you also passed through the 10 o'clock hour and entered the eleventh hour. Since you began this fifth hour at 9:56 AM ST, and have three (3) minutes remaining, you are now three minutes into the eleventh hour. This now gives you the time during which Mars—the ruler of this fifth hour of Wednesday— has dominion: 9:56 to 11:03 AM ST. Without further comment, let's work through the remaining seven periods of the Hours of the Day in this example.

Sixth Hour of the Day: [2.5834 - 60 = -57.4167 + 66.9167 = 9.5000]. Sixth hour period: 11:03 to 12:10 PM.

Seventh Hour of the Day: [9.5000 - 60 = -50.5000 + 66.9167 = 16.4167]. Seventh hour period: 12:10 to 1:16 PM.

Eighth Hour of the Day: [16.4167 - 60 = -43.5833 + 66.9167 = 23.3333]. Eighth hour period: 1:16 PM ST to 2:23 PM ST.

Ninth Hour of the Day: [23.3333 - 60 = -36.6667 + 66.9167 = 30.2500]. Ninth hour period: 2:23 to 3:30 PM.

Tenth Hour of the Day: [30.2500 - 60 = -29.7500 + 66.9167 = 37.1667]. Tenth hour period: 3:30 to 4:37 PM.

Eleventh Hour of the Day: [37.1667 - 60 = -22.8333 + 66.9167 = 44.0833]. Tenth hour period: 4:37 to 5:44 PM.

Twelfth Hour of the Day: [44.0833 - 60 = -15.9167 + 66.9167 = 51.0000]. Tenth hour period: 5:44 to 6:51 PM ST.

As you can see, the twelfth hour of the day ended on the exact minute at which sunset began, according to the Naval Observatory's data; a check on your work that confirms your calculations are correct to this point. This is also the start time of the first hour of the night, which we will now examine in some lesser but sufficient detail.

Move over to the second division on your chart—the one on the right side of the paper—labeled Hours of the Night. Of course, you have all the planets ruling each hour already recorded in the twelve cells, and now simply need to figure out the times when each of those planets begins and ends its rule. As I mentioned, the hour and minute when sunset occurs—in this case 6:51 PM ST—constitutes the hour and minute when the first hour of the night also begins. So add 6:51 PM (ST) to cell 1 of Wednesday as the start-time for the first Hour of the Night of Wednesday.

Since you converted the numbers in your chart into their planetary correspondences earlier, you should see Sun in cell 1. To calculate the time of the Sun's influence, recall that the lengths of the Hours of the Day and Night differ, and will throughout the year, except for the dates on which the Vernal (spring) and Autumnal Equinoxes occur. Since you know there are 66.9167 minutes in a day hour, and you previously subtracted this number from 120, you also know you have 53.0833 minutes in each of the hours of the night for this day, and that this is the figure you will be using to fill in the times in which the planets ruling the hours of the night have effect.

Since I have run through an entire series of calculations with you in calculating the times for the Hours of the Day in this example, it would be excessively redundant to belabor the process you now have firmly in hand. This being the case, we will work through the calculations for the first two hours of the night, and let you fill in the remaining ten. *Remember, in order for your calculations to be correct, you will also have a check here to rely upon: and that is, that the twelfth Hour of the Night in this example will end precisely on the minute the Day Hours began—5:28 AM ST—thus completing one complete day.* So let's do those first two calculations to get you started.

First Hour of the Night: [51.0000 (the exact figure for the time the twelfth hour of the day ended) minus 60 = -9.0000 + 53.0833 = 44.0833]. The time period in which the Sun rules this first hour of the night is therefore, 6:51 PM ST to 7:44 PM ST.

The second hour of the night—the hour ruled by Venus as you can see from your chart—is: [44.0833 - 60 = -15.9167 + 53.0833 = 37.1666. Rounded off by our rule of thumb, we have the time period during which Venus rules as 7:44 to 8:37 PM.

We will mention only one more cell. For cell 8, Sun, the exact start minutes is 2.5831. When our memory cell figure of 53.0833 is added to this figure, we would still be under sixty minutes. Therefore, in this case, it is not necessary to subtract sixty minutes from the exact start time. However, if you do not notice this when you first do your calculation, and you find you have a final end time that is a minus figure, you can just add sixty minutes back again.

The remaining ten hours are calculated in exactly the same way, and will end at exactly at 5:28 AM ST, the exact minute of sunrise of the day being calculated. You are finished. You now have the example Kabbalistic Cycles Chart completed. You not only know the sequence of the planetary rulers for this day, but the exact times during which each of them rules both the Hours of the Day and the Hours of the Night.

A few words of working advice about your daily use of this system:

• When making your Kabbalistic Cycles charts, it is perfectly permissible to do the calculations for one day, and to use those same calculations for an additional two consecutive days. For instance, the times of sunrise to sunset and sunset to sunrise used in the Wednesday example above, can be safely extended into Thursday and Friday. Consequently, you will have a chart with only one set of times for the Hours of the Day and Night, but three days worth of planetary rulers. Why can you use one set of times for up to three days? There are two reasons:

1. The precision of your calculations ensures that although the times of sunrise to sunset and sunset to sunrise most certainly change everyday, those changes over any two consecutive twenty-four hour periods will usually be fairly negligible due to the precision of those calculations. This means that after rounding off, the times over a three-day period will show such slight variation, that other variables such as the clock or watch you use to set the chart up in the first place cannot have such precision to enable you to obtain the 'exact' time that an event occurs in

your life, each and every time. You would need an atomic clock for that!

2. Except at those times of the year when the length of the days and nights change rapidly, such as the first few weeks after either the Summer and Winter Solstice or the Vernal and Autumnal Equinox, the changes in the actual fractions of a second between the times of (up to) three successive days and nights over a given twenty-four hour period are very negligible. When the times do change rapidly as noted above, I recommend doing a chart for no more than two days at a time from one set of sunrise/sunset and sunset/sunrise times instead of three days. Frankly, this is only marginally necessary.

But there are those times, more often than you may like, when life will hurl challenges and surprises at you, and it will always seem to be at the last minute of a given planetary ruling period. Your ideas, thoughts, and actions in dealing with those situations can and will be greatly influenced by just which planet is ruling that particular moment. By calculating a chart for only a two day period during these interludes of rapid time change, you can be reasonably certain that the times being dealt with according to your chart are quite accurate.

• Be sure to keep your charts. Do not discard them after their use when any given three or two-day time period has ended. You will be surprised how many times you will notice in passing some event or condition that mushrooms days later. By checking the time of the event's inception against your old chart for that day, you'll be amazed at how accurate the System was. This will also help you to gain confidence not only in the System itself, but in your ability to use it correctly: a faculty you will develop naturally as you use the Kabbalistic Cycles in daily life.

• Always carry a small pocket notebook and pen or pencil with you. Jot down the date, day, and time some occurrence or circumstance stands out in your mind. Check your Cycles chart for the day in question, and refer back to it again if the situation that caught your eye develops. It does not have to be some earthshaking event in your life, although heaven knows, you do want to use the System for those events! Rather, it can be some small incident or seemingly minor episode that happens to attract your attention.

Most importantly, I recommend this activity because I do not, under any circumstances, want you to *believe* that my Kabbalistic Cycles System works for you! *Always remember that belief is a bridge for fools*, and will damn you quicker than your worst enemy, but with a beguiling smile. You would also do well to remember that *belief is simply what the dictionary defines it to be: an opinion without facts.* Neither you nor I want that.

So we must be vigilant, *work* at using this System, and *put it to the test* as we have rarely done to most other 'tools' we were given at different times in our lives. *We want to replace the belief of the fool, with the fact of the rational, intelligent, thinking, self-determining human being.* In so doing, you will find yourself with advantages not only over others, but over your own formerly believing self, and perhaps even less-than-ambitious nature like never before.

And whatever you do, be sure you keep these small 'Journals.' They are testaments to your own growth and development, as well as reminders of just how effective this System truly is. To this day, I have over three hundred—yes, that's right, over three hundred—of these remarkable, small testaments to the beauty of the Kabbalah and the exactness of its cycles. I will never discard them. And if you begin the practice of using them as I suggest, neither will you.

Before closing this chapter, just a reminder about the Sephiroth Kether, Chokmah, and Malkuth. As there are nine cards of the Greater Arcana of the Tarot that are not used in the Kabbalistic Cycles System it is now time for the reader to know something about the three Sephiroth cited above. Besides the fact that Kether does not possess any planetary attribution, its nature precludes its use in daily life affairs.

Although Chokmah does have the planet Uranus assigned to it by latter-day Kabbalists, as a rule it is not used in Occult and Magical work. What does all of this have to do with our use of the Kabbalistic Cycles System? If you recall, this system is based upon the *Planets of the Ancients*—Saturn, Jupiter, Mars, the Sun, Venus, Mercury, and the Moon. As such, the stellar Sephiroth, Kether and Chokmah, do not enter into its use.

In like manner, Malkuth—the Earth plane of existence in which we live—is the repository of all those influences that are provided by Sephiroths 3 through 9, and which regulate the daily affairs in this, the densest and coarsest realm of matter through the Laws of Nature. As the receptacle, this Sephirah is also omitted.

You finally have it all. You understand that *only the nine planetary attributions—Saturn through the Moon—and the thirteen cards of the Greater Arcana of the Tarot—cards VI through XVII, and card XIX—are used in establishing the Control and Certainty you need in your life.* From a great circular area of concern, we have drawn that area down into a central point, while ensuring you have established a solid foundational subjective synthesis from which to operate the Kabbalistic Cycles System.

Your painstaking work in deriving this System is now complete. As with any mathematical derivation however, this solution set must now be applied to the problem type. That is what we are going to do in the next chapter, proceed with the actual working, so you can begin to control your life and to establish the certitude and results you so richly deserve.

Hours of the Day					Hours of the Night				
PERIODS					PERIODS				

Figure 4.

Sample Blank Chart for the Kabbalistic Cycles System

Wednesday, August 25 through Friday, August 27, 2004
5:28 am Std, 6:51 pm, Std; 803 ÷ 12 = 66.9167 (day) and 53.0833 (night)

Hours of the Day

WED	THURS	FRI	PERIODS
8 Mer	4 Jup	7 Venus	5:28–6:35 am
9 Moon	5 Mars	8 Mer	6:35–7:42 am
3 Sat	6 Sun	9 Moon	7:42–8:49 am
4 Jup	7 Venus	3 Sat	8:49–9:56 am
5 Mars	8 Mer	4 Jup	9:56–11:03 am
6 Sun	9 Moon	5 Mars	11:03–12:10 pm
7 Venus	3 Sat	6 Sun	12:10–1:16 pm
8 Mer	4 Jup	7 Venus	1:16–2:23 pm
9 Moon	5 Mars	8 Mer	2:23–3:30 pm
3 Sat	6 Sun	9 Moon	3:30–4:37 pm
4 Jup	7 Venus	3 Sat	4:37–5:44 pm
5 Mars	8 Mer	4 Jup	5:44–6:51 pm

Hours of the Night

WED	THURS	FRI	PERIODS
6 Sun	9 Moon	5 Mars	6:51–7:44 pm
7 Venus	3 Sat	6 Sun	7:44–8:37 pm
8 Mer	4 Jup	7 Venus	8:37–9:30 pm
9 Moon	5 Mars	8 Mer	9:30–10:23 pm
3 Sat	6 Sun	9 Moon	10:23–11:16 pm
4 Jup	7 Venus	3 Sat	11:16–12:09 am
5 Mars	8 Mer	4 Jup	12:09–1:03 am
6 Sun	9 Moon	5 Mars	1:03–1:56 am
7 Venus	3 Sat	6 Sun	1:56–2:49 am
8 Mer	4 Jup	7 Venus	2:49–3:42 am
9 Moon	5 Mars	8 Mer	3:42–4:35 am
3 Sat	6 Sun	9 Moon	4:35–5:28 am

FIGURE 5.
KABBALISTIC CYCLES SYSTEM CHART FOR THE
PLANETARY HOURS RULING THE DAY SPECIFIED

CHAPTER EIGHT

The Kabbalistic Cycles of Life—
Their Theory and Application

THE THEORY

I n the opening pages of Chapter Seven, we looked at
the nature of cycles, and considered their basis in
human life. We saw how the cycles of frequencies or
patterns of repetition appear everywhere in Nature. We
realized that cycles are *the* fundamental *basis* of Nature. We
came to understand that the ancient astrologers, magicians, and indeed, early occultists knew this. Led by the
earliest of astrologers, an eclectic system of practical
human knowledge that utilizes the cyclic impulses they
found in the heavens was fashioned and synthesized.

Our understanding was broadened when we learned
that they accomplished this not through rumination and
idle speculation about the heavenly influences, but by
observing events in Nature and the changes that occurred
within their own personal lives, and correlating these
events to the changes that seemed to flow from the heavenly arrangements and placements of the Zodiacal Signs
and the planets. Then they merged their astronomical
knowledge with their natural science philosophy and later,
with magical and occult ideas.

This produced an important system that established
rulers for the division of any twenty-four hour period into
Hours of the Day and Night. But always these planetary
rulers had to cycle in the order we discussed. This order
also remained true to their understanding of natural
science and philosophy, as well as to their occult and mag-

ical conceptions, the system as a whole having been exhaustively and extensively tested over the centuries. Of course, these early philosophers knew that the planet ruling the day in general has a powerful effect in this schema; yet this Ruler of the Day influence had not—for some reason—been as clearly defined and integrated into this Hours of the Day and Night system as had the rulers of the hours themselves. That is, there is no precise discussion of the moderating role the planet ruling the day has on the hours which cycle through any given day and its night. Yet, in building our Kabbalistic Cycles System, those of us using this book and abiding by this scheme, have additionally wedded it to the Hebrew oral tradition.

As must be the case in all Science, not only must original principles be retested in the course of seeking further knowledge, but new principles arising from this search must be rigorously tested. If they are true, they will eventually lead to theories capable of yielding repeatable results, enabling one to predict tendencies ahead of time, while also allowing for independent verification. To do so, such new principles must evolve through further hypothesizing and experiment, testing, and retesting.

If we are to take such astrological principles and their underlying occult and magical structures so seriously that we use them to chart the actions, decisions, and the very interactions of our lives, then they too must undergo testing to see if they lead to theories capable of yielding repeatable results that will enable one to predict tendencies ahead of time, while also allowing for independent verification of those theories and the principles upon which they rest.

This is what I was fortunate enough to have been able to do. I *evolved* these original cyclic principles into a new system. A system born from the labor of the ancients, perfected and tested over the centuries, and further coerced from Nature itself by my thirty-two year period of testing, hypothesizing, retesting, and finally theorizing, until the Laws underlying this Kabbalistic Cycles System were finally and fully uncovered.

The resulting system presented in this book is based upon the natural cycles and intellectual discoveries of the ancients, but taken to a new theoretical and practical level here. It is designed for use by those men or women who have the courage to take control of their own lives, and establish the certainty they have every right to in this physical life.

The Kabbalistic Cycles System states and is built upon the fact that as each day has assigned to it a ruling planet which cycles according to the days of the week, and each hour of each day has assigned to it a ruling planet which is also cyclic—since it too repeats its presence and influence during other hourly periods of that same day—then *so too do the Paths have a cyclic nature.*

These Path influences are as much a part and parcel of the overall influence exerted upon any event, condition, or circum-stance in the lives of humankind, as are the influences of the planet ruling the day, and the planet ruling the hour. In fact, it is the Path influences exclusively that tie the effects of the ruling planets of the day and hours together. Further, since each planet provides a characteristic influence that favors certain activities while opposing others by virtue of its very influence, so too do the applicable Paths on the Tree of Life provide cyclic effects depending upon:

- *the two planets they connect—*
- *the times the influences of the two planets so connected provide their influence and—*
- *the symbolic imagery of the Tarot Trump representing the influences provided by those Paths.*

Phrased another way, *while the Planetary ruler of each day—along with the planetary ruler of any given hour during that day—exerts a Sensible (or practical) influence in Malkuth, the Paths of the Tree of Life that connect any two Sephiroth, also provide a Sensible (or practical) influence in the world of Malkuth. This influence is symbolized by the appropriate Tarot Trump assigned to that Path. It is important to realize, that while the card can be thought of as projecting the influence into the world of mankind, it is actually not the card itself that pro-*

vides this influence: it is the nature of the Path that emanates this influence, which is perfectly represented by the symbolic imagery of the Tarot Trump.
*This is the crux of the Kabbalistic Cycles System. It is **the** one single factor that makes it different from any and every type of astrology or other daily planetary-ruling scheme, such as the Rosicrucian system, or any system laid down in any of the magical Grimoires. It integrates all the forces that enter into play in any given hour of any given day, not just those represented by the planet ruling the day, or the planet that happens to rule a particular hour.*
Thus, in an given day, an event that occurs at any given time, will bear the characteristic imprint not only of the planet ruling the day and the planet ruling that particular hour, but the imprint and influence of the Path itself, if there is a Path that connects the ruler of the day with a ruler of a particular hour.

As all of the above italicized statements constitute the very heart and center of the Kabbalistic Cycles System of Self Mastery, I have phrased these core ideas in several different ways, purposely repeating them over and over, in order to catch the different eyes of various readers. Even so, *I strongly recommend you pause at this point, read and reread those sections several times, until you completely understand what they are trying to convey to you.*

*You must understand them clearly from this point on, because at this juncture, the attentive, astute reader should no longer have a need for repetition and rephrasing. Since the remainder of this book will deal with the hard core elements of the Kabbalistic Cycles System in a **direct** manner, only such repetition as is absolutely necessary will used beyond this point. Thus it is strongly recommended that the reader have the above concepts firmly in mind before we proceed with their real life application in the next section.*

THE APPLICATION

In order to apply the derivation of the Kabbalistic Cycles System to the problem set of our life conditions, we will now go through each part of the system, one at a time, discussing each, and finally unifying the components into a cohesive whole at the end of this chapter.

Allow me to make one point clear before we get on with the task at hand. In carefully considering the format for this book, and always trying to make it easier for the reader, *the Sensible Qualities of the Planetary Attributions and the meanings of the Tarot Trumps that correspond to the Paths used in the system will be reproduced here in each appropriate section.* That is, they will be imported from earlier chapters to make them easier to use. I consider this to be a very necessary repetition. There is nothing more frustrating for a reader than having to page back through text looking for information, simply because the author chose to write the book to some deadpan length. Such ill chosen format only breaks the reader's ancillary train of thought, seriously interfering with concentration and understanding. But there is another justification for reproducing the information here. In previous chapters it was provided in order to build your subjective synthesis state. Now it must be *applied* to the Kabbalistic Cycles System in a *practical manner*, and therefore should be readily at hand.

Note also, that *since the Paths have an Occult Concept assigned to them which is truly occult in nature, they have not been included as such. Rather, since the Paths' Sensible Qualities are represented by the Tarot Trumps as explained, those meanings instead will be used to accomplish our objective.*

THE PLANETS RULING THE DAY

As you learned in Chapter Six, each of the Seven Planets of the Ancients rules a given day of the week. Additionally, each of those planets also rules one of the twelve Hours of the Day and twelve Hours of the Night, in a cyclic fashion, according to an assignment worked out by the ancient astrologers and later magicians and occultists, and which we remember by using the simple rule, "3, 4, 5, 6, 7, 8, 9, and back again!"

The problem usually encountered in any hourly system for any day of the week is that the planet ruling the day drops into the background for some reason. In other words, for a Sunday ruled by the Sun, the influence of the Sun is often completely discarded by a given system, while the individual focuses solely on the planet ruling the hour they are interested in.

For example, on a particular Sunday during the tenth hour of the day, the inquirer finds that the planet Mercury is ruling the hour. The tendency in all of the cases I have seen is to disregard the influence of the Sun, and to concentrate solely on the effects of Mercury for determining the action that should or should not be taken! This is comparable to ordering a surf and turf dinner, and throwing away the steak!

The reason for this complete disregard is quite simple. It is a critical error carried over from those early philosophers who devised the Hours of the Day and Night system, but did not clearly define and integrate the effects of the daily Planetary Rulers into that system. For some reason they did not reveal or concern themselves with the moderating role the planet ruling the day has on the hours which cycle through it. Consequently, none of today's systems have bothered to incorporate this consideration into the *components* of their own system, and then unify those components into one cohesive whole. The Kabbalistic Cycles System takes this into account by stating a number of *Fundamental Principles* leading to a complete integration. In addition, an appropriate Commentary expands each Fundamental Principle.

Fundamental Principle 1 — *The planetary ruler of any given day is as important as the planetary ruler of the hour in question. It does not simply act as a backdrop against which the planetary periods exert their influence. Rather, the daily planetary ruler provides both an overall mental tone and behavioral accent for the events that will occur during a given day, in addition to establishing a limiting condition that separates the nature of the events occurring during any day, from the nature of events occurring during any of the other six days of the week.*

Commentary 1 — The planetary ruler of the day provides a mental and behavioral accent to the events occurring during the day it rules. To make the point crystal clear, let's take a single example and follow it through an entire seven-day week.

We begin with any given Sunday. On this day, people usually begin to think in terms of new conditions, new plans, new ideas, new ways of advancing themselves and of making more of their lives. These are plans they intend to launch during the upcoming week. There is a freshness about the new ideas and plans on this Sunday; a vigor and an anticipation with which they begin to plan their efforts so they can carry them out during the coming week (or weeks or months). There is also a 'limiting condition' for each day of the week, as established by its planetary ruler. Now, by a limiting condition, I mean a preset, prescribed boundary of thought or action that is typical for any given day of the week, because it reflects the overall nature of the planet ruling any given day.

On a Sunday for instance, the limiting condition is one of growth since, as a rule, you won't find people thinking about or planning for death, dealing with lawyers, beginning long trips, planning out aggressive acts for the upcoming week, involving themselves in deep study, planning elaborate social affairs, making health spa appointments, and the like. No, the limiting condition for Sunday is typically one of personal, inner, and worldly growth. It is this impulse, brought about by the planetary ruler of Sunday—the Sun—that provides it. Hence this influence must be factored into the planetary influence ruling the hour in question, which we will do in the section on The Planets Ruling the Hours.

The next day, Monday, ruled by the Moon, usually finds those well intended new plans and ideas put on the back burner. Since the Moon rules such mundane matters as business activities and the subconscious, the combination of solely these two areas of lunar influences usually bogs down the individual's good intention of launching new plans "...first thing tomorrow!" Before the day has ended, the average person is too tired to even recall those new plans and ideas from yesterday, let alone attempt to put them into action. *The limiting condition for this day?*

"Business as usual. Get the week off to a good start, and just let me get through today!"
On Tuesday, the day ruled by Mars, an aggressive tone can be found everywhere. People are more edgy, self-absorbed, irritable, yet filled with an energetic impulsiveness—all martial qualities—than they are on Monday. The attitude 'Just leave me alone and let me do my job!' prevails everywhere, in one form or another.

If the martial influence of aggressiveness and uncontrolled physical and mental energy spurs the individual on to put the new plans, ideas, or actions into operation on this day, you can count on those plans or actions being met with *at least* equal opposition. The martial influence will affect everyone. Openness to new ideas and plans is anything but on peoples' lists during this twenty-four period. *The limiting condition for Tuesday is overall aggressiveness or one-pointed self-interest. Do what you know, keep your own counsel, and avoid others as much as possible. And if push comes to shove, push back twice as hard as the other fellow!*

On Wednesday, in general, life has eased up, but things seem somehow fluid. Nothing is really pinned down. You remember your plans now—they took a two-day vacation on Monday and Tuesday—and now you are eager to get them off the ground. Well, sort of eager, because you feel a little unsettled, as if your mind is both here and there all at once. You just can't settle down, mentally and physically. Nevertheless, you do make an effort of some kind to begin your new plan. You speak to your boss about your new idea, make that telephone call to get the preliminary information you need, or any of a host of other actions that has given your mental creation its first glimmer of life outside of your mind.

The limiting condition for Wednesday is simply, do the best you can, put what energy you have into getting your new idea started, and just keep at it — as the time and tide of your daily life allows. As you can see, this limiting condition has infused your idealistic intentions with a sizeable dose of pragmatism, brought on by the fluid nature of the Mercurial influence of this day.

It's Thursday. There is a feeling of expansiveness in the air—and in you! Most people put this down to that pathetic attitude, "The week's almost over! Then I can do what I want for two days! (Things I won't remember, can't afford, and don't really care about, but hey! It's what *I* want to do!)" But you know better. You can feel the growth and expansive impulses coming from Jupiter, the ruler of this day. And you make the most of it. Well, almost, because you still feel a little fluid, but a heck of a lot less so than yesterday!

So you acquire that additional information you need for your new idea or plan, get some further thoughts on the matter across to your boss, or put phase two of your plan into physical operation in some way. You're feeling much better about yourself, and indeed, better about your new goal! But still, you didn't do all you could have done, and you know it. Nevertheless, it's a step in the right direction, and so you just enjoy your good feelings about yourself and your accomplishments to date for the rest of the day. *The limiting condition? An expansiveness and beneficence that, while certainly helpful, can induce more of a happy-go-lucky, carefree, 'good feeling about me' attitude than you ideally want.*

It's Friday already. There's a buzz all around you from everyone. All are looking forward to their weekend of fun and games and—no work! There is an 'enjoy it while you can and the heck with everything else' attitude in everyone, and this includes you! And why shouldn't it? After all, you deserve it! Look at the hard week you just put in! But then, come to think of it, there is that damn, pesky new idea and plan that had you floating up to the ceiling last Sunday. Or was it the Sunday before?

Still, you're feeling very good about yourself, and intend to pamper yourself today, take some extra time off, and start the weekend as early as you can—even while still at work. To set your mind at rest however, you do manage to break through this luxurious feeling of self-worth and even beauty, and manage to get a little something extra accomplished on that new plan or goal. Now, you are *really* feeling good about everything! *The limiting condition here? Self-indulgence at the expense of accomplishing what you know you must, in order to move ahead with your life.*

It's Saturday. What a glorious day—or is it? There's a sense of heaviness behind the glow you had yesterday when you so looked forward to the weekend. Oh, it's not going to stop you from enjoying the day as much as you can. But somehow, you just don't feel as energetic as you did on Thursday and Friday, so you settle for a little less. Maybe ordering in a pizza while watching the games on television, or just going to the mall, getting that new gizmo you wanted, then back home to see what's on the boob tube for the night.

That softball game, that cozy dinner out with you-know-who, or that grass that needs to be cut, well, they can wait! Oh, don't let me rain too heavily on your weekend parade! You do enjoy yourself to some degree, yes. But, well, it's just not what you had in mind yesterday. And while you're 'enjoying' yourself, that damn, miserable new idea, plan, or goal, is chipping away, bit-by-bit at the edges of your mind, reminding you of all that you failed to do to get it going throughout the past week. So much for fun and games on your glorious weekend. *The limiting condition for Saturday of course, is inertia, stasis, a heaviness in physical, mental, and emotional matters, and accountability—as in that new plan which has all but fallen by the wayside.*

You are back to Sunday. Now. What was that new idea or goal you had? Oh yes! Now you remember! Better get to fine tuning it so you can really get it off the ground—this week! You see the problem.

Does this negative scenario of mine about the planetary influences projected by the planets of the Sephiroth that rule the days of the week upset you? It should, because you know I'm right! Look at your own life right now, and honestly tell yourself that I am nothing but a pessimist, focusing on only the negative. You might be saying that you can do what you want, and that "No planet affects me as much as he says it does! I've got free will and can do what I want—next week!"

Or will you find that the above pattern has been all too often repeated in your weekly and daily life? Does this mean the planetary influences are damning you to a life of frustrated inactivity, and will continue to do so? Does this mean that you have no free will and cannot push through it all to manifest what you want? The answers to these questions are of course, "No," and "Push all you want. It will get you about as far as you've gotten up to now!"

I tell you now, that *while a number of these planetary properties and their limiting conditions seem tough, they function as do any other phenomena in this universe: as a two-edged sword. But quite obviously, as with the growth accent of Sunday, not all of the planetary properties or their limiting conditions are negative. You saw that in your study of the Sensible Qualities of the planets of each Sephirah!* Without your conscious knowledge of them however, and incorporating them into your state of subjective synthesis, then yes, like most of those around you, you will most probably continue to be their puppet and plaything throughout your life, accomplishing very little, living a life of quiet desperation.

But, armed with the knowledge of the planetary properties and their positive and negative limiting conditions, you can use them as you see fit by pushing intelligently and willfully. And **THAT** *is the difference!* As you will see, if all that existed were the planetary rulers for each of the seven days of the week, then yes, life would generally be more of an uphill struggle than it is now. But as you will come to understand, these daily planetary rulers and their influences are attenuated, lessened, or stepped-down through their interaction with the planets that rule any given Hour of the Day or Night.

Further, the Path influences attenuate these raw daily planetary rulers even further, lending full control over their use, so you can consciously and willfully use them to your advantage during any hour of any day. *This is our next task. First to gain insight into the effects produced by the planets, and secondly, to understand how these plane-*

tary effects interact with the influences provided by the Rulers of the days of the week.

THE PLANETS RULING THE HOURS

Fundamental Principle 2 — *When a Daily Planetary Ruler exerts its influence on a specific Hour of the Day or Night, that effect is attenuated according to the nature of the planet ruling during that hour. Only in the case of a particular Hour of the Day or Night being ruled by the same Ruler that rules the day, is the pure effect of the planet ruling the day in full force.*

Commentary 2 — The effects of the planet ruling any given day are significantly moderated by a different planet ruling a given hour. For instance: On a Sunday, the Sun's influence, which provides the overall tone and behavioral accent of the events of the day, will be considerably dampened during a Mercury hour. That is, the issues that are dominated by Mercury will stand out as matters of principal concern. Yet always, there will be a solar tone and accent to them. Let's take an example.

The Sun's influence on any given Sunday has you in the growth mode. You are busy ruminating about your plans at first, but only mentally. You are toying with them, sizing them up in your mind to see if see if you can pin them down. Suddenly, during an hour ruled by Mercury, you pick up a piece of paper and a pen or pencil, and begin to make of list of the details, figure out what steps to take, set down a list of actions and the priority they must be taken in, and so on.

As you can see, the overall growth influence of the day is definitely still in effect, but now the *immediacy* of the situation is directed by Mercury. You will find that during this hour your mind is clear and incisive, and the details are flowing easily to you. Much more than, say, during a Venus hour, which would govern the more pleasurable, flights of fancy tendencies that could very well work their way into your plans! This is a simple example, but it does illustrate the point.

Missing however, are the other salient, hidden forces we discussed earlier: the effects of the Paths, and the Tarot which serve as representations of the Paths' forces, and just how they will effect your overall plans. But for now, it is only important that you understand that the planetary ruler of any given hour of any particular day does indeed moderate or attenuate the overall effects of the planet ruling that day, providing those two rulers are different. Only during an hour ruled by the same planet that rules the day, will the full effect of the planet ruling the day be in effect, which will be explained in detail below.

In this example, if you were to sit down with a pencil and paper during a solar hour on a Sunday, and attempt to detail your plans, you would find your mind given over to elaborate, volatile, buoyant, less than practical scenarios that would add unnecessary details and complexities to your goals. In short, working on your beloved plans during a day and hour ruled by the Sun is like throwing gasoline on an already raging fire, as when the fires of your mind are burning so brightly on this new plan of yours. The same holds true for any other day of the week. A given hour ruled by the same planet that rules the day, will accentuate the effects of that ruling planet.

THE PLANETS RULING THE DAY AND HOURS, AND THEIR INTERACTION

Fundamental Principle 3 — *A proportionality of effect enters into the interaction between the ruler of a given day and the ruler of a given hour when those two planets are different. There is also such a proportionality constant involved when the ruler of a given day and the ruler of the hour are the same. When the hour and day planet are the same, instead of seeing a double effect, the effect experienced will be increased by a factor of four. When the hour and day planet are different, the effect of the planet hour will be four times as great as the effect of the planet day.*

Commentary 3 — It is a curious fact that the planet ruling any specific day does not have a more profound effect on an hour ruled by a different planet, seeing that the ruler of the day has jurisdiction over the entire twenty-four hour period. But it does not. In fact, as was pointed out in Fundamental Principle 2, the Ruler of the hour greatly modifies the effect of the planet governing the day.

From all of the experimental data I collected throughout the years of uncovering the laws of the Kabbalistic Cycles System, I found there is a fourfold effect produced during those hours in which the planet ruling both the hour and the day is the same. That is, as given above, the effect of the same planet governing both the day and hour is four times as strong as when a different planet governs during that or any other hour of that day.

By contrast, the effect produced when a different planetary force is in effect for any hourly period is somewhat like the reciprocal of this. This means that during the day ruled by the Sun, Mercury ruled hour in the above example, Mercury's effect is approximately four times as great as is the Solar influence and its limiting condition. This is why you can more or less effectively override the dominant mental and behavioral tone established for any day of the week by the planet ruling that day. You simply wait until an appropriate hour ruled by a planet that provides the influence you want, and then proceed to do what you feel must be done. Of course, it's not as simple as this, or else we would have no need of such a complex system as the Kabbalistic Cycles.

So now what? Now that you know you can attenuate the powerful influence of the ruler of any day of the week by waiting for an appropriate hour, just *what* do you do with this? I mean, just *exactly how* do you use it to your best advantage? If these were all the requirements you had to contend with in order to establish control over your affairs and gain the control and certainty over your own life that you so desperately need, then surely your life—and the lives of all those occultists, magicians, astrologers, and anyone who delves into such matters—would be heaven on earth right now! But it is not, is it?

Why is this? Because while you can use this basic knowledge to set to work, there are so many phases to any plan or idea, and so many possible variations in knowing when to do this, and when to do that, that are simply not addressed by any astrological chart—whether Natal, Pro-gressed, or Horary—or any of the reigning hourly systems that are in use today.

For example: After evolving your new plan or idea on that first Sunday, and having had a rather miserable week owing to the general effects of the planets, the following Sunday—after thinking it all out and realizing what hap-pened—you (finally) got around to it—again—and during a Mercury hour of that second Sunday, pinned down the details of your new plan. You're ready to launch it. One question: *when*?

You know of course, you can override the effects of any day by selecting an appropriate hour so that hour's planet will provide the fourfold effect you need. But do you do that on a Monday, during, say, a Jupiter hour? Or how about on a Tuesday, during an hour ruled by Jupiter? Or maybe on a Wednesday during an hour of Jupiter or even an hour ruled by the Sun? Surely, from the Planetary Attributions you studied here, those planets have very favorable mundane characteristics!

Yet again, Thursday during a Jupiter hour might be ideal. But come to think of it, not as ideal as Friday, with its powerful Venus influence, moderated just so perfectly, by taking your plans to your boss or the bank loan officer during a Jupiter or—hey! maybe better yet—during one of that day's Solar hours! OK, you make a decision, and do it the same way you have done before to a hundred different plans designed to increase your self-growth and improve your worldly position over the years.

Yet the results you got from those past efforts, and now from this new effort in which you just fell flat on your face, have never been any better than the odds of chance. Come to think of it, you're now wondering if those results were even as good as the laws of chance! At this point, you're seriously considering if you shouldn't just trudge ahead, stick to the Exoteric ways of the world, and let all this occult nonsense be damned! And you've hit the nail on the head, at least as far as realizing that what you know just doesn't work.

The reason for your latest failure and for the failure of all those other hourly and astrological systems out there *is that they simply did not take the process far enough. In Nature, things are always connected. Even in Quantum Mechanics, we have realized that at some fundamental level, all things are connected.* The famous Butterfly Effect which originally caused so many physicists to snicker, if not outright laugh, doesn't have those particular know-it-alls laughing anymore.

This quantum-based idea states that due to the interconnectedness of all things at a fundamental level, a butterfly flapping its wings in Brazil, can cause a tornado in Illinois. It is the same here. *All of these cyclic planetary forces are connected to each other, but this connection has never been addressed before, and this connection occurs through the Paths of the Tree of Life, and only through those Paths, as the genius of the Kabbalists established in the underlying theory of the Kabbalah and the glyph of the Tree centuries ago.*

THE CONCEPT OF 'FLOW' ON THE TREE OF LIFE

In the study of Magic, Mysticism, and other branches of Occultism, there is a general concept of movement or flow, as I term it, that is found throughout the literature. It can be seen in one form or another in such diverse sources as the writings of Tibetan Mysticism, to tenets of Blavatsky's Theosophy; from the original Egyptian magical papyri, to the later eclectic Egyptian synthesis of its own magical system with those of other races, to the Graeco-Egyptian expansion and logical refinement of the Egyptian magical systems; from the *Corpus Hermeticum*,[40] the actual basis of all genuine Hermetic Magic, to the Kabbalistic writings of Arthur Edward Waite and Eliphas Levi; from the Order Documents of the Hermetic Society of the Golden Dawn, to the philosophic basis of Alchemy.

This idea of 'flow' is a corollary, literally, a logical deduction of the ancient spiritual injunction, "Godhead descends into Manhood, and Manhood ascends into Godhead," a point briefly discussed earlier. It is through this flow that the ten properties of Godhead stream or surge through the ten Sephiroth of the Tree of Life into the world

of humankind, which blesses us with the glories and treasures of Creation.

The ancient injunction is also an invitation for humankind to make the ascent consciously, and to travel from
Malkuth to the Godhead of Kether. Both ways, from Godhead to Manhood, and from Manhood to Godhead, involve a metaphorical 'movement' or 'flow,' which is
actually *a change of state from one position to another*. And in
keeping with the duality which exists throughout all of
manifest Creation, there is an inherent and necessary
struggle for humankind when ascending the Tree, Sephirah by Sephirah, while the descent of Godhead into its
own Creation is a phenomena of no resistance, owing to
the nature of Godhead, and the fact that this IT brought
forth all things from Itself through the mechanisms of the
Kabbalistic doctrine that we study.

It was the realization of this concept of flow that—after
many years of struggling to uncover the laws behind what
was developing into the Kabbalistic Cycles System—
finally welded all of the other parts together. After this
realization occurred to me, I began to use a type of metaphorical logic applied to the Tree and its Paths.

This metaphorical reasoning went something like this.
If the effortless movement of the blessings of Godhead
flow into Creation *down*, then by extension, the struggle
mirrored in humankind's *ascent* up the Tree would have to
be reflected through the Paths, since they are the constructs used in ascending, as can be found virtually in all
Kabbalistic literature. Conversely, these same Paths must
be the mechanisms through which the blessings from the
IT flow down into Malkuth.

If this is so, then mundane attributions assigned to
these Paths which are contained in their Tarot Trump
assignments would be both the connecting and balancing
links between the Planetary Rulers of the Day and Hours
of the Day and Night. And if this is true, then the Sensible
or more mundane forces of the Paths as represented by the
symbolism of the Tarot Trump cards must also *correspond
to this directional flow.*

Assuming there are only two possible positions for the Tarot when placed upon the Tree, then 'flow down the Tree' must correspond to the effortless flow of God's blessings to us, mirrored through the cards. 'Flow up the Tree' would necessarily have to correspond to our struggle to climb the Tree. The mirroring of this ease of descent and struggle of ascent would have to be represented both pictorially and literally by the *orientation* of the Tarot Trump in question. That is, it would have to take the upright position for flow down the Tree, and the reversed position for flow up the Tree.

As it turned out, this speculation was correct. But there was still one more card to play, as it were. *What determined flow up the Tree and flow down the Tree, since the Planetary Rulers of both the Days and of the Hours clearly had a significant role in the process?* A year later, it hit me. *Flow must be from the hour into the day, and not from the day into the hour!* And this was found to be exactly the case. It became the final thread that wove the Kabbalistic Cycles System together. Allow me to explain this discovery in terms that will be meaningful to you, and that will enable you to work this system with perfect certainty and precision. This will be done in the next and final section of this chapter.

FINAL UNIFICATION OF THE KABBALISTIC CYCLES SYSTEM
THE PATHS, THEIR TAROT ATTRIBUTIONS, THE PLANETARY RULERS, AND 'FLOW' ON THE TREE

To the reader who has made it this far, I say, congratulations! You made it! What now follows is the complete unification, or more precisely, the complete integration of the Kabbalistic Cycles System. As you will soon see, your perseverance will pay off. With what you will learn in this and the following sections, you will be able to obtain complete control over the affairs of your life, and reach that level of certainty which can only come from such complete control. Now we continue with the work at hand.

As you now know, *cards Zero (0) through Five (V), and cards XVIII, XX, and XXI of the Greater Arcana are not used.* As a consequence, we do not concern ourselves with their corresponding nine Paths: (11) Aleph, (12) Beth, (13) Gimel, (14) Daleth, (15) Heh, (16) Vav, (29) Qoph, (31) Shin, and (32) Tav.

Instead, the remaining thirteen Paths are the only ones employed, always keeping in mind their Tarot attributions. Corresponding with this information will be kept the Planetary influence of each connected Sephirah. Finally, the Planetary Ruler of the Day of the week is wedded to our final considerations.

Therefore, the following is a concise summary of all pertinent information:

Days of the Week

Sunday (Sun)
Monday (Moon)
Tuesday (Mars)
Wednesday (Mercury)
Thursday (Jupiter)
Friday (Venus)
Saturday (Saturn)

Sephirah/Planets

Binah → Saturn
Chesed → Jupiter
Geburah → Mars
Tiphareth → Sun
Netzach → Venus
Hod → Mercury
Yesod → Moon

Paths and Their Connections

Path 17 — **Lovers** —	connects Binah (**Saturn**) with Tiphareth (**Sun**)
Path 18 — **Chariot** —	connects Binah (**Saturn**) with Geburah (**Mars**)
Path 19 — **Strength** —	connects Geburah (Mars) with Chesed (Jupiter)
Path 20 — **Hermit** —	connects Chesed (**Jupiter**) with Tiphareth (**Sun**)
Path 21 — **Fortune** —	connects Chesed (**Jupiter**) with Netzach (**Venus**)
Path 22 — **Justice** —	connects Geburah (**Mars**) with Tiphareth (**Sun**)
Path 23 — **Hanged Man** —	connects Geburah (**Mars**) with Hod (**Mercury**)
Path 24 — **Death** —	connects Tiphareth (**Sun**) with Netzach (**Venus**)

Path 25 — **Temperance** —   connects Tiphareth (**Sun**) with
                              Yesod (**Moon**)
Path 26 — **Devil** —   connects Tiphareth (**Sun**) with
                              Hod (**Mercury**)
Path 27 — **Tower** —   connects Netzach (**Venus**) with
                              Hod (**Mercury**)
Path 28 — **Star** —   connects Netzach (**Venus**) with
                              Yesod (**Moon**)
Path 30 — **Sun** —   connects Hod (**Mercury**) with
                              Yesod (**Moon**)

You are also aware that flow down the Tree is a reflection of God's—the ITS—movement from Itself downward into ITS Creation. And as such, this effortless, perfect movement is, in a metaphorical sense, deemed as 'good' or 'positive,' even in those daily affairs of humankind that we involve ourselves in on a moment-to-moment basis while in Malkuth. Please be careful here. Although this downward flow is termed metaphorical to aid your human comprehension, it is realistically a functional metaphor. That is, the classification of the downward flow as being good or positive actually does work in the mundane affairs of men and women when used in the Kabbalistic Cycles System. As such, it is truly functional.

And finally, you understand that there are only two possible positions for the Tarot when placed upon the Tree, since the cards not only represent the forces of the Paths, but also indicate the flow either down or up the Tree, *according to the flow which is **always from the hour into the day**.* Since *flow down the Tree* must correspond to the effortless flow of God's blessings to us, as mirrored through the cards, this flow would have to be represented in the orientation of the card assigned to the Path in question as the *upright position. Flow up the Tree*—again, *from the hour into the day*—would of necessity, have to correspond to our struggle to climb the Tree, the struggle being represented by the orientation of the card such that it is in a *reversed position* on the Path to which it corresponds.

(Note here, to be explained and exampled below, that the list of Paths and Their Connections, just listed, was written to serve as a shorthand summary. When Paths are taken into consideration, reading from left to right will read as a positive flow *from hour into day.* Reading from right to left will exhibit a negative flow *from hour into day.*)

All of the above is only an abstract of the knowledge of the Sephiroth, Planets, Paths, and the Tarot, and this newly *applied* concept of Flow on the Tree. While it is important, meant for you to study carefully, there is nothing like directing this knowledge into examples that will breathe the life of understanding into your new knowledge. To do this, we will now look at each Path that is used in the Kabbalistic Cycles System, its Tarot Trump association, the orientation of its Card, the Planetary jointure each Path makes through its particular Sephirothic connection, and the concept of flow as it is applied to the entire system. It is also necessary from this point onward to work from the inside out, owing to the central importance of the Tarot attributions and their orientation to reflect flow on the Tree. What do I mean? We will explore the Sephiroth-Path connections from the point of view of the Tarot card attributions, seeing that these Path influences are the strongest forces involved. And why are they the strongest forces involved? Because in point of fact—

Fundamental Principle 4 — *the Path influences attenuate the planetary influences connected by a given Path even more so than does a different planet ruling an hourly period on any given day.*

Commentary 4 — As you found out, the ratio for the planetary attenuation effect is on the order of 4:1. For example, during a Venus hour on the day ruled by Jupiter—Thursday—the effect of Venus is four times as great as the influence of Jupiter during that hour. The same holds here. There is a further attenuating effect provided by the Path, which is on the order of 8:1. In the last example this would mean that while the effect of Venus will be four times greater than that of Jupiter's, the effect of the Path—(21) Kaph, connecting the two planets, and to which Trump (X) The World is assigned—will be eight times greater than the effect provided by Venus!

I know what you're thinking. If this is all true, why not just throw away the influences of the planet ruling the day and hour, and just use the Path influence? The answer is that it takes all three effects—the planet ruling the day, the planet ruling the hour, and the Path influence (where applicable), to produce a *complete result*. In those numerous cases where there are no Paths connecting the planet ruling the day with a planet ruling any given hour, there is a very easy rule you will learn later on, that works every time. Now, onto the business at hand.

PATH-TAROT WORKING DETAILS, PLANETARY ATTRIBUTIONS, AND EXAMPLES OF USE OF THE THIRTEEN PATHS OF THE KABBALISTIC CYCLES SYSTEM

Path 17—Tarot Card: VI The Lovers (Positive) **Downward Flow** = Saturn (Binah) Hour into Sun (Tiphareth) Day. (Negative) **Upward Flow** = Sun (Tiphareth) Hour into Saturn (Binah) Day. *Tarot Attributions:* Card in **upright** position (Downward Flow): a trial in life or an experiment of a personal nature that you will successfully conclude; the emergence of a new affection or object of devotion, whether it be a person or new interest of some type. Card in the **reversed** position (Upward Flow): a failed life-trial or experiment; the loss of affection for a person or interest.

Influences of Planets connected by the Path: **Saturn**—issues relating to financial debts; the repayment of these debts; the acquisition of real estate; death; crops and agriculture; lassitude; inertia; lack of individual will; activities that require intensive thought followed by a period of consistent action; an influence that is good for legal matters in which justice is sought, and which involves the authorities: such as government offices, both state and federal, as well as police, judges, courts; also a good influence for bringing issues to the attention of those who have the power to decide an outcome favorable to the petitioner; excellent for literary work requiring deep insight; a positive period for attempting sales and the advancement of products through advertising by means of printed media; beginning or advancing any scientific pursuit; an excellent influence under which to engage in deep thought regarding any issue. This Saturanean influence is extremely adverse for seeking favors or recognition from those who can grant them. It is also adverse for: making investments, whether in the stock market or in any kind of business; beginning agricultural projects such as planting or seeding. It is also a very ill time for making new acquaintances, and is extremely adverse for beginning a marriage, the use of any medical remedy for body or mind, or attempting any cures of the body or mind by any metaphysical system. Additionally, it is very adverse for surgery of any kind, and a very unfortunate hourly influence under which to enter into a contract of any kind.

Influences of Planets connected by the Path: **The Sun—** power and success in life; Life itself; illumination; mental power and ability; as with Jupiter under Chesed, also money; robust physical, emotional, and mental health; growth at the personality, character, and psychic levels; dealing with superiors of all kinds, and in any situation; asking for favors from people in authority; seeking the approval, recommendation, or help from others in any proposal whatsoever, be it of a business or personal nature; composing important letters that produce in the mind of the intended recipient a picture of the writer as a confident, balanced, individual whose request for aid, introductions, or favors, should be immediately granted. This is also an excellent influence under which one can act in noble and high-minded ways that will build up his or her public esteem and prestige. This influence however is adverse for involving oneself in illegal plans, actions, or activities of any kind whatsoever. Curiously, it also provides a negative influence for beginning or launching a new business, a new plan, or a new idea, owing to its underlying Elemental Attribution which is always shifting, changing in force and form, as the Sun itself, the most Sensible of this Sephirothal influence that has further descended into the realm of matter. By the same rationale, it is likewise adverse for signing contracts of any kind, and for entering into any partnerships, mutually beneficial arrangements or agreement—whether of a social, business, professional, or personal nature—or for entering into any kind of relationship in which there is a political element of any kind. Additionally, this planetary influence is also quite adverse for marriage, for making any new investments of any kind, for purchasing or liquidating real estate holdings, and for all forms of surgery.

Example of Use 1: You are looking to make a real estate investment. Someone approaches you out of the blue, on—curiously enough—a Sunday, during a Saturn Hour with what sounds like an ideal offer. Should you take it? Yes! The downward flow of the heavy-handed but stabilizing influence of Saturn will blend with the growth desires stimulated by the Sun, to make this a very profitable investment indeed. The Path's influence will powerfully serve to bring about a very successful conclusion to the transaction, one you will long remember and be grateful for.

Example of Use 2: The same offer above comes to you on a Saturday, during a Sun Hour. Flow is up the Tree, and hence the Tarot Card, The Lovers, is reversed. Should you now enter into this deal? Run from this same offer as fast as you can because some new variable will be operating in the background that will bring total and complete failure to the venture, and total loss of your investment.

Example of Use 3: Remember that plan for personal growth you worked on earlier in this chapter? You started to lay the plans for it during a Mercury Hour on that Sunday, due to the intellectual influences *typically* provided by Mercury, and the growth impulses fostered by the Sun. And of course, you remember the problems you had during the week, getting it launched. Well, as you will find out when we discuss Path 26, there were other reasons that launch did not go so very well. It was not simply due to the planetary rulers setting the tone of each day, it was primarily due to the upward flow on the Tree. But now you know better, so you use the heavy-handed, stabilizing

influence of the Saturn Hour during this new Sunday to
not only detail your plans, but to set down the steps necessary to hurl them at the world during the upcoming week.
And you *will* succeed. Take that to the bank!

Example of Use 4: Take those same plans from Example 3, and go to work on them during a Saturday (Saturn
Day) during an hour ruled by the Sun. See the problem? Of
course you do. There is an upward flow from the planet
ruling the hour, into the planet ruling the day. Result:
about as good as when you evolved your ideas during the
Mercury Hour of this day, which was another upward
flow. They will fail, for one reason or another.

Path 18—Tarot Card: VII The Chariot (Positive)
Downward Flow = Saturn (Binah) Hour into Mars
(Geburah) Day. (Negative) **Upward Flow** = Mars
(Geburah) Hour into Saturn (Binah) Day. *Tarot Attributions*: Card in **upright** position (Downward Flow): victory,
conquest, overcoming odds and obstructions, but only
after battle. Card in the **reversed** position: defeat after
battle; obstructions to plans and actions; plans and actions
defeated by either internal or external obstructions and
obstacles, but once again, only after battle.

Influence of Planets Connected by the Path: **Saturn**—as in
Path 17, the following Saturn properties apply: issues relating to financial debts; the repayment of these debts; the
acquisition of real estate; death; crops and agriculture;
lassitude; inertia; lack of individual will; activities that
require intensive thought followed by a period of consistent action; an influence that is good for legal matters in
which justice is sought, and which involves the authorities:
such as government offices, both state and federal, as well
as police, judges, courts; also a good influence for bringing
issues to the attention of those who have the power to
decide an outcome favorable to the petitioner; excellent for
literary work requiring deep insight; a positive period for
attempting sales and the advancement of products
through advertising by means of printed media; beginning
or advancing any scientific pursuit; an excellent influence
under which to engage in deep thought regarding any

issue. This Saturn influence is extremely adverse for seeking favors or recognition from those who can grant them. It is also adverse for: making investments, whether in the stock market or in any kind of business; beginning agricultural projects such as planting or seeding. It is also a very ill time for making new acquaintances, and is extremely adverse for beginning a marriage, the use of any medical remedy for body or mind, or attempting any cures of the body or mind by any metaphysical system. Additionally, it is very adverse for surgery of any kind, and a very unfortunate hourly influence under which to enter into a contract of any kind.

Influences of the Planets Connected by the Path: **Mars**—determination; perseverance; vigor; aggression; construction or destruction according to purpose; vitality; endurance. This martial planetary influence is excellent for dealing with material pursuits and matters requiring physical —as opposed to mental—energy; it is also a fortuitous time for dealing with sensual affairs of every type, problems of a mechanical nature, or working out the intellectual details of new ideas that will lead to new, mechanical inventions. Athletes, bodybuilders, and weightlifters will find this an excellent period in which to develop and shape their physical form, while effectively and safely exerting the maximum amount of energy in that physical development. The influence also provides for experimental scientific activities as opposed to purely theoretical investigations. It exerts a very adverse effect in asking for favors, or for dealing with any beneficent matters of a personal nature whatsoever. It is also a very adverse influence under which to seek or make new acquaintances with the intention of seeking favors from them at the time, or at some point in the future. It is also a very unfortunate time in which to deal with any and all legal matters, including those involving judges, courts, or attorneys in any way, as well as for gambling, speculation of any type, entering into marriage, or having surgery—whether outpatient or that requiring even the briefest period of hospitalization. The emotions are extremely volatile under this influence, particularly those of an aggressive, hostile, or violent nature. It is a time best spent alone, dealing exclusively with matters that the influence favors.

Prefatory Note: as mentioned earlier in the Chapter Six, the influence of this Path, and Path 27, The Tower, are the most difficult of the Paths. In this case, Card VII of the Greater Arcana, applied to Path 18, warns that plans made, opportunities that arise, and the actions taken under its influence, will have an extremely grim, major component to them. I also mentioned that of these two cards, this card (VII) The Chariot, is perhaps surprisingly the hardest of the two to work with, even in its upright position. It bespeaks of a long, arduous struggle which will take a heavy toll on the individual, even though he or she will become victorious, as indicated by the Card being in the upright position; that is, when flow is down the Tree, from a Saturn Hour into a Mars Day. The reader having been reminded of this, and realizing that there will be times in life when it is strictly necessary for one to work under this terrible influence, let's take a look at some examples.

Example of Use 1: It's Tuesday, and things at your place of employment have not been going well. The economy is still spiraling downward, despite the inflated figures and the grinning, lying-through-their-teeth reassurances the anchors of the Nightly Business Report have been feeding you for the past five years. You get to work, and your boss calls you into his office. You notice it's during an hour ruled by Saturn. He asks you to sit down, and then he drops the bomb: a cutback is coming, and you will probably be among those who gets a pink slip, with no chance of being called back to the company. There is no employment left in your area, all the companies have been laying people off for the past year. This means a move with money you don't have, to another city where new employment is a crapshoot at best, and immediate bills that cannot be paid. Your weekly paycheck was the only thing keeping you (and perhaps your family) marginally afloat. You realize all of this as his words are sounding like hollow echoes in your ears, and you panic.

Somehow, through all the terror coursing through your mind and emotions, you recall this Path influence. You know you stand a chance—but only a chance—if you can turn it around. You calm your mind and emotions, take a deep breath, and say, "What if I make myself more valuable to the company? Like, maybe learning two other jobs that are now done by others who *will* be getting cut? I'm also willing to put in ten more hours a week without pay, if that will help! I'm stretched so thin now, I'd go under for sure if I lose this job!"

He looks at you, realizing that the others who *will* be laid off are in the same situation you're in. But he is not talking to them during this hour. He is talking to *you*. The Path influence is attenuating the raw, destructive energy of Mars ruling the day, and bolstering the fourfold more powerful Saturn influence of 'this being a good influence for bringing issues to the attention of those who have the power to decide an outcome favorable to the petitioner.' He looks at you carefully, and says, "OK, I'll tell you what. You start learning those other two jobs today, and be prepared for a fifty-hour week starting now. But realize, I'm only going to pay you for a forty-hour week. If you show me that you can cut the mustard, I'll *try* to keep you on." He continues, stressing the point, "Understand this: there are *no* guarantees, but I'll do the best I can to keep you on. Agreed?" At this point, you *must* agree.

You will struggle, and for a long, very unstable, extremely emotional upsetting time. But—and this is the important point and the influence of this Path—he will keep you, while all those around you are worrying about their unemployment insurance running out. Further, after the business storm clears, you will be the one that will not only receive a very significant raise in pay, but will be promoted to boot. That is *if* the company can stay afloat during this period. Now do you see how this Path works, even when its positive influence is in effect? I trust you do, because this is as clear as I can make it.

Example of Use 2: It's a Saturday, the conditions at your place of employment are as in **Example of Use 1,**

above. Knowing this, you decided to go into your office on your own time, and clear up some paperwork. It's really a self-reassuring attempt on your part meant to ease your fears of your impending—perhaps inevitable?—discharge. You are not looking for praise or accolades from anyone. You are just concerned about the stability of your employment, and in the back of your mind you are thinking that such actions just might help your situation.

Coincidentally, your boss is in his office. He hears you come in, and seizes the opportunity to have a private talk with you. This will be the same one he had in Example 1, but this time it's occurring on a Saturday. You note the hour is a Mars Hour, flow is up the Tree, and Card VII of the Tarot, The Chariot, is reversed. Do yourself a favor. Listen to him politely, immediately return home, and start preparing for what *is* now inevitable unemployment. It doesn't matter one iota that your boss told you the same things he (would have) told you on that Tuesday during a Saturn Hour when flow was down the Tree from the Saturn Hour into a Mars Day. In this example, it occurred with the Mars Hour flowing into the Saturn Day, and the card is reversed. You will lose your job. The best thing you can do in this situation is try to get over the shock as soon as you can, and get a jump on all of those others who will be trying to find employment in the area in which you live. Start looking for new work on Monday.

Example of Use 3: You have taken a hard look at yourself in that new full-length mirror you recently purchased, and you definitely did not like what you saw. You still can't believe that your belly actually does arrive at a destination five minutes before you do, with your jowls a close second. And that slight pallor about you looks none too good, either. You knew you were out of shape, but still, you have been taking nightly walks. Well, sort of frequent walks, and watching your carbohydrates, and eating less. Surely all of that activity and care should have helped to keep the physique in decent shape, but obviously it didn't!

You are aware you're getting older and you know the excess weight is not good for your health. It's a Tuesday, and a Saturn Hour is in force. Flow is down the Tree, from the Hour into the Day. You've had enough. The video you sent for on that whiz bang home exercise machine that promises a complete workout in twenty minutes a day, four times a week, is staring you in the face again. Or maybe it's the memory of that new gym that opened up down the block that keeps popping back into mind. So you go for it. You order the machine or sign up for a year's membership during this hour.

Since you now plan for important matters using your newly acquired knowledge of the Kabbalistic Cycles System, you begin your grim workout regimen under a similar or different set of favorable influences. Guess what? Yes, you will struggle. You will see just how hard keeping to a workout schedule really is, and how determined you have to be in order to recapture something of your human figure. But I have news for you. After this battle, you will be victorious!

You will become the new you—imaged by the aggressive, energetic influence of Mars, and the grimly determined impulse of Saturn during your hour of decision. And yes, the Path influence represented by Card VII The Chariot, did turn out to be correct. It was a struggle to say the least. But you succeeded, and through the overall influences of these Sephiroth and their Path connection, you also learned something more about yourself, something you didn't anticipate when you took responsibility for your health and appearance. That is, as with *all* things in this life: *it's up to you, and no one else.* You've gained immeasurably with your insight into self-motivation, self-respect, and self-discipline. So the hard fought battle gave you more than you bargained for—but at a price no one who has not taken to this Path influence could ever understand.

Example of Use 4: The same scenario plays out as in Example 3 except it occurs during a Saturn Day, Mars Hour, and flow is up the Tree. In other words, the negative aspect of Card VII The Chariot applies, since the card occupies the reversed position. In this case, you would simply note the impulses, forget about the exercise machine or club membership, and wait until a more favorable day and time set of influences, and explore this pressing issue again. If you do this, you will be surprised to find that some completely new idea for effectively dealing with your unhealthy situation just seems to pop into your mind, or that you just happened to see some new device on television that targets your problem. And you can count on the decision/action combination you take at that time to succeed, because it will!

Path 19—Tarot Card: VIII Strength (Positive) **Downward Flow** = Mars (Geburah) Hour into Jupiter (Chesed) Day. (Negative) **Upward Flow** = Jupiter (Chesed) Hour into Mars (Geburah) Day. *Tarot Attributions*: In the **upright** position: metaphysical or spiritual force and strength; inner strength which overcomes danger and adversity. The strength through which the Holy warrior battles against overwhelming odds, and victoriously subdues and overcomes a great threat. Subjugation of opposition through spiritual power. In the **reversed** position: power and strength, but physical in nature. Endurance and determination in matters requiring physical strength, and the physical prowess through which these qualities are sustained. (Watch! Flow is opposite of what you might think.)

Influence of the Planets Connected by the Path: **Mars**—determination; perseverance; vigor; aggression; construction or destruction according to one's purpose; vitality; endurance. This martial planetary influence is excellent for dealing with material pursuits and matters requiring physical—as opposed to mental—energy; it is also a fortuitous time for dealing with sensual affairs of every type, problems of a mechanical nature, or working out the intellectual details of new ideas that will lead to new, mechanical inventions. Athletes, bodybuilders, and weightlifters will find this an excellent period in which to develop and shape their physical form, while effectively and safely exerting the maximum amount of energy in that physical development. The influence also provides for experimental scientific activities as opposed to purely theoretical investigations. It exerts a very adverse effect in asking for favors, or for dealing with any beneficent matters of a personal nature whatsoever. It is also a very adverse influence under which to seek or make new acquaintances with the intention of seeking favors from them at the time, or at some point in the future. It is also a very unfortunate time in which to deal with any and all legal matters, including those involving judges, courts, or attorneys in any way, as well as for gambling, speculation of any type, entering into marriage, or having surgery—whether outpatient or that requiring even the briefest period of hospitalization. The emotions are extremely volatile under this influence, particularly those of an aggressive, hostile, or violent nature. It is a time best spent alone, dealing exclusively with matters that the influence favors.

Influence of the Planets Connected by the Path: **Jupiter**— abundance; plenty; money; all aspects and types of growth and expansion; visions; dreams; spirituality as a way of life. This Jupiter influence is very good for beginning a new venture, a new plan, or a new idea of any kind, for working out the details of new plans and ideas, and for the making of contracts or agreements, regardless of their nature. It is an excellent influence under which to study and gain new knowledge, as it is for involving oneself in educational matters of any kind. It is a very fortunate influence under which to marry, and is a very beneficent period for making new acquaintances, borrowing money, and dealing with powerful or prominent people who can be of genuine benefit to your plans, ideas, and desires. It is likewise an excellent influence for purchasing or selling real estate, asking for favors directly from virtually any-one, and for indulging in all forms of speculation for profit. This influence also has a spontaneous, instinctive, and involuntary characteristic that must be guarded against, lest the individual becomes careless in weighing and analyzing situations. Yet even so, the outcome of most activities that take place under this Jupiteranean power are benefic and positive.

Examples of Use 1: You are deeply involved in a money making project that if successful, will put you on easy street for the rest of your life, or at least provide the financial freedom you have always wanted. The project has required an enormous amount of your time, physical stick-to-it-ness as well as mental exertion, more nights without sleep than you care to remember, and has drained all of your liquid assets. You are at the end of your rope. You've had enough. No one cares enough about your new project to even look at it, let alone take it and you seriously, and you are about to throw in the towel and chalk the entire matter up to a hard earned lesson in life.

It's a Thursday during an hour ruled by Mars, and you receive a phone call from someone who heard of your new invention, product, process, or software, take your pick. He wants you to be at his office or plant the following Monday morning, bright and early, to give him a demonstration and full explanation. You know this is the break you've been waiting for, but you are beyond physical and mental exhaustion. You have to go to your regular job tomorrow, and take care of a hundred other duties this weekend, which you have already put off much too long. To top it all off, this new prospect is in the next state. You are flat broke. You can't even afford an airline ticket, and certainly don't have the time to drive the distance to meet with him.

Yet you know that this downward flow on the Tree, through the Path of Strength, is marshaling an inner strength you never knew you possessed, and it is propelling you to somehow overcome what you are certain is the last obstacle standing between you and your dreams fulfilled. You realize that the beyond physical strength welling up from some hidden depth within you is indeed that strength through which the Holy warrior battles against overwhelming odds, and victoriously subdues and overcomes a great threat. It is truly rooted in some genuine spiritual power or psychic force within you.

Through your own will and determination, and yet by way of something else you sense surging through your nature, you find yourself 'in mode' to fight on. You call in sick at work the next day, throw together a presentation Friday night and Saturday, borrow the money you need for the airline ticket, and find yourself at this prospective client's office at 8:15 AM on Monday morning. Will you succeed? Of course!

You'll have to do your best, as there are no sure things in anything in life without one's best efforts, but with the forces of these planets and their Path behind you, succeed you will, in a way beyond simple emotional gratification. It has also honed your psychic faculties, and you experience new depths and power in your own genuine, spiritual nature. A strange inner transformation, precipitated by a series of mundane concerns and events, has occurred. You are the winner on all Fronts!

Example of Use 2: Once again the same series of events outlined in the above example, except now they play out on a Tuesday during a Jupiter Hour. Hence, the flow is up the Tree. That is, from the Jupiter Hour into the Mars Day. Tarot Card VIII Strength is in the reversed position, due to the upward flow. In this reversed position, the card stands for power and strength, but physical in nature. It highlights endurance and determination in matters, but those matters that require physical strength and physical prowess through which the qualities of endurance and determination are sustained.

Since the physical aspects are stressed here, your preparations for this meeting may contain the same elements as in the previous example, but they will lack the psychic or spiritual component needed to close the deal, and you will feel this lack during the preparations. Besides your preparations harboring this void, the delivery of that presentation and the response of your interested client, will also be missing this key ingredient. While you may not lose out immediately, the client will express a somewhat feigned, halfhearted interest at first, which you will clearly sense. At some point, the deal will eventually fall through, in which case, you may very well have to abandon your further efforts to get this project off the ground.

A very tenuous aspect always appears with the Strength card in the reversed position, but I have given you about as clear an example of its strange influence as I can in this instance.

Example of Use 3: You have been thinking seriously about ways to advance yourself or about advancing some personal interest of yours—one that requires a long term commitment. You realize such an effort will demand a great deal of expended physical energy over time, and even more mental energy. Say you are thinking of going back to college to finish your degree or acquire an advanced one, or of making of a long term contract of either a business or personal nature, such as marriage. It's a Thursday, during the Mars Hour, and what you consider to be the perfect opportunity to fulfill this inner need presents itself to you. Flow is down the Tree, and the Strength card of the 19th Path is thus invoked. Should you go for it? Absolutely. While the more mundane influences of Mars and Jupiter will most certainly enter into the matter very strongly, the balance of this 19th Path will mediate their influences in such a way, that the source of *real* energy behind the venture—the psychic force or spiritual power—will guide and support you throughout the entire project: from its wishful beginning, through to its successful conclusion.

Example of Use 4: The same as in the example above, except the opportunity presents itself during a Mars Day, during a Jupiter Hour. As such, flow is up the Tree, and Card VIII Strength of the Tarot is in the reversed position. As occurred in **Example of Use 2**, the occasion that presents itself will be filled with purely physical energy and drive, but lacking any appreciable spiritual energy or psychic content whatsoever. Thus it will eventually fail outright over time, or produce such unfavorable results that you wind up dropping the matter or backing out of it in some way. Again, use care with this reversed card influence.

Path 20—Tarot Card: IX The Hermit (Positive) **Downward Flow** = Jupiter (Chesed) Hour into Sun

(Tiphareth) Day. (Negative) **Upward Flow** = Sun (Tiphareth) Hour into Jupiter (Chesed) Day. *Tarot Attributions:* In the **upright** position: deliberation due to watchful attention, or a feeling of caution; a warning of some kind, that things are not as they seem. Also, issues, matters, or exercises for developing the psychic faculties and *genuine* spiritual development are stressed by the card in this position. In the **reversed** position: excessive self-admonition or over cautiousness in important matters; imprudent actions; ill-advised activities; indiscreet behavior.

Influences of the Planets Connected by the Paths: **Jupiter**—abundance; plenty; money; all aspects and types of growth and expansion; visions; dreams; spirituality as a way of life. This Jupiteranean influence is very good for beginning a new venture, a new plan, or a new idea of any kind, for working out the details of new plans and ideas, and for making contracts or agreements, regardless of their nature. It is an excellent influence under which to study and gain new knowledge, as it is for involving oneself in educational matters of any kind. It is a very fortunate influence under which to marry, and is a very beneficent period for making new acquaintances, borrowing money, and dealing with powerful or prominent people who can be of genuine benefit to your plans, ideas, and desires. It is likewise an excellent influence for purchasing or selling real estate, asking for favors from virtually anyone directly, and for indulging in all forms of speculation for profit. This influence also has a spontaneous, instinctive, and involuntary characteristic that must be guarded against, lest the individual becomes careless in weighing and analyzing situations. Yet even so, the outcome of most activities that take place under this Jupiter power are benefic and positive.

Influences of the Planets Connected by the Paths: **The Sun**—power and success in life; Life itself; illumination; mental power and ability; as with Jupiter under Chesed, also money; robust physical, emotional, and mental health; growth at the personality, character, and psychic levels; dealing with superiors of all kinds, and in any situation;

asking for favors from people in authority; seeking the approval, recommendation, or help from others in any proposal whatsoever, be it of a business or personal nature; composing important letters that produce in the mind of the intended recipient a picture of the writer as a confident, balanced individual whose request for aid, introductions, or favors, should be granted immediately. This is also an excellent influence under which one can act in noble and high-minded ways that will build up his or her public esteem and prestige. This influence however is adverse for involving oneself in illegal plans, actions, or activities of any kind whatsoever. Curiously, it also provides a negative influence for beginning or launching a new business, a new plan, or a new idea, owing to its underlying Elemental Attribution which is always shifting, changing in force and form, as is the Sun itself. By the same rationale, it is likewise adverse for signing contracts of any kind, and for entering into any partnerships, mutually beneficial arrangements or agreements—whether of a social, business, professional, or personal nature—or for entering into any kind of relationship in which there is a political element of any kind. Additionally, this planetary influence is also quite adverse for marriage, for making any new investments of any kind, for purchasing or liquidating real estate holdings, and for all forms of surgery.

Example of Use 1: You have been looking for a chance to get in on the ground floor of a new business, or jump to a new position in your firm, or go off on your own and found your own company. Or maybe you have an opportunity to unload that old building or acre of ground that has been in your family for generations, and is now yours to do with as you please. It's a Sunday, and although no one usually concerns themselves with such matters on this day, a situation arises during the Jupiter Hour that will enable you to get started in this new direction you want to take. You have to deal with another individual to do so however, and a meeting is set between the two of you during a Sun Hour later in the evening, and The 20th Path of

The Hermit is invoked thereby (because the issue *began* in a Jupiter hour.)
What can you expect? First of all, your sense of caution will be alerted. It may be a tone in the other person's voice; or a slight skepticism you thought you noticed when you told him the price for the old building, or piece of ground; or that you are interested in jumping to the new position in the firm; or the like. The two of you finally meet during the Sun Hour, and both of you are a bit edgy: him for his reasons, you for yours. The meeting seems to go well, and you walk away content. Have you succeeded? I mean, have you gotten your way fully? Will your way truly work out in your best interests? The answer? Yes, to all.

In fact, when you look back over the situation, *you will see that it was your very caution that prompted you to act this way or that, say just the right thing or keep your mouth shut at just the right moment, or in some manner communicate a non-verbal message, in a certain way, that brought you the success you wanted in the matter.* Count on it. You have a new, desirable situation on your hands now, and one that will bear the mark of permanency.

Example for Use 2: As in other examples, the same set of circumstances occur, but on a Thursday, during a Sun Hour. Flow is up the Tree, and Card IX is therefore in the reversed position. What will happen? There is a feeling of cautiousness within you. This is normal for you of course, but somehow this time it seems excessive. You're really on guard. Try as you might, you can't put your finger on it exactly, but somehow, you are very suspicious of the individual and this upcoming meeting. Nevertheless you and he meet. What will the outcome be for you?

You will find that the *excessive state of caution will completely destroy your best efforts.* Your expectations in this matter will come to naught. Not immediately or in a direct manner, but rather slowly, over a lengthy period of time. This is the worst part of the upward movement of flow on this Path. A significant amount of time is lost in 'appearance,' causing other opportunities to be lost by virtue of your occupation with the matters at hand that began under the auspices of this influence. Like all upward flow movements along the Paths, this movement should be strictly avoided.

Example for Use 3: You've let it be known that you're interested in running for a local office, or for a position in your hobby club, church, or some organization in which you sincerely feel you can do more good than the individual who now occupies that chair. Nothing has come of your declaration over the months, and you've all but forgotten about it. Suddenly, on a Sunday evening, during a Jupiter Hour, you get a telephone call from the chief organizer or head of your group, organization, church, or town council.

Unknown to you, the right people have decided that you are the right man or woman for the job, and the voice on the other end of the telephone asks you to write a letter to so-and-so tonight, formally stating your qualifications, and outlining your plans for improving the club or organization. A note of caution rears up in your mind, principally because no one made you aware that they took the statements you made months ago seriously. But you are also aware of the planetary and Path influences, and that while such matters are typically negative under a Sun Day influence, this influence is moderated by the authority of the Jupiter Hour to a fourfold extent, while the Path influence provides an eightfold positive effect on the issue because of Tarot Trump IX being in the upright position.

So you courteously thank the caller, hang up, and set to work under this hour to produce the best written proposal that you can. Never mind it takes you half the night. The important thing is that you began the action under this influence, and as such, your written declaration will carry the imprint of the influence being exerted at this time. Will you get the position? Without question. In fact, it is amazing to note that your writing exercise will be coolly directed by the cautionary note this Path influence produces. That is, the Path influence will act in such a way as to make sure your statements and claims can be verified by others, and that they ring true about who you are and what you have accomplished to date. And always, your projected image will be in the best possible light. In fact, you will find that you are in for a very positive and lasting experience after you are appointed to the position in question.

Example of Use 4: The same telephone call arrives but on a Thursday, during a Sun Hour. All conditions and requests from the caller are as in the previous example, and you set to work during this hour. The result? As always, the upward flow will damn your best efforts. In this instance, that overly cautious attitude of yours will wind its way into your letter, and in some way, strike a discordant note within the mind of the reader. This note of disbelief will color his mind. As in other reversed examples, you will fail to obtain what you want, but only after a lengthy period of time in which other genuine opportunities presented themselves, and which have been lost due to the delaying aspect of this influence.

Path 21—Tarot Card: X The Wheel of Fortune (Positive) **Downward Flow** = Jupiter (Chesed) Hour into Venus (Netzach) Day. (Negative) **Upward Flow** = Venus (Netzach) Hour into Jupiter (Chesed) Day. *Tarot Attributions*: In the **upright** position, the card symbolizes beneficence; expansiveness; growth; money; good luck; good fortune; success. In the **reversed** position: ill fortune; the reversal of dame fortune; hardship; loss; contraction; struggle; failure.

Influences of the Planets Connected by the Paths: **Jupiter—** As before, this planetary force provides for abundance; plenty; money; all aspects and types of growth and expansion; visions; dreams; and spirituality as a way of life. This influence is also very good for beginning a new venture, a new plan, or a new idea of any kind, for working out the details of new plans and ideas, and for making contracts or agreements, regardless of their nature. It is an excellent influence under which to study and gain new knowledge, as it is for involving oneself in educational matters of any kind. It is a very fortunate influence under which to marry, and is a very beneficent period for making new acquaintances, borrowing money, and dealing with powerful or prominent people who can be of genuine benefit to your plans, ideas, and desires. It is likewise an excellent influence for purchasing or selling real estate, asking for favors from virtually anyone directly, and for indulging in all forms of speculation for profit. This influence also has a spontaneous, instinctive, and involuntary characteristic that must be guarded against, lest the individual becomes careless in weighing and analyzing situations. Yet even so, the outcome of most activities that take place under this Jupiter power are benefic and positive.

Influences of the Planets Connected by the Paths: **Venus**—Unselfishness; Love, but of a sexual nature; beauty of form, and the appreciation of that beauty; the emotions of the conscious level of our being; women; music; self-indulgence; extravagance; all material and sensual affairs; music; art; the theater; any form of behavior or expression that supports sensuality. It is also a very fortuitous influence under which to begin any new enterprise or project, whether sensual or business in nature. It is also an excellent influence in which to make new acquaintances, but only those that are met through spontaneous social contact. It is also a very favorable influence for entering into marriage, to borrow or loan money, and to host social gatherings and parties, but only those affairs that are meant for pure enjoyment. It is very positive for speculating in stocks, bonds, or in any new business proposition. It is important to note here that due to the Venusian planetary influence of this Sephirah, almost any activity or action that is begun or ended while this influence is in operation, will bear very significant, desirable, or fortunate results. It is an influence that, in effect, blesses and magnifies activities of almost any kind, but especially those of a sensual and material nature. There are a few very adverse aspects of this influence, such as dealing with social underlings or subordinates; beginning long trips to remote locations; using social means to harm enemies or competitors; or to attempt using social functions as a means of gaining a business or personal advantage at the expense of a collaborator or fellow worker.

Example of Use 1: It's a Friday. You've put in a hard week, and intend to relax by going out for the night. Maybe it will be dinner, some shopping, and a movie. You're in a very positive frame of mind, and enjoy being around people, perhaps more on this day, than on any other. You're enjoying your dinner, paging through a self-help book you've been trying to get through for the last month, when a stranger suddenly walks up to you and says, "Excuse me! I couldn't help notice that book you're reading! I've been doing my best to understand it, but I'm hung up on a few points, and don't know anyone else who's reading it. Do you mind if I ask you a question or two?"

Surprised, you look at the very attractive woman or man standing at your side. The smile is infectious, and you are beginning to feel something in the pit of your stomach that you haven't felt since your high school days—butterflies! "Why, I'd be delighted to help if I can! Won't you join me? It would make matters a lot simpler for both of us!" The adorable woman (or handsome man) smiles broadly, and almost too eagerly replies, "Thank you! I'd love to!"

As he or she slides onto the seat across from you, you happen to glance at that small Kabbalistic Cycles chart you've been using as a makeshift book mark, and find that it's a Jupiter Hour! That's right! Card X The Wheel of Fortune is at work, with all of the joy, excitement, and fulfillment that it brings, and of course, it's in the upright position. What are the details of this happy situation, how do they unfold, and where do they lead?

I'll let the reader fill in the blanks from this point on. But I will say that such a situation will turn out splendidly for both of you, in all areas of life, even so far as eventually making the situation permanent. An idealized example? Something you only find in the movies or in a book? Don't count on it! Not when it comes to the downward flow of a Jupiter Hour into a Venus Day! The most amazing, charming, happy, and exciting events are realized under this influence. On *this* you can count!

Example of Use 2: Of course, all of elements in the above example are in play once more. Except the day is Thursday. You are feeling 'expansive'—if a bit fluid—but generally, pretty good. And you are paging through that darned self-help book as you're having an impromptu dinner out, trying to have your Friday a day early because of other commitments tomorrow night. To your delight, the same scene unfolds, and that gorgeous (or handsome) stranger approaches you, as if the scene were written into a movie.

But you notice that it's a Venus Hour, and flow is up the Tree. Card X The Wheel of Fortune is reversed. Does this mean that the oh! so tempting situation is doomed to abject failure, and will fall apart before you've had a chance to fantasize until your heart's content? Surprise! In this case, not exactly so! What do I mean? It is strange, but *this card is so powerful, that even in its reversed position—that is, in a flow up the Tree from a Venus Hour into a Jupiter Day— the card produces indirect beneficent results.* How can this happen in this idealized example?

That beautiful woman or handsome man will either be with a friend, or will introduce you to his or her spitting image, or will suggest the two of you go shopping together, take in that movie, or any of a host of possibilities in which you will end up having the same experience you did in the case of Example 1 above. In any event, it will be through his or her influence that you will be encouraged to either go somewhere you would not normally go yourself, or change the established sequence of doing things you had originally planned to do that night, or some such variation on the theme. And it will be through such changes that the good of this card will come to you, even though the flow is upward. In short, the benefits of the card will flow to you—albeit indirectly—as though the flow were downward on the Tree and the card were in the upright position. That is, from the Hour into the Day.

Why is this the case here? I put it down to a 'Tension of Creation' as I term it, in which the Great Benefic Jupiter interacts with a very earthy, mundane Venus, in order to bring about a new creation, regardless of the direction of flow. Yet, as you saw, the upward flow does have a skewing effect, in that it complicates and blinds the initial force flowing from Jupiter. Still, the combination of these two planets ever pushing toward physical pleasure, completion, and beneficence in the material world, overcomes the normally deleterious effect of upward flow, although in an indirect and sometimes very confusing manner.

The admonition to the reader in such a case of reversed flow, is to be exceptionally alert to the events issuing from the initial condition that arises under this reversed card influence.

Example of Use 3: You want to beautify your home. Too long have you lived in a dingy, shabby square or rectangle, the ceiling of which you rarely look at, and whose floors you try your best to ignore. The dirty, worn out carpeting has really been bothering you for years. With age, you've come to understand that your surroundings have a definite, powerful bearing upon your mood and emotions. And in turn, these emotions have a direct effect upon your feelings about yourself, your life, and—come to think of it—how you feel about others, even after you leave that closed geometry you call home.

So now you are going to do something about it, and not in some cheap, slipshod way, either! You've been saving for awhile, getting ideas, and really making a concerted effort to change your world from the outside in, instead of only the inside out, as has been your philosophy until now. This time you pull out your trusty, Jim-dandy Kabbalistic Cycles chart and consciously decide on the time to go shopping and spend all that hard earned money to make your dwelling a place you can truly live in.

And guess what time you select? Of course! A Friday, during a Jupiter Hour, when the flow is down the Tree, and the Wheel of Fortune Tarot Trump is in the upright position! Just the influence needed to make you feel luxurious, and to attract those fineries that extend this luxury to your home by selecting just the right items for your new décor. The shopping spree begins as planned, and lasts throughout the day. Of course, you are aware by now that the important influence is the one under which an activity begins, since that influence is carried through to successive hours as long as the *intent* is there.

While you're hard at work selecting this and paying for that, an art print catches your eye. You thought of buying a few inexpensive pictures to brighten up those dark, empty spaces on your walls, but you had no idea you would find such a beautiful, delightful print that simply brings out the very best in your emotional nature. It is breathtaking and—you can afford it! You happily add it to your swelling collection, and after a hard ten or so hours shopping, you head home and spend the next two days putting your new treasures in place.

As the weeks pass, you notice not simply an improvement in your overall attitude toward yourself and others, but a calmness and peace of mind that refreshes you from the outside in, and the inside out. You sleep more soundly, have more energy, and are much more positive and optimistic. As if this wasn't enough, you notice you are more creative, think more clearly, and appreciate Life in all of its manifestations more than you ever have before. Is all this possible? Can all of these benefits truly spring from doing something as simple as redecorating, and doing it under the auspices of this planetary combination/Path influence? You better believe it is!

The long and the short of it is this. You can either work with the forces of the Tree and Nature, or work against them, according to that famous of all rationalizations: 'I'll do what I want when I want. I have absolute Free Will!' Either way, you will get results. The question is, what kind? The answer to that you will know and be more than happy with if you follow the Kabbalistic Cycles System being taught here.

Example of Use 4: All of the conditions of the previous example are once more in effect, except you decide to do

212 Joseph C. Lisiewski, Ph.D.

all of that shopping on a Thursday, during a Venus Hour. The flow is against you. Nevertheless, you will experience the same good results, but in an indirect way. It may be that you have to visit more stores, can't quite find what you're looking for, have to make changes in the original designs you had your heart set on, or any of the infinite possibilities that underlie any experience. But still, as hard as it may be for you to believe right now, you will wind up with the very same beneficial results. Results that will produce the exact same effects in you as those that were generated by the easy experience when the flow was down the Path. It's just the way it works.

Path 22—Tarot Card: XI Justice (Positive) **Downward Flow** = Mars (Geburah) Hour into Sun (Tiphareth) Day. (Negative) **Upward Flow** = Sun (Tiphareth) Hour into Mars (Geburah) Day. *Tarot Attributions*: In the **upright** position, the forces of this card translate into harmony, justice, and stability. Poise, equilibrium, and balance are also supported, as both attitudes and actions. In the **reversed** position, the card's forces indicate conflict and injustice, along with general instability, imbalance, and intolerance.

Influences of the Planets Connected by the Paths: **Mars**— determination; perseverance; vigor; aggression; construction or destruction according to purpose; vitality; endurance. This martial planetary influence is excellent for dealing with material pursuits and matters requiring physical —as opposed to mental—energy; it is also a fortuitous time for dealing with sensual affairs of every type, problems of a mechanical nature, or working out the intellectual details of new ideas that will lead to new, mechanical inventions. Athletes, bodybuilders, and weightlifters will find this an excellent period in which to develop and shape their physical form, while effectively and safely exerting the maximum amount of energy in that physical development. The influence also provides for experimental scientific activities as opposed to purely theoretical investigations. It exerts a very adverse effect in asking for favors, or for dealing with any beneficent matters of a personal nature whatsoever. It is also a very adverse influence under which to seek or make new acquaintances with the intention of seeking favors from them at the time, or at some point in the future. It is also a very unfortunate time in which to deal with any and all legal matters, including those involving judges, courts, or attorneys in any way, as well as for gambling, speculation of any type, entering into marriage, or having surgery—whether outpatient or that requiring even the briefest period of hospitalization. The emotions are extremely volatile under this influence, particularly those of an aggressive, hostile, or violent nature. It is a time best spent alone, dealing exclusively with matters that the influence favors.

Influences of the Planets Connected by the Paths: **The Sun**—power and success in life; Life itself; illumination; mental power and ability; also money; robust physical, emotional, and mental health; growth at the personality, character, and psychic levels; dealing with superiors of all kinds, and in any situation; asking for favors from people in authority; seeking the approval, recommendation, or help from others in any proposal whatsoever, be it of a business or personal nature; composing important letters that produce in the mind of the intended recipient a picture of the writer as a confident, balanced, individual whose request for aid, introductions, or favors, should be immediately granted. This is also an excellent influence under which one can act in noble and high-minded ways that will build up his or her public esteem and prestige. This influence however is adverse for involving oneself in illegal plans, actions, or activities of any kind whatsoever. Curiously, it also provides a negative influence for beginning or launching a new business, a new plan, or a new idea, owing to its underlying Elemental Attribution which is always shifting, changing in force and form, as the Sun itself, the most Sensible of this Sephirothal influence that has further descended into the realm of matter. By the same rationale, it is likewise adverse for signing contracts of any kind, and for entering into any partnerships, mutually beneficial arrangements or agreements—whether of a social, business, professional, or personal nature—or for entering into any kind of relationship in which there is a political element of any kind. Additionally, this planetary influence is also quite adverse for marriage, for making any new investments of any kind, for purchasing or liquidating real estate holdings, and for all forms of surgery.

Example of Use 1: *Note: Please pay special attention to this example. It contains a number of elements that are all too often found in challenging life-situations. While the example might sound obtuse at first, your careful study of it will probably reveal that it is more characteristic of 'sudden happenings' than you might like to readily admit. Be aware also, that the general components of this example are applicable to many different situations in which you are forced to cooperate or act, usually, against your will or better judgment.*

You were about to embark on a new program designed to increase your psychic faculties. Yes, you were going to choose a more obvious, favorable time in which to begin this lengthy program of inner self-development, but some circumstance or another has literally forced you to begin it on a Sunday. You know all too well that the Solar influence of the day does not favor starting any new plan. Yet you also know that the energy and dynamic nature of Mars is there to aid you, especially since the circumstance that has forced you into this position is one that has angered you greatly.

You can feel the martial force urging you to begin your new plan during its influence. It power, overriding that of the Sun's influence of the day by a factor of four, gives you the confidence to proceed. You further feel that the injustice of the situation foisted upon you is also being met by the martial forces, and in your heart, you know your course of action is being set for you by the very forces of the Tree. You start your program of inner development during this day's Mars Hour, and immediately begin to direct your psychic energy at the root of the threat to its very cause. Path 22, with its downward flow from Mars into the Sun aids you. Its force of justice opposes the threat, while balancing your psychic exercise in such a way that the full force of equilibrium and equity of this Path at first curbs, and then in the twinkling of an eye, dissolves the threat, while immobilizing its very source.

Is all of this really possible? Can the influence of this planetary/Path combination aid you to such an extent in a matter in which you are totally innocent and without blame? Oh yes, most definitely. This is a very strange Path, and one that is not to be taken lightly. It has special uses as has been intimated here in this simple example, beyond its more mundane uses as will be seen in **Example for Use 3.** Your further study of Kabbalah will reveal more of this Path's austere and justice-oriented nature to you, while the force of the Path itself guides you in its righteous use.

Example of Use 2: The conditions of the previous example prevail, but they have been unleashed upon you on a Tuesday. You are tempted beyond belief to assume a defensive posture by using the influence of this 22nd Path of Justice. Or perhaps the idea of using the full force of the Path offensively, to strike back at the source of the threat by beginning your new psychic development program under its influence and directing the force toward the threat, has you by the throat. You know better, but your rage and fury—themselves the direct impulses of Mars pouring into you in an uncontrolled way through the upward flow of the Path—have blinded your better judgment, and you proceed during a Sun Hour.

The result? Imbalance all around. What you unleash will rebound upon you, adding immeasurably to the miseries of the threat, to bring you to your figurative and literal knees. Once again you have a choice. Either learn to live and work in cooperation with the Laws of the Holy Tree of Life, or be damned by them. It is as straightforward as this.

Example of Use 3: You've been meaning to cut back on your alcohol consumption for some time now. Not that it's really out of hand, but you have noticed that you usually have two drinks at lunch time—or has it grown to three?—and the 'after work' cocktail has turned into four—or is it five?—over the course of the evening, whether you're simply watching television or finishing that woodworking project in your basement. Come to think of it, you once had a life during the weekdays. You normally only 'threw back a few' on the weekends while watching the games, or going out with so-and-so for a social evening. But never mind, you're still at your job, well liked by everyone, and a pretty good 'Joe' or 'Cindy.' After all, life is tough, pressures abound from all sides, and everyone's stress levels are more often than not off the scale. "Still, maybe I'd better stop or at least cut way back…"

Your train of thought is suddenly broken by alternating blue and red flashing lights in the rearview mirror that are reflecting into your eyes. The meaning of the lights hits you like a brick across your forehead. Before you can slow down, those lights become accompanied by the wail of a siren. It's the police. You pull over to the side of the road, the officer emerges from his vehicle, stands off to the side of your car door, and in a voice somewhere between somber and curious, says, "Good evening sir (or madam)! I couldn't help notice you swerved across the center lane a few times. Have you been drinking tonight?" Your heart—now in your throat—skews your normally resonant voice. "I've been at my friend's watching the game (or playing Canasta). I did have a drink or two, but that was hours ago. I was thinking about something on the way home, and guess I wasn't watching where I was going! I'm sorry!"

The police officer looks you squarely in the eye and replies, "Please step out of your vehicle, sir (or madam)! I have to determine if you are driving under the influence." Shocked beyond belief, you comply. You know you had six drinks at least, and now the martial rage at your own behavior is driving your blood pressure through the roof. You can feel the pulsing in your neck as the officer gives you a field sobriety meter and asks you to blow into it. Your mind is racing, as feelings of guilt and fear course through your veins—right next to all of that alcohol.

The officer takes the meter from you, shines his flashlight on it, and says, "Well, it looks like this is your lucky night! You measure an alcohol level just .02 under the legal limit. If I were you, I'd get back in my car and head home immediately, and say a prayer. Because I can tell you, from the way you were driving, I suspected you would read at least .15 on my meter. Take this as a warning, and learn to control your drinking!"

When you get back home, after calming down, you happen to think of the cycles, and take a look at your latest chart. To your absolute disbelief, you find the cop stopped you during a Mars Hour on this Sunday, the flow down the Tree was with you, and you escaped a very expensive and socially damning nightmare that could have ruined the rest of your life. But how could this be? How could the force of Justice that lies behind the 22nd Path have aided you? You were irresponsible in your drinking, and you know it.

But then, you were questioning yourself as you were driving home. You began to see what you were doing to yourself and to others through your negligent behavior. Did the concept of Justice and balance behind this Path help you? What do you think? You will find many strange and wonderful effects, and no end of guidance, through the diligent use of the Tree and its components. As your author, I strongly suggest that you listen to that counsel closely, and give thanks for the blessings that the Tree can—and will—confer upon you, *when you work with it correctly, knowledgeably, and in good conscience.*

Example of Use 4: The same conditions in **Example of Use 3** are in operation. You have even been questioning yourself in the exact same manner as in that example, when the flashing lights of the police car attracted your attention. The only difference is, in this case, it is a Tuesday, and the hour during which you have been pulled over is a Sun Hour. Flow is now up the Tree, and the Tarot Trump of the 22nd Path is in the reversed position: imbalance, conflict, instability, and injustice abound. The raw aggressive energy of Mars is mediated by the Sun, yes, and by a factor of four.

Joseph C. Lisiewski, Ph.D.

But there is a grimness in the eightfold impact the Path is exerting in the matter. This time the officer is belligerent. Maybe he had a hard day, and has had enough of drunks running around the highways, and has even targeted you. You wonder, as he puts the handcuffs on your wrists, if in his foul mood he might have somehow made that sobriety meter read a little higher—like the 0.15 reading it registered this time, and which you certainly feel like inside.

There's no way out of it now. You are under arrest for DUI. You won't be arraigned until tomorrow morning, which means you'll spend the night in jail, right alongside the dregs of society—and *you* are now one of them. You'll also miss work tomorrow, and everyone will soon know why. And what about the bail? Who is going to put up the $5,000 to get you out of the cell you're sharing with that big fellow Bubba, who keeps staring at you so affectionately? And where will the money come from for the lawyer fees? And of course, it will be in all the newspapers tomorrow, under the 'Local Arrest' section. What about jail time? It was only your first offense, but the Law has been cracking down hard lately, especially in your town? Now what?

What happened? You had those same noble thoughts about cutting back or outright quitting your drinking that you would have had if the incident occurred on a Sunday during a Mars Hour as given in the previous example. Why didn't it work for you this time? I'll tell you why. The properties of this Path are very explicit here. In the case of reversed flow, imbalance, injustice, conflict and instability will dominate any situation, and as you found out, that includes a feedback effect that this Path actually has on itself! That's right. Upward flow on this Path causes a reflection of the Path forces upon itself, so that it destabilizes its own effects when the card is in its reversed position. It is as if it were a double-negative. And in fact—it is. You're in for a bad time of it now, and the final conclusion to your DUI will be very severe indeed. You will be extremely fortunate if you do not have to serve any jail time, because the influence of upward flow on this Path is merciless in the extreme, and that is as mild as I can put it. But look on the bright side. If you ever needed a reason to give up the booze, now you have it.

Path 23—Tarot Card: XII The Hanged Man (Positive) **Downward Flow** = Mars (Geburah) Hour into Mercury (Hod) Day. (Negative) **Upward Flow** = Mercury (Hod) Hour into Mars (Geburah) Day. *Tarot Attributions:* In the **upright** position, the card symbolizes the acquisition of knowledge that eventually matures into wisdom. The process is slow however, and as with life in general, requires sacrifices on the part of the individual for that knowledge to ripen into wisdom. Discernment is also indicated when this card is in the upright position. In the **reversed** position, the forces of the Path stress self-centeredness, and an exclusive concern for one's own self at the obvious expense of others. It also denotes slyness and deceptive behavior designed to have one accepted by some group, or the masses themselves.

Influences of the Planets Connected by the Paths: **Mars**— As you know by now, this planet rules determination; perseverance; vigor; aggression; construction or destruction according to purpose; vitality; endurance. This martial planetary influence is excellent for dealing with material pursuits and matters requiring physical—as opposed to mental—energy; it is also a fortuitous time for dealing with sensual affairs of every type, problems of a mechanical nature, or working out the intellectual details of new ideas that will lead to new, mechanical inventions. Athletes, bodybuilders, and weightlifters will find this an excellent period in which to develop and shape their physical form, while effectively and safely exerting the maximum amount of energy in that physical development. The influence also provides for experimental scientific activities as opposed to purely theoretical investigations. It exerts a very adverse effect in asking for favors, or for dealing with any beneficent matters of a personal nature whatsoever. It is also a very adverse influence under which to seek or make new acquaintances with the intention of seeking favors from them at the time, or at some point in the future. It is also a very unfortunate time in which to deal with any and all legal matters, including those involving judges, courts, or attorneys in any way, as well as for gambling, speculation of any type, entering into marriage, or having surgery—whether outpatient or that requiring even the briefest period of hospitalization. The emotions are extremely volatile under this influence, particularly those of an aggressive, hostile, or violent nature. It is a time best spent alone, dealing exclusively with matters that the influence favors.

Influences of the Planets Connected by the Paths: **Mercury** —this Mercurial influence is very positive for dealing with intellectual discernments; scientific thought; mathematics; writing of all kinds; logic; reason; using and accelerating the analytical faculty of the conscious self; thinking; speaking, whether in public or private. Additionally, as with Netzach and Venus, the Mercurial influence of Hod is very beneficial for art, music, and the theater; for literary work of any kind; to design or begin new advertising efforts; to plan new projects or involvements; to launch new business plans; to make new acquaintances in business or academic circles, and to begin new business relationships. It is an excellent influence under which one can successfully initiate contracts, but short-term ones only. It is also an excellent time for reading or buying new books that can be of great help to the individual in an intellectual, life-sustaining, or life-enhancing way; also for dealing with business or academic journals, papers, or researching documents, such as land and property Title and Deed searches. This influence also favors educational matters of every type, as well as the buying and selling of printed material. It imparts a very benefic influence for taking any medicine or beginning any system of mental cure. It is an excellent influence for mystical, metaphysical, or magical study, under which profound insight into occult, esoteric, mystical, or magical concepts can be achieved, the essence of which can then be used for intellectual self-growth, the attainment of considerable material benefit, or both. It is also a positive influence for speculating and taking chances in a business or proposition that at other times may appear unsound or chancy. This is also an excellent influence under which important letters can be written. This Mercurial influence has some serious negative aspects as well, such as dealing with enemies in any legal manner; entering into marriage, or seeking favors from people in authority. It is equally adverse for either purchasing or selling real estate holdings, and is a period in which the individual can become the target of fraudulent or even illegal schemes. In general, it is an influence under which the truthfulness of all statements coming from anyone must be carefully evaluated, despite the overall positive aspects this influence exerts.

Example of Use 1: There's fire in your eyes, and a burning desire in your soul for that special knowledge you've been trying to get all of your life. Maybe it's the mastery of advanced mathematics, physics, or chemistry. Or maybe even getting serious about that amateur astronomy interest of yours that—as with that two thousand dollar telescope you just couldn't live without two years ago—has been relegated to the back of your mind and its counterpart, your closet. Or perhaps it's something as innocuous as getting that golf game of yours up to par where you want it. Or maybe it's pushing past an obstacle in attaining a certain psychic or spiritual state through a special meditation you've only been toying with thus far.

Whatever the specifics, the Mercurial forces are prompting you to do something serious about it on this Wednesday, and you notice that the Hour in which this burning ambition came to you is ruled by Mars, and hence the energy behind your determination. Flow is down the Tree, from the Mars Hour into the Mercurial Day. You can feel it surging within you. As you begin to set about getting into that course of study, to meditate, to grab that golf bag and head out to the course, or grab that telescope and start your trek to the darkest field you can find, you feel somber. Not sad, but realistic in a fresh and insightful way.

You know that all of those past harebrained attempts at mastering this passion of yours were just insignificant ego-

driven games, aimed at appeasing some impulse that arose
from who knows where. As the memory stream of broken
self-promises flows smoothly past your mind, you vow
that this time you are not going to let yourself down. And
under the aegis of this planetary/Path combination, you
won't! Because now, during this time, and under these
particular influences, you realize that mastery means just
that: the attainment of knowledge and skill that far outdis-
tances mere proficiency.

Perhaps the first serious glimmers of wisdom are making their way across the now receding ego-generated
darkness of your mind. You are slowly become aware that
this effort will take time. It won't be accomplished in a
day, a week, a month, or even a year. Rather, it will require
a constant, steady effort. You will have to give up other
desires for this time, but you wisely understand the necessity of this. The going will be rough, as it is in attaining to
all new knowledge or acquiring new abilities, but you are
intent on seeing it through this time. And as long as you
begin your plan actively under these influences, you will
attain that which you desire.

Along the way, you will gain deep insight into your
intellectual motives, thinking processes, and reasoning
abilities. Along with these benefits, don't be surprised to
find that you have also acquired an improved memory, a
heightened ability to visualize images, and a clearer mind.
Yes, you can put it all down to starting your activity under
this Mars–Mercury–23rd Path influence—and you will be
glad you did!

Example of Use 2: Your drive and determination to
attain mastery in your special interest is there just as in the
example above, but with one very important exception: it
has entered your mind and emotions during a Mars Day,
during a Mercury Hour. Flow is up the Tree, and the orientation of Tarot Trump XII The Hanged Man, is in the
reversed position. Will your praiseworthy desires and
newly initiated attempts utterly fail—this time? Not in the
way you might think.

Due to the reversed flow, you will find yourself gradually decreasing the demands you place on attaining mastery. Little by little, you will settle for less and less, so that the 'mastery' you eventually gain will more or less resemble some state of proficiency as opposed to the state of mastery you originally intended to reach. Settling for less is a reflection of the general attitude of the masses in all things—those masses you might sneer at, or even despise. Yet here you have adopted their justification in settling for scraps, and have rationalized away your 'need' for mastery.

In effect, you have turned that need into the convenience of proficiency. Neither will you gain any deep insight into your intellectual motives, thinking processes, and reasoning abilities under this influence. Nor will there be any evidence of an improved memory, a heightened ability to visualize images, or a clearer mind. No, there won't be any of these things. But then again, it may be all right after all. It simply depends on who you are, and what you want to do with your life. Here's where that oft-touted, never understood construct of Free Will, will come to the fore. It will reassure you that your justifiable rationalization for settling for less makes perfect sense. Or does it? But then after all, it really is up to *you*.

Example for Use 3: You've been doing well lately, in all areas of your life, and especially in the financial arena. Your job is secure despite the economic climate, you've made some investments that have paid off handsomely, and all in all, you're enjoying your prosperity and the new life it has given you. You feel really good about yourself. Well, almost. For some odd reason, you discover you have an altruistic component to your character, that out of necessity, you have been suppressing for years. But now, since you're in a stable position, you are beginning to listen to it and have decided to follow its promptings. You want to do something meaningful that stands out, even if only in some small way. But this must make a difference in an intellectually satisfying and emotionally gratifying way, as opposed to just keeping the new drug design department of Eli Lilly & Company burning their midnight oil in their 'noble' efforts to keep America healthy.

You initially tried to dismiss this desire as a purely ego-driven reaction to your financial success—a type of guilt reaction, if you will—but it just won't go away. This inner need refuses to dry up and let you enjoy your quarterly dividends from those needless, nonsensical investment norms of bigger, faster, more expensive, more of the same insanities that keep this great land of opportunity on the move.

You have been in love with books since you were a kid. But more than this. You are fascinated by the printing process and publishing business, having always considered them to be truly noble: one of the highest expressions of humankind's activities. A few months ago, you hear about an investment opportunity in a small publishing house. You investigated it thoroughly. It is old fashioned. Its small mechanical presses, skilled printing professionals, and hardheaded owner still sew the pages before they put a cover on them. Although they only publish one hundred different titles and add a mere ten more a year to their list, their reputation has grown over the past twenty-five years they have been in business, and their books sell as fast as they can print them.

The owner would like to move up to the ranks of a medium-sized press, publishing between two hundred to three hundred books a year, and adding as many as twenty new titles to his yearly credit. He realizes he will need new some computer aided equipment to do this, but only so much as is absolutely necessary to make this upward move. He refuses to give in to the computer teckie irrationally driven point-and-click mentality, and has drafted a business plan that not only keeps the press in the old fashioned mechanical type era, but maintains a medium-publisher profile permanently.

You like everything about the company but just haven't given it much thought. It's a Wednesday, ruled by Mercury, the planet that governs such matters so powerfully, and the hour is ruled by Mars. You're aware of this as the telephone rings. Guess who? It's the owner of that small publishing firm. He asks you if you're interested, because he too wants to move on, with or without you. But you and he hit it off very well, and knowing the hour and the Path influence, you agree, and write him your check for one-fifth ownership.

The result? You will not only be intellectually and emotionally gratified in the extreme by this decision and action, but will make a handsome profit as well, over time. There won't be any quarterly dividends for awhile, and there will probably be an additional minor sum you will have to contribute due to a sudden or surprise equipment cost increase. But besides the profit, you'll end up learning something about the publishing game, because the owner and you will hit it off so well, he'll start to educate you about all ends of the business. You will also acquire a deep appreciation for craftsmanship, and for the type of people who care about what they do for a living.

The interiorization of this experience will rub off on you, adding to further success in your own work. Your love for the printed word and its manifestation in book form will skyrocket, bestowing an intellectual and emotional satisfaction that is so deep, it may very well change the way you view yourself and the world around you. All of these things are not simply possible, but well nigh inevitable, when the influence of the 23rd Path is applied to matters ruled by the joined Mars-Mercury planetary pair.

Example of Use 4: All original conditions remain the same, except that telephone call arrives during a Mars Day, Mercury Hour, and flow is up the Tree. Hence the 23rd Tarot Trump is in the reversed position. Under this influence, the best you can expect is a shell of the result achieved in **Example of Use 3,** above. Things will begin to go wrong immediately after you cut the check.

It could be that some other investors pull out at the last minute, requiring more investment from you than you feel comfortable with, and you will have to back out. Or the scanty computer equipment needed to achieve the next level in growth is no longer available, and requires newer teckie nonsense with all of its bells and whistles, along with high priced teckies to run it, who turn out to be modern day 'craftsmen' who can't even spell the word quality, let alone produce it. Or you could become greedy at the eleventh hour, and insist on this or that which strains the relationship between the owner and you, or makes demands that in some way eventually causes a decrease in the quality of the final product.

In the end, as an example, the publishing house decides to stop stitching the pages, and simply glues them to the cover like other trade paperback houses do. Or they are forced to use cheaper ink, smaller type, or some variation that turns out a product that only the masses will understand and appreciate. In the end, old customers will fade away, and orders will drop. But never fear! Those masses with their teckie mentalities will replace them. Oh, you'll make some profit, but the intellectual and emotional gratification will be worth about as much as a two-dollar bill. Heed this example well. This is a very empty Path when flow is up the Tree, and I strongly advise you not to do anything important when its influence is in effect.

Path 24—Tarot Card: XIII Death (Positive) **Downward Flow** = Sun (Tiphareth) Hour into Venus (Netzach) Day. (Negative) **Upward Flow** = Venus (Netzach) Hour into Sun (Tiphareth) Day. *Tarot Attributions:* In the **upright** position, the card can refer to physical death. Also, to some kind of end (as in an important matter, issue, or relationship), or to a massive, nebulous change or transformation in the individual, comparable to the end of a part of the self as occurs, for example, in the Attainment of the K&C of the HGA. In the **reversed** position: corruption; disintegration; decomposition through putrefaction; stasis.

Influences of the Planets Connected by the Paths: **The Sun**—As before, this planet provides power and success in life; Life itself; illumination; mental power and ability; as with Jupiter under Chesed, also money; robust physical, emotional, and mental health; growth at the personality, character, and psychic levels; dealing with superiors of all kinds, and in any situation; asking for favors from people in authority; seeking the approval, recommendation, or help from others in any proposal whatsoever, be it of a business or personal nature; composing important letters that produce in the mind of the intended recipient a picture of the writer as a confident, balanced, individual whose request for aid, introductions, or favors, should be immediately granted. This is also an excellent influence under which one can act in noble and high-minded ways that will build up his or her public esteem and prestige. This influence however is adverse for involving oneself in illegal plans, actions, or activities of any kind whatsoever. Curiously, it also provides a negative influence for beginning or launching a new business, a new plan, or a new idea, owing to its underlying Elemental Attribution which is always shifting, changing in force and form, as the Sun itself, the most Sensible of this Sephiroth's influence that has further descended into the realm of matter. By the same rationale, it is likewise adverse for signing contracts of any kind, and for entering into any partnerships, mutually beneficial arrangements or agreements—whether of a social, business, professional, or personal nature—or for entering into any kind of relationship in which there is a political element of any kind. Additionally, this planetary influence is also quite adverse for marriage, for making any new investments of any kind, for purchasing or liquidating real estate holdings, and for all forms of surgery.

Influences of the Planets Connected by the Paths: **Venus—** Unselfishness; Love, but of a sexual nature; beauty of form, and the appreciation of that beauty; the emotions of the conscious level of our being; women; music; self-indulgence; extravagance. Also on the mundane level, this influence governs all material and sensual affairs; music; art; the theater; any form of behavior or expression that supports sensuality. It is also a very fortuitous influence under which to begin any new enterprise or project, whether sensual or business in nature. It is also an excellent influence in which to make new acquaintances, but only those that are met through spontaneous social contact. It is also a very favorable influence for entering into marriage, to borrow or loan money, and to host social gatherings and parties, but only those affairs that are meant for pure enjoyment. It is very positive for speculating in stocks, bonds, or in any new business proposition. It is important to note here that due to the Venusian planetary influence of this Sephirah, almost any activity or action that is begun or ended while this influence is in operation, will bear very significant, desirable, or fortunate results. It is an influence that, in effect, blesses and magnifies activities of almost any kind, but especially those of a sensual and material nature. There are a few very adverse aspects of this influence, such as dealing with social underlings or subordinates; beginning long trips to remote locations; using social means to harm enemies or competitors, or to attempt using social functions as a means of gaining a business or personal advantage at the expense of a collaborator or fellow worker. *Please Note: As mentioned in the previous Commentary for this card, this Path is not as difficult as it sounds. In reality, its meanings usually refer to the evolution and development of the Self through the process of self-growth, the means used to achieve this state notwithstanding. It is a hard path in terms of process, but its end results are stunning and utterly glorious.*

Example of Use 1: It's a Friday, and the Sun is ruling the hour when you arrive home. Flow is down the Tree and positive. Likewise, Tarot Trump XIII is in the upright position. As you approach the front door, you wish that when you walk inside, your wife, husband, or significant other would be happy to see you, throw his or her arms around you, tell you how excited they are to have you all to themselves during the upcoming weekend, and then lay out a set of plans for the two of you that would have you jumping up in the air and clicking your heels. But you know better. The life you have been sharing for these past few years has been anything but happy. Where is the Sun's influence of Life, Light, and growth together, as a couple? Where is that Venus influence of unselfishness, physical lovemaking, and luxury, the two of you shared throughout the first several years of your marriage or relationship? What has happened to all of those good times?

As you walk through the door, you see the answer to all of these questions in the form of packed luggage piled neatly in the center of the living room. Before you can take stock of the situation, your partner emerges from the adjoining room, and says, "It's best this way for both of us. I've had enough, and I think you have too! I'm leaving. My attorney will contact you on Monday, and we can start divorce proceedings," or similar words depending upon the exact type of relationship the two of you had.

Yes, the Sun's influence—so life-giving—and the force of Venus—so nurturing and pleasure seeking—have been scattered by the harsh realities of the 24th Path. You make a fainthearted attempt to stop him or her from leaving, but your former partner just throws a sideways glance at you as if to say, "Please don't keep this charade up. It's over, and we both know it!" And so you step aside as the taxi pulls up to the front door, the driver puts the luggage into the cab, and you watch the most important part of your life disappear down the driveway, and out of sight.

Between the tears, there is a deep, inner sense of relief, but something you just can't handle at the moment. So your let the immediacy of the situation's impact overtake you, and spend the weekend in your own type of hell. You are alone, unable or unwilling to speak to anyone about the shattered thing you now call your life. The months drag on, and your lawyers have been lining their pockets with you and your former partner's hard earned money, and you are still numb inside.

A few more months pass, and something has happened. You've accepted the situation, and as your former partner's glance had conveyed to you, you now realize ending the relationship was the best thing for both of you. You start to live again, although the idea of dating just doesn't quite appeal to you yet. That is, not until that fateful Friday, during a Jupiter Hour with its downward flow, when the 21st Path's influence has you sitting in that restaurant with that self-help book, and that beautiful woman or handsome man approaches you with a few questions about that same book she or he is reading!

See how it works? The Path of Death is indeed a hard one, and I am not trying to lighten it by creating some cheap, ego-bolstering rosy picture, painted with the soothing colors of lies. No, believe it or not, this is how the initial and final effects of this Path work out in the end. Something very good happens as a consequence of the 'death' of some situation or condition. And that something is always a new, life-enhancing experience that brings about magnificent personal growth.

From your own hell to your own purgatory, and finally into your own heaven on earth, is the experience and reward of this Path. Don't fear it. Struggle with it, try to avoid it if you can and if you so choose. But equally, accept it when it strikes unexpectedly, and seems to kill your soul. Accept it because a new day will dawn, and it will once again be filled with the glories of the Sun and the joys of Venus, issuing forth in some unseen, hidden way.

Example of Use 2: The conditions of the above example are in effect once again, except in this case, you returned home from some activity or other on a Sunday, during a Venus Hour. Flow is up the Tree, from the hour into the day, and hence the 13th Tarot card is in the reversed position: the forces of corruption, disintegration, decomposition through putrefaction, and stasis are in full effect. You walk in, find your partner watching television or otherwise occupying themselves, and begin the same meaningless diatribe that helped extinguish the fire your relationship once knew.

Sooner than later, each of you is off on your own in the same house, doing what pleases you, and avoiding each other at all costs. This evening—like all other evenings— passes uneventfully, and neither of you care. Sex is a thing of the past. Both of you receive more mental stimulation from watching the Weather Channel than from each other, and life drags on, and on, and on, and on. Stagnation and the putrefaction it produces leads to the complete decay of human feelings and joy, and has destroyed both of you.

But it has progressed so far that neither of you care about ending it. Both of you have been engulfed by the miasma of complacency. There is nothing for either of you to look forward to except an old age that will finally—and mercifully—put both of you out of your joint misery.

Notice how your fear of this card in its upright position—when flow is down the Tree from the Sun Hour into the Day of Friday—might have dwindled considerably within you as you read the above. Ask yourself this. Of the two examples given here for this card, which one would *you* rather experience? I bet I know, even if you are not yet ready to admit it to yourself.

Example of Use 3: It's a Friday, and knowing the planetary influence is favorable for succeeding in almost any activity, you decide to open the doors of your new business. After all, it's the start of a busy, buying weekend, and you have your new store located in the very heart of the busiest section of the mall! What better time to start such an enterprise! Sure, you decided you're going to open during a Sun Hour. Flow will be down the Tree, the Tarot card will be in the upright position, and the 24th Path of Death will be invoked. Who cares? You have Free Will, remember?

All that nonsense of Kabbalistic Cycles you unfortunately read and became so angry over, doesn't mean a damn thing, and you know it! Just some jerk's stupid idea. "Hell, I don't need any idiot telling me my marketing research and plans are dependent upon some ridiculous planet or Path scheme or whatever it was about anyway! *I* decide what *I* do, and take full responsibility for it!" Well, bully for you! because that's just what you must do when the business axe falls, and your new store—right in the center of the busiest section of the mall—fails big time!

Oh, you'll scramble, change stock, sales people, give away door prizes and cut your prices to the bone—right before you close the doors and worry about facing the bank loan officer next week to tell him you can't make that business loan payment. Time will pass, and after much agony and soul searching, you'll eventually see something you completely missed before, or be offered to get in on a new venture, and—maybe even using this stupid Kabbalistic Cycles System—will go in for it during a fortunate time. Surprisingly, the money for it will come out of nowhere, the new business will flourish, and after licking your wounds, you'll start making that profit you always dreamed of. Count on the essence of this experience happening, because it will.

Example of Use 4: You're opening your new store in the last example on—of all days—a Sunday, during a Venus Hour. Of course, all that business consultation you paid for through the nose tells you that despite appearances, people's last minute weekend buying habits are what you are going after to get your business off with a bang. As the months pass, you did everything that you did in the above example, but business has been slow. (static) No matter what you try, your sales limp along, allowing you to barely make your monthly business loan payments, your payroll, add some new merchandise here and there, and ever so slightly eke out the most marginal living for yourself. Eventually, the shifting scales will go completely against you, and your business will fail. There will be harsh consequences as a result that will spread into your personal life as well, from which it will take you in all probability, years to recover. Such are the implications and effects arising from this card in the reversed position.

Path 25—Tarot Card: XIV Temperance (Positive) **Downward Flow** = Sun (Tiphareth) Hour into Moon (Yesod) Day. (Negative) **Upward Flow** = Moon (Yesod) Hour into Sun (Tiphareth) Day. *Tarot Attributions:* In the **upright** position: the impulse to unite or wed seemingly disparate concepts, ideas, or actions in a positive and beneficial way; the use of temperate or measurable means and ways in thoughts and actions; a balanced approach to a problem, and the judicious implementation of its solution. In the **reversed** position: disparate concepts, ideas, or actions that cannot be conjoined or united; disagreement; loggerheads; an extreme approach to a problem and its unbalanced implementation, which not only does not resolve the original problem, but which creates additional problems as a result of the extremist measures employed.

Influences of the Planets Connected by the Paths: **The Sun**—power and success in life; Life itself; illumination; mental power and ability; as with Jupiter under Chesed, also money; robust physical, emotional, and mental health; growth at the personality, character, and psychic levels; dealing with superiors of all kinds, and in any situation; asking for favors from people in authority; seeking the approval, recommendation, or help from others in any proposal whatsoever, be it of a business or personal nature; composing important letters that produce in the mind of the intended recipient a picture of the writer as a confident, balanced, individual whose request for aid, introductions, or favors, should be immediately granted. This is also an excellent influence under which one can act in noble and high-minded ways that will build up his or her public esteem and prestige. This influence however is adverse for involving oneself in illegal plans, actions, or activities of any kind whatsoever. Curiously, it also provides a negative influence for beginning or launching a new business, a new plan, or a new idea, owing to its underlying Elemental Attribution which is always shifting, changing in force and form, as the Sun itself, the most Sensible of this Sephirothal influence that has further descended into the realm of matter. By the same rationale, it is likewise adverse for signing contracts of any kind, and for entering into any partnerships, mutually beneficial arrangements or agreements—whether of a social, business, professional, or personal nature—or for entering into any kind of relationship in which there is a political element of any kind. Additionally, this planetary influence is also quite adverse for marriage, for making any new investments of any kind, for purchasing or liquidating real estate holdings, and for all forms of surgery.

Influences of the Planets Connected by the Paths: **The Moon**—Women; the personality; modifications; rapid changes; fluid conditions, ever cycling between extremes. As with Hod's projection, Mercury, educational efforts of all kinds are also ruled by this planet, it being the projection of Yesod into our universe. Additionally, this lunar influence provides a positive impulse for the planting of seeds, beginning journeys by water, or making new acquaintances in a social, business, or academic setting. It is also an excellent influence for all literary work, for entering into the sacrament of marriage, for taking any medicine, or to begin any mystical or metaphysical system of body or mind treatment in which a direct, complete cure is sought. This Lunar influence of Yesod is also very positive for surgery of all types, and for dealing with metaphysical, mystical, and magical studies. This fluid, creative, Lunar influence provides an energy dynamic backdrop against which most activities and aspirations indulged in during the time of its reign will prove both prolific and productive.

Example of Use 1: You've been laid off permanently, and have been searching for work without success, that is, until last Friday. You finally have a real chance to land a new job, but it's in a totally different field. The ten years you spent as a machinist are now past, and you're facing a new position as a satellite dish installer. This new company is desperate for people, and so they entertain your application. But desperate or not, they are reluctant to hire you outright, owing to the investment they must make by putting you though a six-month training program, and are somewhat worried that your past skills just won't cross over to their type of work. They want a letter of recommendation from your former employer.

It's now Monday, Sun Hour. Knowing the Path influence of this hour/Path combination, you approach your former employer for that letter during this Sun Hour and Moon Day. Flow is downward, from the hour into the day, and he agrees. You take your letter to your prospective employer, give it to him, and are asked to wait outside while he reviews it and discusses it with his plant superintendent and his own boss. An hour or so later he emerges from his office, smiles broadly, extends his hand to you and says, "Congratulations, Mike! You're just the kind of guy we've been looking for! We had no idea that a machinist had such skills! Welcome aboard! Can you start tomorrow?"

What happened? This particular influence unites or weds seemingly disparate ideas, actions, or situations in a balanced, complimentary way. Your former employer wrote that letter stressing your mechanical skills, reasoning abilities, mental clarity and gift of logic, loyalty, determination, and agreeable nature in such a way, that this new company could not help but hire you. Impossible, you say? I have seen similar situations arise a thousand times under these influences. Such are the forces that emanate from the downward flow of this Path.

Example of Use 2: It's Sunday. That job interview you had last Friday has you nervous. This is your last chance to get a job in your area, and you've got to land it! You can't wait until tomorrow to ask your former employer for that letter of recommendation. So out of sheer anxiety, you give him a call during a Moon Hour, flow upward, from the hour into the Sun Day, and timidly ask if he will do you this favor, and that you need the letter for tomorrow. He feels guilty for having had to let you go, and so eagerly agrees to write the letter and has it ready for you by noon tomorrow.

You pick up the sealed letter, take it to your prospective employer, and are asked to wait outside as before. Two hours later your soon to be new boss (you hope) comes out of his office and states, "I'm sorry, Mike. While your letter of recommendation was good, it really only accents your machinist abilities and the talents that go with it. We just can't take a chance. Sorry. Good luck to you on your job hunt!" The effects of this Path in its upward flow have done it again: failed to unite conflicting opposites. And now you are stuck with the results.

Example of Use 3: You need a raise. The cost of living has gotten to you at last. You can barely meet your bills now, and are at your wit's end. But there is a wage freeze at your place of employment. Indeed, they have downsized, and those left feel fortunate they still have jobs. In short, your interests and those of your company's could not be more different. But you are forced to take a chance, and so during a Sun Hour on a Monday, with its downward flow and upright 14th Tarot Card of Temperance, you approach your boss, plead your case, and remind him—nicely, of course—of all the overtime you gave, gratis, and the volume of work you have been putting out these past three months. He listens, says he will take it up with higher management, and summarily dismisses you.

Two days later he calls you into his office, asks you to sit down, smiles, and delivers the verdict. "Joe, I can't believe it myself, but you got that raise you need! I explained how well you've been doing, and what an asset you are to the company, and asked them to do their best to show their gratitude, even during these rough times. And they went for it! Your raise begins immediately, and will show up in your next paycheck! Congratulations!" As you can see, even extreme cases of disparate interests and conflicting desires can be reconciled through this 25th Path, if you know how to use it properly. And now you do!

Example of Use 4: During a chance meeting with your boss at the local sports grill, while he was feeling no pain and was lucid enough to remember, you asked him for that raise as you did in the example above. But this time it was on a Sunday, during a Moon Hour, flow upward, the card Temperance reversed. Oh, he took your case to the higher-ups as he said he would, and after due consideration they refuse your request. "We have to look out for all of our employees' interests these days, not just Joe's alone," your boss tells you when he delivers the bad news. "Joe's interests are at odds with the company's right now. Maybe when things get better we'll consider it." That was their final words. As usual, this Path's upward flow damned the reconciliation of opposing interests. It happens every time.

Path 26—Tarot Card: XV The Devil (Positive) **Downward Flow** = Sun (Tiphareth) Hour into Mercury (Hod) Day. (Negative) **Upward Flow** = Mercury (Hod) Hour into Sun (Tiphareth) Day. *Tarot Attributions:* In the **upright**

position: an eventual beneficial or favorable result arises from a seemingly deleterious event or situation. In the **reversed** position: that same situation produces a unfavorable or very unsatisfactory result, or is concluded in some negative and possibly harmful manner.

Influences of the Planets Connected by the Paths: **The Sun**—power and success in life; Life itself; illumination; mental power and ability; as with Jupiter under Chesed, also money; robust physical, emotional, and mental health; growth at the personality, character, and psychic levels; dealing with superiors of all kinds, and in any situation; asking for favors from people in authority; seeking the approval, recommendation, or help from others in any proposal whatsoever, be it of a business or personal nature; composing important letters that produce in the mind of the intended recipient a picture of the writer as a confident, balanced, individual whose request for aid, introductions, or favors, should be immediately granted. This is also an excellent influence under which one can act in noble and high-minded ways that will build up his or her public esteem and prestige. This influence however is adverse for involving oneself in illegal plans, actions, or activities of any kind whatsoever. Curiously, it also provides a negative influence for beginning or launching a new business, a new plan, or a new idea, owing to its underlying Elemental Attribution which is always shifting, changing in force and form, as the Sun itself, the most Sensible of this Sephirothal influence that has further descended into the realm of matter. By the same rationale, it is likewise adverse for signing contracts of any kind, and for entering into any partnerships, mutually beneficial arrangements or agreements—whether of a social, business, professional, or personal nature—or for entering into any kind of relationship in which there is a political element of any kind. Additionally, this planetary influence is also quite adverse for marriage, for making any new investments of any kind, for purchasing or liquidating real estate holdings, and for all forms of surgery.

Influences of the Planets Connected by the Paths: **Mercury** —this Mercurial influence is very positive for dealing with intellectual discernments; scientific thought; mathematics; writing of all kinds; logic; reason; using and accelerating the analytical faculty of the conscious self; thinking; speaking, whether in public or private. Additionally, as with Netzach and Venus, the Mercurial influence of Hod is very beneficial for art, music, and the theater; for literary work of any kind; to design or begin new advertising efforts; to plan new projects or involvements; to launch new business plans; to make new acquaintances in business or academic circles, and to begin new business relationships. It is an excellent influence under which one can successfully initiate contracts, but short-term ones only. It is also an excellent time for reading or buying new books that can be of great help to the individual in an intellectual, life-sustaining, or life-enhancing way; also for dealing with business or academic journals, papers, or researching documents, such as land and property Title and Deed searches. This influence also favors educational matters of every type, as well as the buying and selling of printed material. It imparts a very benefic influence for taking any medicine or beginning any system of mental cure. It is an excellent influence for mystical, metaphysical, or magical study, under which profound insight into occult, esoteric, mystical, or magical concepts can be achieved, the essence of which can then be used for intellectual growth, the attainment of considerable material benefit, or both. It is also a positive influence for speculating and taking chances in a business or proposition that at other times may appear unsound or chancy. This is also an excellent influence under which important letters can be written. This Mercurial influence has some serious negative aspects as well, such as dealing with enemies in any legal manner; entering into marriage, or seeking favors from people in authority. It is equally adverse for either purchasing or selling real estate holdings, and is a period in which the individual can become the target of fraudulent or even illegal schemes. In general, it is an influence under which the truthfulness of all statements coming from anyone must be carefully evaluated, despite the overall positive aspects this influence exerts.

Example of Use 1: Remember that example in the earlier part of this chapter where the planetary force of Sunday put you in a growth mode? You took to working out the details during a Mercury Hour in that example, but accomplished very little on your goal during the ensuing week: each day had its particular limiting condition, as you'll recall. The following Sunday rolled around, you were painfully reminded of your failure to do something significant toward your goal during the past week, and started again in a new, bright-spirited way. No matter. Unless you apply your knowledge of the Kabbalistic Cycles on this next Sunday, you'll fail again because as you know by now, the problem was the flow on the Tree. During a Mercury Hour on Sunday in that example, flow was up the Tree, the card is reversed, and the negative influences of the Tarot in question manifest. In this case, card XV Devil, meaning essentially, failure.

Example of Use 2: This time, it's a Wednesday. You look at the your Kabbalistic Cycles chart, and see that the hour you wish to get that Sunday-designed plan of yours off the ground is a Sun Hour. That means flow is down the Tree, the Tarot card is upright, and all is well, but is it really? Consider the card's influences again, in *both* the upright and reversed positions. Unless you want to struggle for a considerable length of time and have a real fight on your hands, and this, after getting more kicks in the teeth than you can count, don't use this Path of the Devil at all. It has its purpose in magical work, but for daily mundane use, I strongly recommend you stay away from it regardless of its flow. It's just too difficult a Path to work with when it comes to normal, daily matters.

Examples of Use 3 & 4: Quite simply, there aren't any for the reasons given above. Avoid this Path influence and of course, the planetary influences connected by it in this instance. It will bring you nothing but trouble.

Path 27—Tarot Card: XVI The Tower (Positive) **Downward Flow** = Venus (Netzach) Hour into Mercury (Hod) Day. (Negative) **Upward Flow** = Mercury (Hod) Hour into Venus (Netzach) Day. *Tarot Attributions:* In the **upright** position: devolution; downfall; degeneration; decadence; disaster; calamity; tragedy; woes; catastrophe, disruption. In the **reversed** position: the same, but to a lesser degree. *Please Note*: There are no examples listed for this Path. I will simply repeat the admonition below, given for this card in the chapter of the Tarot. As with card XV The Devil and its 26th Path, this 27th Path—and the planetary influences it connects during its rule—are to be strictly avoided. But unlike the 26th Path, the admonition given here is done so in the *strongest* possible sense. *Anything done during either the upward or even downward flow of the Path governed by The Tower, will bring ruin to you, your work, and your plans.* Simply reread the Commentary below, and learn from it. I cannot stress this enough! (Although for myself, I do not consider the Path of the Devil to be as severe in daily matters as those of the Tower and the Chariot, I yet place it here for other occult reasons that cannot be addressed in this book. For the reader's safety and peace of mind, then, I have listed the Tarot card of the Devil along with the Chariot and the Tower, for the reasons just given.) *Commentary: Card XVI—along with card VII The Chariot and card XV The Devil—and their Paths, are by far the most difficult and dangerous Paths on the Tree. As you will see when working the Cycles System, their influence is to be watched for carefully at all times, and absolutely avoided if at all possible!*

Path 28—Tarot Card: XVII The Star (Positive) **Downward Flow** = Venus (Netzach) Hour into Moon (Yesod) Day. (Negative) **Upward Flow** = Moon (Yesod) Hour into Venus (Netzach) Day. *Tarot Attributions:* In the **upright** position: happy expectation; joyful expectancy; happy prospects; an exciting future filled with many possibilities. In the **reversed** position: happy expectations and joyful expectancies are disappointed or thwarted; emptiness; effeteness.

Influences of the Planets Connected by the Paths: **Venus—** Unselfishness; Love, but of a sexual nature; beauty of form, and the appreciation of that beauty; the emotions of the conscious level of our being; women; music; self-indulgence; extravagance. Also on the mundane level, this influence governs all material and sensual affairs; music; art; the theater; any form of behavior or expression that supports sensuality. It is also a very fortuitous influence under which to begin any new enterprise or project, whether sensual or business in nature. It is also an excellent influence in which to make new acquaintances, but only those that are met through spontaneous social contact. It is also a very favorable influence for entering into marriage, to borrow or loan money, and to host social gatherings and parties, but only those affairs that are meant for pure enjoyment. It is very positive for speculating in stocks, bonds, or in any new business proposition. It is important to note here that due to the Venusian planetary influence of this Sephirah, almost any activity or action that is begun or ended while this influence is in operation, will bear very significant, desirable, or fortunate results. It is an influence that, in effect, blesses and magnifies activities of almost any kind, but especially those of a sensual and material nature. There are a few very adverse aspects of this influence, such as dealing with social underlings or subordinates; beginning long trips to remote locations; using social means to harm enemies or competitors, or to attempt using social functions as a means of gaining a business or personal advantage at the expense of a collaborator or fellow worker.

Influences of the Planets Connected by the Paths: **The Moon**—Rules women; the personality; modifications; rapid changes; fluid conditions, ever cycling between extremes. As with Hod's projection, Mercury, educational efforts of all kinds are also ruled by the Moon, it being the projection of Yesod into our universe. Additionally, this lunar influence provides a positive impulse for the planting of seeds, beginning journeys by water, or making new acquaintances in a social, business or academic setting. It is also an excellent influence for all literary work, for entering into the sacrament of marriage, for taking any medicine, or to begin any mystical or metaphysical system of body or mind treatment in which a direct, complete cure is sought. This Lunar influence of Yesod is also very positive for surgery of all types, and for dealing with metaphysical, mystical, and magical studies. This fluid, creative, Lunar influence provides an energy dynamic backdrop against which most activities and aspirations indulged in during the time of its reign will prove both prolific and productive.

Example of Use 1: I'll bet the business that poor guy opened under the Death card's influence in **Example 3** of Path 24 is still fresh in your mind. Good! Because if he would have opened that same business on a Monday during a Venus Hour so flow was down the Tree from the Hour into the Day, I could have guaranteed that poor guy his enterprise would have taken off like a rocket. And if his product line in any way appealed to women, was in education—as in books—or was in art supplies, paintings, or even a bookstore that carried a line of art and the more literary type of publications, or items that strictly appeal to one's sense of luxury and extravagance and not necessity—that same individual would be a most happy business man (or woman) indeed!

Example of Use 2: Now, if that same aspiring businessman would have opened that business of his on a Friday during a Moon Hour, in which flow is upward on the Tree, to say that his happy expectations and joyful expectancies will soon be disappointed, would be to make an understatement. No matter how hard he tries, regardless of stocking his new store with the exact same merchandise as he did above, and which appeals to women, or contains a line of art and literary books, or items of pure luxury and extravagance, his venture will fail abysmally. The upward flow of this Path is very severe in its pronouncements. Additionally, one should use extreme care when deciding to simply be out and about for social reasons during this influence. It is extremely negative for indulging in any social matters whatsoever.

Example of Use 3: You've decided to pop the question. After years of the dating scene, you've had about all you care for of the empty-headed, gold-digging, utterly vain and absolutely egotistical, available women out there. Oh, they're available, as you come to realize in your thirtieth year of life. Available for a quick trip to the altar, a quicker trip to the divorce court, alimony, child support, and all of the other wage attachments that will have you living in a one-room efficiency apartment for the next twenty-odd years. But this last lady you've been seeing for the past year and a half is different. Very different.

You both hit it off, and in every conceivable way are the compliment of each other. It couldn't be better if you designed it yourself. And you've been wondering about her little signals. Is she trying to tell you to either put up or shut up? (Ask me, you dummy, or just go away and let me move on!) Are these the meanings behind that coyness and those few slight remarks favoring marriage she has been making lately? Enough is enough, you make your decision, and on this Monday evening during a surprise dinner you take her to, you pop the question. Of course, it's a Venus Hour, and the flow is down the Tree. The result? Remember the endings to those delightful fairy tales you enjoyed so much as a kid? "And they lived happily ever after." Because if you propose during this influence, both of your lives will be long, fruitful, and very happy together. And I wouldn't make such a sweeping statement if I wasn't absolutely certain of it.

Example of Use 4: It's a Friday, the hour of which is ruled by the Moon. Nevertheless, you can't really believe all the cycles stuff, and you ask her the big question. Surprise! She accepts! See? All of that running the important affairs of your life by some insane idea some author cooked up to rationalize away his own life is just that: a bunch of nonsense, and you just proved it.

The scene fades, and somewhere between the end of your first year to the middle of your third year of marriage, you're looking for a good divorce lawyer to protect you as much as possible, while trying to figure out how you will pay the child support and 'temporary' alimony, and keep body and soul together. Is this *really* possible? Are there such forces out there that can—that did!—affect your life so drastically simply because you ignored the times of their influence? Guess it's time to fall back on your Free Will rationalization, and think it through for yourself. After all, you'll have plenty of time, sitting alone in that one-room efficiency apartment. You certainly won't have any money to be out and about now, not with all that child support and 'temporary' alimony to pay.

Path 30—Tarot Card: XIX The Sun (Positive) **Downward Flow** = Mercury (Hod) Hour into Moon (Yesod) Day. (Negative) **Upward Flow** = Moon (Yesod) Hour into Mercury (Hod) Day. *Tarot Attributions:* In the **upright** position: bliss; happiness; contentment; joy; desires and goals achieved; wants satisfied; appeasement in general. In the **reversed** position: the same, but to a lesser extent.

Influences of the Planets Connected by the Paths: **Mercury** —this Mercurial influence is very positive for dealing with intellectual discernments; scientific thought; mathematics; writing of all kinds; logic; reason; using and accelerating the analytical faculty of the conscious self; thinking; speaking, whether in public or private. Additionally, as with Netzach and Venus, the Mercurial influence of Hod is very beneficial for art, music, and the theater; for literary work of any kind; to design or begin new advertising efforts; to plan new projects or involvements; to launch new business plans; to make new acquaintances in business or academic circles, and to begin new business relationships. It is an excellent influence under which one can successfully initiate contracts, but short-term ones only. It is also an excellent time for reading or buying new books that can be of great help to the individual in an intellectual, life-sustaining, or life-enhancing way; also for dealing with business or academic journals, papers, or researching documents, such as land and property Title and Deed searches. This influence also favors educational matters of every type, as well as the buying and selling of printed material. It imparts a very benefic influence for taking any medicine or beginning any system of mental cure. It is an excellent influence for mystical, metaphysical, or magical study, under which profound insight into occult, esoteric, mystical, or magical concepts can be achieved, the essence of which can be then used for intellectual growth, the attainment of considerable material benefit, or both. It is also a positive influence for speculating and taking chances in a business or proposition that at other times may appear unsound or chancy. This is also an excellent influence under which important letters can be written. This Mercurial influence has some serious negative aspects as well, such as dealing with enemies in any legal manner; entering into marriage, or seeking favors from people in authority. It is equally adverse for either purchasing or selling real estate, and is a period in which the individual can become the target of fraudulent or even illegal schemes. In general, it is an influence under which the truthfulness of all statements coming from anyone must be carefully evaluated, despite the overall positive aspects this influence exerts.

Influences of the Planets Connected by the Paths: **The Moon**—exerts its influence upon: women; the personality; modifications; rapid changes; fluid conditions, ever cycling between extremes. As with Hod's projection, Mercury, educational efforts of all kinds are also ruled by the Moon, it being the projection of Yesod into our universe. Additionally, this lunar influence provides a positive impulse for the planting of seeds, beginning journeys by water, or making new acquaintances in a social, business, or academic setting. It is also an excellent influence for all literary work, for entering into the sacrament of marriage, for taking any medicine, or to begin any mystical or metaphysical system of body or mind treatment in which a direct, complete cure is sought. This Lunar influence of Yesod is also very positive for surgery of all types, and for dealing with metaphysical, mystical, and magical studies. This fluid, creative, Lunar influence provides an energy dynamic backdrop against which most activities and aspirations indulged in during the time of its reign will prove both prolific and productive.

Example of Use 1: For four long years—maybe longer depending upon your major and financial situation—you've struggled to get through college, produced the GPA you needed to get into a good graduate school program, and have all of those applications to grad school sitting on your desk, ready to be filled out. Of course, this means you'll no longer starve either, because a reasonable stipend goes along with your fully paid graduate education—right up to that Doctorate degree. I'll bet you know what is coming next. Yes, you guessed it. Be sure to fill out all of those applications during a Mercury Hour, on the day ruled by the Moon, when the flow is down the Tree.

The influence of this 19th card that symbolizes the forces of this 30th Path, will truly produce happiness, contentment and joy, and all of your desires and goals achieved. Don't be one bit surprised if all of the schools you apply to accept you, and even go out of their way to recruit you. They could even reach the point of fighting each other, offering you competitive package after package, just to make sure you come to their school. And why not? You deserve it. Just use this so very fortunate Path correctly, and you will be ever so very, very glad you did!

Example of Use 2: The same as above, but due to one thing or another, you are forced to fill those applications out on a Wednesday, during a Moon Hour. However, flow will be up the Tree, and the 19th Tarot Trump, the Sun, will be in the reversed position, indicating happiness, joy and contentment to a lesser degree, but still, the receipt of your heart's desires. Will you have the same positive experiences as when the flow is down the Tree through this Path during a Mercury Hour and Moon Day? For all intents and purposes—yes! The schools may not fight over recruiting you, but their offers for funding your education and giving you a good stipend will be almost as good as in the previous example. In short, you'll be happy and content but to a lesser degree. Why is this? Because this 30th Path is the mirror image of the Path of the Tower. That 27th Path which is so hard regardless of the direction of flow, is offset completely by this wondrous, exciting, life-sustaining and fulfilling connection between Mercury and the Moon. Don't miss out on using it, until your heart's content.

Example of Use 3: Your company has called a very important business meeting, and you've been asked to work out a new plan for increasing your department's efficiency. But more than that, the Vice President of Operations told you that it has to be extremely good. Why? Because they want to adapt it to the other departments as well. Since your department is leading the entire company in productivity right now, they figure you know something they don't, and want you to share it with the other department heads so the entire company will benefit.

Work out your plan diligently, by all means. But if you have anything to say about it, schedule the meeting for a Monday, during a Mercury Hour, when you have the downward flow of the Tree with you. You'll be absolutely amazed how well your ideas will be received and implemented. And, of course, you will receive some type of reward for it: whether a raise, a promotion, or a bigger expense account. You will benefit from this Path and its downward flow, and in a big way. So use it well.

Example of Use 4: The same demands are made upon you as above, but this time, whether due to others' scheduling or you being pushed, you have to schedule the meeting on a Wednesday during a Moon Hour and of course, flow is upward on the Tree, from the Hour into the Day. As in the above example, your results will be almost as good. There might be a little reserve at first in implementing your ideas, a snag here, a catch there, but implemented they will be, and some 'lesser' reward will be given you as a result. Again, you simply cannot go astray when using the influences of this 30th Path.

SUPPLEMENTARY GUIDELINES FOR EFFECTIVELY USING THE KABBALISTIC CYCLES SYSTEM

In closing this chapter, I thought it best to provide the diligent reader with some added guidelines that may clear up any unanswered questions he or she may have. They are simple and short, and are the inevitable conclusions of all that has been given throughout this book. Nevertheless, in learning any new subject, questions and uncertainties abound—as well they should in the mind of a conscientious student. I trust the following will be of help to you:

• Earlier I said that in those numerous cases where there are no Paths connecting the Planet ruling the Day with a Planet ruling any given Hour, there is a very easy rule that works every time. Here it is. *On any given day, when the hour you are interested in is not connected to the ruler of that day by a Path, simply use the influence of the hour in question.* For example: It's a Thursday, ruled by Jupiter. The hour, however, is ruled by Mercury, and a business, academic, or mystical issue arises. Should you wait for another time to act on or evaluate the issue? Of course not! Simply use the influence of the hour in question, since the hour's influence moderates the effect of the planet ruling the day by a factor of four.

• How do you use the combined influence that arises when the same planet is ruling both the day and the hour you are interested in? Say, on a Thursday ruled by Jupiter, during an hour ruled by Jupiter? Or a Friday, during a Venus Hour? That's easy. *Don't!* As it turns out, this double effect is very deleterious to all issues governed by the ruling planet. It is curious in the extreme, but instead of this combined influence strengthening the force exerted on the matter by the planet, it actually provides a destabilizing effect. Does this instability hold throughout the entire hourly period in question? No. It oscillates between a very positive and very negative effect, but at different times during that hour. Since you will never know when the positive or negative effect is dominant unless you test it out, you are better off waiting for another hour. If you enjoy intelligent experimenting as I do however, go ahead and use this powerful, unstable influence. I assure you, you will learn much!

Aside from these two minor instructions given above, you are now ready to employ the Kabbalistic Cycles System to your heart's content. And if you give it a fair trial, I am more than confident you will use it on a daily basis throughout the rest of your life.

EPILOGUE

In writing this book, it was my intention to give you a new, tried and proven system you could use to remove the mass of confusion that dominates the use of occult methods for achieving certainty and control over your life. Additionally, I sought to add a unique method to the literature of the field which, over time, will bear itself out as a method that can be applied in an infinite number of ways to various occult, metaphysical, mystical, and—most of all—magical practices. It is my sincere wish that you, the astute reader who has gone through so much by diligently studying this work, will benefit from it in your daily, work-a-day world to such an extent that you will bless the day you found it, or indeed, it found you!

All of us are thrown into this world without a blueprint or guide for life. As this salient, hard fact dawns on us, there are those of us who simply will not and cannot accept the diatribe of the Sunday morning religionist, the armchair philosopher, or the well meaning know-it-all whose life is anything but an example of what he or she preaches. To those determined to live their lives their way, by their own Will, I salute you and pray that I have presented you with a genuine tool with this book—a tool that will provide you with all of the Control and Certainty in your life that you so richly deserve simply by virtue of your Human Birthright.

REFERENCES

Chapter One

1. Coué, Emile. *Self-Mastery Through Conscious Autosuggestion*. 1922. Reprint, Kessinger Publishing, Kila, Montana. 1997.
2. Lisiewski, Joseph, Ph.D. *Ceremonial Magic & The Power of Evocation*. The Original Falcon Press, Tempe, Arizona. 2004.
3. Haanel, Charles F. *The Master Key System*. Kallisti Publishing, Wilkes-Barre, Pa. 2000.
4. Hyatt, Christopher S., Ph.D. *Undoing Yourself with Energized Meditation and Other Devices*. The Original Falcon Press, Tempe, Arizona. 1982.

Chapter Two

5. Ellis, Albert, Ph.D. and Robert A. Harper, Ph.D. *A New Guide to Rational Living*. Wilshire Books Co., No. Hollywood, California. 1975.

Chapter Three

6. *Walking With Cavemen*, Discovery Channel, televised June 15, 2004.
7. Horney, Karen, M.D. *Self-Analysis*. W.W. Norton & Co., New York. 1994
8. James, William. *Psychology. The Briefer Course*. Dover Publishing, Inc., New York. 2001.
9. Brenner, Charles, M.D. *An Elementary Textbook of Psychoanalysis*. Bantam Doubleday Dell Publishing Group, Inc., New York. 1995.
10. Glickman, Rosalene, Ph.D. *Optimal Thinking. How to be Your Best Self*. John Wiley and Sons, Inc. New York. 2002.
11. Wenger, Win, Ph.D. and Richard Poe. *The Einstein Factor. A Proven New Method for Increasing Your Intelligence*. Prima Publishing, Roseville, Ca. 1996.
12. Tracy, Brian. *Maximum Achievement*. Simon & Schuster, New York. 1993.
13. Bacovin, Helen, translator. *The Way of a Pilgrim*. (see 14)

14. Bacovin, Helen, translator. *The Pilgrim Continues His Way.* (Both titles under same cover.) Image Books/Doubleday, New York. 2003 ed.

Chapter Four

15. *American Heritage College Dictionary, 3rd ed.* Houghton Mifflin Company, Boston. 1993.
16. Carnegie, Dale. *How to Win Friends and Influence People.* Reissue edition, Pocket Books, New York. 1990.
17. Copelan, Rachel. *How to Hypnotize Yourself and Others.* Barnes & Noble Books, New York. 1982.
18. Greer, John Michael. *The New Encyclopedia of the Occult.* Llewellyn Publications, St. Paul, Minnesota. 2003.
19. Agrippa, Henry Cornelius of Nettesheim. *Three Books of Occult Philosophy.* Translated by James Freake, edited and annotated by Donald Tyson. Llewellyn Publications, St. Paul, Minnesota. 1993.
20. Rolleston, Frances. *Mazzaroth—The Constellations, Parts I–IV, including Mizraim: Astronomy of Egypt.* Weiser Books, York Beach, Maine. 2001.
21. Lewis, H. Spencer, F.R.C., Ph.D. *Self Mastery and Fate with the Cycles of Life.* The Rosicrucian Press, Ltd., San Jose, California. 1st ed. 1929, 26th ed. 1971.
22. Wilhelm, Richard, translator. *The I Ching, or Book of Changes.* Princeton University Press, 3rd ed. 1967.
23. Waite, Arthur Edward. *The Pictorial Key to the Tarot.* Weiser Books, York Beach, Maine. 2000. (Original edition 1910.)

Chapter Five

24. Regardie, Israel. *A Garden of Pomegranates. An Outline of the Qabalah.* 2nd ed. Llewellyn Publications, St. Paul, Minnesota. 1994.
25. Matt, Daniel C. *The Essential Kabbalah—The Heart of Jewish Mysticism.* Castle Books, New Jersey, 1997 ed.
26. Fortune, Dion. *The Mystical Qabalah.* Ernest Benn Limited, London. 1957.
27. Kaplan, Aryeh, translator and commentary. *Sefer Yetzirah. The Book of Creation. In Theory and Practice.* rev. ed., Samuel Weiser, Inc., York Beach, Maine. 1997.
28. Scholem, Gershom, editor. *Zohar. The Book of Splendor. Basic Readings from the Kabbalah.* Schocken Books, New York. 1977.
29. Reuchlin, Johann. *De Arte Cabalistica. On the Art of the Kabbalah.* University of Nebraska Press, Lincoln, Nebraska. 1993.

30. Levi, Eliphas. *The Book of Splendours. The Inner Mysteries of Qabalism. Its relationship to Freemasonry, Numerology, and Tarot.* Samuel Weiser, Inc., York Beach, Maine. 1984.

31. Levi, Eliphas. *The Mysteries of the Qabalah or Occult Agreement of the Two Testaments.* Samuel Weiser, Inc., York Beach, Maine. 2000.

32. Waite, Arthur Edward. *The Holy Kabbalah. A Mystical Interpretation of the Scriptures.* Carol Publishing Group. 1995.

33. Fortune, Dion. *The Mystical Qabalah.* Ernest Benn Limited, London. 1957. pg. 197.

Chapter 6

34. Waite, Arthur Edward. *The Pictorial Key to the Tarot.* Weiser Books, York Beach, Maine. 2000. (Original edition 1910.)

35. Mathers, S.L. MacGregor. *The Tarot: Its Occult Significance, Use in Fortune-Telling, and Method of Play.* Sq. 16 mo., London, 1888.

36. Levi, Eliphas. *Magical Ritual of the Sanctum Regnum, Interpreted by the Tarot Trumps.* Translated by W. Wynn Westcott, M.B. Kessinger Publishing Co., Kila, Montana. 1997.

Chapter 7

37. Lewis, H. Spencer, F.R.C., Ph.D. *Self Mastery and Fate with the Cycles of Life.* The Rosicrucian Press, Ltd., San Jose, California. 1st ed. 1929, 26th ed. 1971.

38. Agrippa, Henry Cornelius of Nettesheim. *Three Books of Occult Philosophy.* Translated by James Freake, edited and annotated by Donald Tyson. Llewellyn Publications, St. Paul, Minnesota. 1993.

39. Ibid, page 371.

Chapter 8

40. *Hermetica, volumes 1 through 4 (Corpus Hermeticum). The Ancient Greek and Latin Writings which contain religious or philosophic teachings ascribed to Hermes Trismegistus.* Introduction, Texts, and translation by Walter Scott. Kessinger Publishing Group, Montana.

MORE BOOKS ON MAGIC

CEREMONIAL MAGIC & THE POWER OF EVOCATION

by Joseph C. Lisiewski, Ph.D.

Introduced by Christopher Hyatt, Ph.D. & S. Jason Black

Ceremonial Magic lays bare the simplest of Grimoires, the Heptameron of Peter de Abano. Its Magical Axioms, extensive Commentaries, copious notes, and personal instructions to the reader make this a resource that no serious student of Magic can afford to be without. It is all here, as in no other Grimoire. Use its instructions and the world of evocation and personal gratification are within your grasp!

ISRAEL REGARDIE & THE PHILOSOPHER'S STONE

by Joseph C. Lisiewski, Ph.D.

Introduced by. Mark Stavish

Dr. Lisiewski delves into the hitherto unknown role Israel Regardie played in the world of Practical Laboratory Alchemy: not the world of idle speculation and so-called "inner alchemy," but the realm of the test tube and the Soxhlet Extractor. For the first time Dr. Regardie's private alchemical experiments are revealed as is his intense interaction with Frater Albertus of the Paracelsus Research Society and with the author himself.

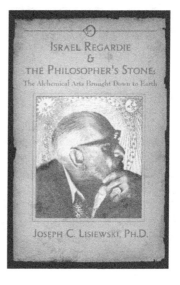

MORE BOOKS ON MAGIC

KABBALISTIC HANDBOOK FOR THE PRACTICING MAGICIAN

by Joseph C. Lisiewski, Ph.D.

Foreword by Christopher S. Hyatt, Ph.D.

For the practicing Magician, the Kabbalah is the backdrop against which his thoughts, ideas, ritual and ceremonial work are placed, and is the archetype which breathes life into secret occult practices. Yet none of the numerous books on 'Qabalah' give those 'on-the-spot' correspondences, attributions, and key concepts in a 'user-friendly' style. Until now.

THE COMPLETE GOLDEN DAWN SYSTEM OF MAGIC

by Israel Regardie

Foreword by Christopher S. Hyatt

Dr. Regardie's classic, final testament to the Golden Dawn includes extensive instruction on astrology, tarot, alchemy, Kabbalah, Enochiana, and much, much more.
Beautifully illustrated throughout, with many color plates, and an extensive index, *The Complete Golden Dawn System of Magic* is the easiest edition to study. An essential text in any library of magical works.

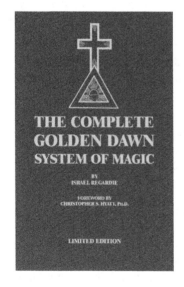

MORE BOOKS ON MAGIC

CONDENSED CHAOS
An Introduction to Chaos Magic
by Phil Hine

Foreword by Peter J. Carroll

"The most concise statement of the logic of modern magic. Magic, in the light of modern physics, quantum theory and probability theory is now approaching science. We hope that a result of this will be a synthesis so that science will become more magical and magic more scientific."
— William S. Burroughs, author of *Naked Lunch*

"... a tour de force."
— Ian Read, *Chaos International*

PRIME CHAOS
Adventures in Chaos Magic
by Phil Hine

An overview of the fastest-growing school of modern occultism: Chaos Magic. Simple, effective techniques of ritual magic, sorcery, invocation, possession and evocation. *Prime Chaos* also explores some of the lighter—and darker—aspects of modern occultism, and presents new ideas for developing magical techniques.

"I wish I'd written this book!"
— Peter J. Carroll, author of *Liber Kaos* and *Psybermagick*

THE *Original* FALCON PRESS

Invites You to Visit Our Website:
http://originalfalcon.com

At our website you can:

- Browse the online catalog of all of our great titles
- Find out what's available and what's out of stock
- Get special discounts
- Order our titles through our secure online server
- Find products not available anywhere else including:
    - One of a kind and limited availability products
    - Special packages
    - Special pricing
- Get free gifts
- Join our email list for advance notice of New Releases and Special Offers
- Find out about book signings and author events
- Send email to our authors
- Read excerpts of many of our titles
- Find links to our authors' websites
- Discover links to other weird and wonderful sites
- And much, much more

Get online today at http://originalfalcon.com

Made in the USA
Las Vegas, NV
18 August 2024

94005037R00144